Me, an Evangelist?

Me, an Evangelist?

Every Christian's Guide to Caring Evangelism

William J. McKay

Stephen Ministries • St. Louis, MO

Scripture quotations are from the NEW REVISED STANDARD VERSION BIBLE. Copyright © 1989, by the Division of Christian Education of the National Council of the Churches of Christ in the USA. Used by permission.

First printing, August 1992

Library of Congress Catalog Card Number: 92-064384
ISBN: 0-9633831-0-8

Printed in the United States of America

8   7   6   5   4   3
03 02 01 00 99 98

To
Martha, Eliza, and Noel

With thanks for the many ways
God loves me through you

Table of Contents

Acknowledgements i

Foreword iii

1. Taking the Fear Out of Evangelism 1

2. Evangelizing the Evangelists 15

3. Growing in God 27

4. Process-Oriented Evangelism 37

5. Building an Evangelizing Relationship 55

6. Listening: The Most Important Evangelizing Skill 69

7. Empathic Evangelism 83

8. Holistic Evangelism 89

9. Evangelizing in Crisis 97

10. Uncovering God-Sized Needs 111

11. Five Ways to Describe Sin 123

12. Eight Ways to Talk about Jesus 135

13. Guidelines for Effective Witnessing 149

14. How to Be an Assertive Witness 161

15. How to Use the Bible in Evangelizing 171

16. The Power of Prayer in Evangelism 181

17. The Basics of Process-Oriented Inviting 195

18. Saying Yes to God 207

19. How to Invite Someone to Church 215

20. How Will *You* Be a Caring Evangelist? 225

Acknowledgements

This book combines the work of many minds and many hands. The Spirit fit together diverse talents to create the final product. May it serve to glorify Jesus.

While I cannot name all who deserve recognition, there are several who must be acknowledged.

Kenneth Haugk taught me much of what I know about caregiving and showed me how to communicate practically in order to equip all God's people to serve as ministers. I enjoy the privilege of having Ken as a teacher, leader, and friend. At great personal sacrifice, he and Joan Haugk began Stephen Ministries, the organization that made Caring Evangelism possible. Many of the basic concepts in this book, including the central theme of process-oriented care, are built on Dr. Haugk's work.

I have the privilege of serving at Stephen Ministries with an extraordinarily talented group of people. My pastoral staff colleagues, David Paap and Gary Voss, contributed many of the ideas in this book. They, together with Kathie Bender and Lee Griess, refined Caring Evangelism at numerous workshops, and consistently gave of themselves to promote a project that would have someone else's name on it. This book would have been impossible without their contributions.

Kari Vo served as a gifted writer, editor, grammatical consultant, source of ideas and examples in the book, and kind critic. Kari and her husband Chau personify Caring Evangelism in their work with the Vietnamese community in St. Louis. I learned a lot about Caring Evangelism from Kari, and many parts of this book came directly or indirectly from her.

Elizabeth Wright is a talented artist who serves at Stephen Ministries. The art work that graces the cover and inside of this book (as well as all the other Caring Evangelism materials) captures the ideas of freshness and personal growth that I want Caring Evangelism to convey, and gives ample evidence of Elizabeth's considerable gifts.

Over the years God has blessed me with very capable administrative assistants and secretaries: Wendy Volkert, Ann Roser, Cheryl Oberdieck, Gayle Bogs, Tammy Isaac, Trish Moore, Jennifer Boehlke, Paul Lauer, Elizabeth Cook, and Marj Maynard. Their ideas, edits, typesetting, administrative abilities, patience, extra work to meet deadlines, and Christian care fueled the development of this book and the entire Caring Evangelism curriculum.

Many others at Stephen Ministries contributed to this project. Marlene Muller's knowledge of publishing made this look like a real book. Ellen Hynes helped keep us all working together. R. Scott Perry and Laura Carpenter were able editors. The rest of the people I need to thank are, I regret, too many to name here. God knows who they are, and they know their work goes to the glory of God.

William J. McKay
July, 1992

Foreword

I've spent the greatest part of my life developing ways to "equip the saints for the work of ministry, for building up the body of Christ" (Ephesians 4:12). So I am overjoyed to introduce this book, which prepares God's people for the greatest service of all—that of fulfilling Christ's Great Commission, to "go therefore and make disciples of all nations" (Matthew 28:19).

What a breath of fresh air this book is for evangelism! William McKay has combined a deep compassion for people's needs with a thoroughly scriptural understanding to create a book that every Christian can welcome with open arms.

Open arms and also with a sigh of relief. Many Christians hear Jesus' Great Commission and want to obey, but they've never found a way of evangelizing that was natural and effective for them. *Me, an Evangelist?* is written for all those people who never thought they could be evangelists.

Me, an Evangelist? will introduce you to a way of evangelizing that flows naturally out of your God-given care and concern for others in ways that make both of you feel comfortable and respected as persons. You will learn to share God's Good News in truly caring ways that demonstrate Christ's love as clearly as you speak about it.

As a clinical psychologist, I especially commend to you the chapters on listening, crisis care, and process-oriented evangelism. As a pastor, I am delighted to recommend Bill McKay's sensitive treatment of "Five Ways to Describe Sin" and "Eight Ways to Talk about Jesus," as well as the chapters on prayer and inviting others to begin a relationship with Jesus.

As a reader I'm pleased to report that Bill has made a very substantial book amazingly quick and easy to read. For every topic—listening, building relationships, knowing when and how to witness—there are clear explanations and plenty of examples. In addition, the story line that continues from chapter to chapter will keep you turning the pages to find out what happens next.

Best of all, as you read you will develop the caring and sharing skills you need to communicate Christ's love effectively to others. As you put these skills into practice, evangelism can become a truly joyful, comfortable experience for both you and those you evangelize.

One final word. This book stands on its own, and it is also an integral part of the course "Caring Evangelism: How to Live and Share Christ's Love." If reading this book makes you want to equip the saints to fulfill the Great Commission, check out the Caring Evangelism Course. It is a top quality tool for training Christians to serve as everyday evangelists in their daily lives.

I commend this book to you and pray that it is a blessing to you personally and for your caring evangelizing.

Kenneth C. Haugk

Chapter 1

Taking the Fear Out of Evangelism

I remember the first time Margaret came to church. It was Easter morning a year ago. I was serving as an usher, helping latecomers find places to sit. The service had just started when Margaret stepped in through the doorway.

I almost didn't recognize her. She had her hair done in a new style, and she was wearing a lovely, bright red and white dress. It was the first time I had ever seen Margaret wearing bright colors.

She looked a little confused, not really sure what to do next. Then she saw me and smiled. I walked over, and took her arm, and led her to a place by my wife, Sarah.

"You look beautiful," Sarah said.

"Just like the maples in your yard last fall," I added.

Margaret pretended to be grouchy as she responded, "Just show me what I'm supposed to do here."

I quickly found someone else to do the ushering. Sitting with Margaret was far more important for me. We turned to the right page in the hymnal and started singing "Jesus Christ Is Risen Today."

That was a red-letter day in Margaret's life, and in mine. Although she hadn't set foot inside a church in 40 years, Margaret is now a growing Christian.

As strange as it sounds to me to say it, my wife Sarah and I were Margaret's evangelists. God worked through us to bring Margaret to church that morning, and to bring her to faith in Jesus.

I never thought I would say I was an evangelist. I always

thought evangelism was for religious fanatics . . . or for Christians who had gifts I didn't have. But my relationship with Margaret showed me that God can use any Christian as an evangelist. It must be true because God used me!

It all started in the middle of the night two years ago when I heard an ambulance pull up in front of Margaret's house across the street. I looked out my bedroom window and saw the paramedics run inside. Shortly afterward the ambulance raced away. Margaret's husband Roy had had a heart attack. Two days later he died.

I didn't know Margaret and Roy Lewis very well then. We had been neighbors for 20 years, but somehow we never really got to know each other. Our lives were too different. Sarah and I spent most of our free time with the kids or over at the church. I don't know what Margaret and Roy did.

Sarah told me about Roy's death the next afternoon when I got home from running some errands. She said, "I feel like we ought to do something . . . say something . . . I don't know. But Mrs. Lewis is over there all alone. I don't think anyone's staying with her. Do you think maybe I could make a little extra for dinner tonight, and you could take it over for her?"

Two hours later, feeling terribly awkward, I was standing on her front step with a dish of chicken casserole in my hand. I pressed the bell once and waited, then a second time. No response. As I was about to give up, the door opened.

She had obviously been crying. Her eyes and nose were red, and she clutched a damp handkerchief. I mumbled something about how we had been thinking about her, and we thought maybe she might not feel like cooking . . .

Just briefly, her eyes lit up. Then she stood back from the door and said, "Thank you. That is very kind of you. Please come in, Mr. Simons."

I went inside and stood by the sofa. While she put the casserole in the kitchen, I looked around the room.

Embers glowed in the fireplace. Along either side of the fireplace were rows of shelves, floor to ceiling, filled with well-worn books. I walked over and started reading titles off the spines. I don't think I'd ever seen so many books of poetry in one place. There were also classic novels, books about philosophy, history, art, music. I took a volume off the shelf; *Leaves of Grass,* by Walt Whitman. On the inside cover was "Margaret Tyler" in small but graceful handwriting. I thumbed through the book and saw underlining and notes written in the same hand.

I put the book back on the shelf as Margaret came back in. She sat down in a chair by the fireplace and said, "I appreciate your coming over, Mr. Simons. It was very thoughtful of you and your wife."

"Please, call me Andy," I said. "I'm sorry about your husband. It must be very painful for you."

She nodded, then looked down. "You may call me Margaret," she said. "We knew it was coming—the doctor said that another heart attack would kill him. Somehow I just didn't expect . . ."

She turned her head away for a moment. The light from the lamp caught the few strands of gray in her black hair, which was pulled back in a tight bun. Her fingers twisted the material of her plain dark green skirt.

"I didn't know he was so ill," I said. "I never thought . . ."

"No," she said, turning back to me. Her face was calm, though sad. "No one knew. We tend to keep to ourselves." She closed her eyes for a moment. "Or at least we did. Now it's just me."

I didn't know what to say, so I just kept quiet. Then a few seconds later I asked, "When is the funeral? I don't want it to seem like I'm inviting myself, but, if you don't mind, maybe I and my family could come to the funeral."

She looked up quickly as if I had broken her train of thought. "Oh," she said. "You would have been more than welcome, but I'm afraid there will be no funeral. Roy's body was cremated this morning. I went to say good-bye one last time."

I felt surprised. Before I thought to stop myself I said, "You mean you didn't have a service or a pastor there or any friends?"

"No," she said, looking straight into my eyes. "No, we don't see the need for such things. Or, at least now I don't."

We talked for a little while longer—she talked about her garden, and I asked if she might like to come over for a barbecue sometime. She said she thought she would.

As I stood to leave I looked again at the bookshelves. As I walked home it dawned on me that, among all those books, I hadn't seen a Bible or any book about religion. Somehow that made her seem even more alone to me.

That evening Sarah and I sat on the sofa and talked about my visit with Margaret.

Sarah said, "This seems to have gotten you down."

"Maybe a little bit," I answered. "I think you were right— Margaret's all alone over there. She didn't say anything about friends or relatives coming to see her. She even seemed a little surprised to see me."

"That's too bad," Sarah said. She leaned back against me and sighed.

"And the thing I keep thinking about is how she doesn't even have God to help."

Sarah lifted her head and looked at me. "How do you know? Did you ask her?"

"No. Are you kidding? It's just that I never see her going to church, and she said that they didn't believe in funerals. I can't imagine how alone I'd feel in that situation if I couldn't even turn to God."

The answer was simple to Sarah. "Why don't you invite her to come to church with us or offer to introduce her to Pastor Ed? Maybe she would appreciate that at a time like this."

I shook my head. "No way," I said. "I've never been one of those religious fanatics, and I'm not going to become one now. She's got enough problems without me bothering her about religion." I stood up and walked over to the window.

I felt like I had to justify myself. "I know they keep talking about evangelism at church, but that kind of thing just isn't for me. I don't want to be like those obnoxious, pushy evangelists who came through the neighborhood last week."

Sarah stared at me, her eyebrows raised. "I wasn't saying we should do anything pushy."

"Well, I just don't feel comfortable talking about religion," I said defensively. "I think religion is a very personal thing, and I'd rather live my faith than talk about it all the time and be a hypocrite. We can think of something else to help Margaret. But don't ask me to be an evangelist. It's just not me."

Needed: A Caring Way of Evangelizing

As Christians all of us are called by Jesus to share the Good News of God's love with others. Jesus said, "You will be my witnesses." He also said, "Go and make disciples." Why then are so many Christian people like Andy? Why are so many reluctant, scared, or even embarrassed to tell others about the life-changing love God has showered on them?

When it comes to Jesus' commands about evangelizing, many questions come up. Is Jesus asking us to ignore or run rough-shod over other people's feelings, needs, and concerns? Do we have to become aggressive or confrontational in order to follow Jesus' command? The biblical answer is clear. Jesus said, "This is my commandment that you love one another . . ." (John 15:12). Paul said that love is patient, kind, humble, trusting, hopeful, and dependable (1 Cor. 13:4-8).

Clearly, Christians need to find a caring way of evangelizing we can feel good about, one that will make it possible for those of us who never thought we could be evangelists to live and share Christ's love effectively with others.

A good way to start is by understanding problems that have kept Christian people from evangelizing. We also need to know why people who are not Christian often resent being evangelized and reject the Gospel message. Once we understand better some of the major struggles people have with evangelism, we will be ready to find a way of evangelizing that will be natural for us and that will gently and lovingly communicate God's love to others.

Eight Common Reasons Why Christians Don't Evangelize

Following are eight common reasons people give for not evangelizing.

1. Fear of the "E-Word"

Many people shy away from anything that has the word *evangelism* in it. When they see or hear that word they turn and run. Some have even said, "Why don't you call Caring Evangelism something different? The word *evangelism* will scare people off."

The word *evangelism* certainly doesn't deserve such a bad reputation. It's actually a wonderful, joyful word that comes from two Greek words, *eu,* which means "good," and *angellion,* which means "message" or "news." The ancient Greeks used the word *evangelism* to mean giving people back home the good news that their city's troops had won a battle. They also used this word to describe other kinds of good news that brought joy to the hearer.

So how did the word *evangelism* get such a frightening reputation? There are many possible answers. Some hear the word *evangelism* and think of dishonest television evangelists who seem more interested in getting viewers' money than in telling people about Jesus. Others remember evangelists who tried to bully them with threats of burning in hell. Maybe you've known people who were considered pests at school or at the office because they were always confronting people about their religious beliefs. You may have had people come to your home uninvited, then refuse to leave until you did what they wanted you to do—praying or making a decision. You may even remember times when someone tried to force you to evangelize, to share the Gospel in ways that made you feel uncomfortable and frightened.

These experiences can leave Christian people afraid of the "E-word" and very unwilling to evangelize. We need a way of evangelizing that overcomes these negative stereotypes, one that is not pushy or obnoxious, but instead caring and sensitive to others' feelings and needs.

2. Limiting Evangelism to Activities That Feel Unnatural

Another reason many Christians don't evangelize is because they think the only way to evangelize is to do things that just don't feel natural to them. They believe they have to knock on doors of people they don't know, pass out tracts on street corners, invite everyone they meet to church, or witness to people in pushy, arrogant ways. But these activities aren't natural or comfortable for them, and they'd rather not evangelize at all if it means having to do these things.

Actually there are many different ways to communicate the Good News of God's love, through words *and* actions. We need a way of evangelizing that is natural for us, and that feels comfortable for the people we evangelize also.

3. Fear of Rejection

Often it's not easy to talk about something as important as our beliefs about God. When we do, we reveal a great deal about who we are and what is really important to us. Evangelizing means making ourselves vulnerable, telling the other person about our pain and struggles, and how God has come through for us during tough times.

That can be frightening. What if the person we share with ridicules us, or disagrees, or tells us our beliefs are immature or ill-informed? Being rejected is very painful. In fact, it's so painful that many simply never risk it.

We need a way of evangelizing in which we build trusting relationships with others—one where we get to know others so well that we can witness and invite in ways they will welcome instead of rejecting. In spite of our best efforts at sensitivity and care, whenever we risk giving ourselves deeply to others we face the possibility of rejection. We need to trust the Holy

Spirit who calls us and strengthens us for evangelizing, and we need to know that our sisters and brothers in Christ will care for us when we feel down.

4. Insecurity about Our Own Life in Christ

There are no perfect Christians, only sinners who have been forgiven by Jesus. All Christians still have room to grow in faith, obedience, and discipleship.

This truth can make us feel insecure about evangelizing. We may ask ourselves, "What right do I have to tell others about Christianity when I don't seem to be able to live it very well myself?" We may be afraid others will see our all-too-human imperfections and call us hypocrites. We may even be afraid that others will say, "If *that person's* a Christian, there must not be much to Christianity."

But we don't need to live like the greatest Christian saint before we begin evangelizing. Our evangelism must make it possible for us to be honest, to admit that we are imperfect persons. We need a way of evangelizing in which God uses us as we are—our struggles and weaknesses, as well as our joys and strengths—to bless others.

5. Not Wanting to Look Like a Fanatic

Many Christians remember occasions when they've been embarrassed by religious people who shoved their brand of religion down everyone else's throats. Actions like these can give Christianity a bad name. Believers who watch this happen may promise themselves that they will never be *that* kind of Christian.

Some are so afraid of looking like fanatics that they don't say a word about God just to make sure their friends, neighbors, or co-workers don't identify them with pushy religious fanatics they've met in the past. Unfortunately, this stifles evangelism.

But evangelism doesn't have to be like that. Instead of alienating people, we can present God's love in ways that interest them. We need a form of evangelism in which we live out Christ's love, rather than just talking about it. As we show how God loves, as we model the self-sacrificing love of our Savior, people will not be put off. God's love shining through us will interest and attract them.

6. We Simply Don't Know How

Many in the church have never learned the basics of evangelizing. They don't know the answers to questions like:

- How do I tell someone about Jesus?
- What exactly is God's Good News?
- What if the person wants to know more?
- How does a person become a Christian?

Many Christians don't know how to begin, and if they ever got started, they wouldn't know what to do next. So they avoid evangelism, even though sometimes they'd really like to tell someone how important Jesus is in their lives.

We need a way of evangelizing that is *practical,* one that will work in the real world. We need to learn specific skills for caring and sharing Christ's love with others, so that we know what we're doing and feel comfortable about it.

7. Insecurity

Many Christians feel insecure about their knowledge of the Christian faith. They are afraid that if they evangelize, someone might ask a question they can't answer, which would embarrass them. They may even worry that, if they don't have all the right answers, the other person will lose interest in Christianity. They don't want to turn anyone away from God, so they don't evangelize at all.

Some Christians suffer from an even deeper insecurity. They avoid evangelizing because they're afraid that someone might ask a question that would make them doubt their own faith.

We need an approach to evangelism that helps us with insecurity—one that equips us with the basic truth about Jesus and shows us how to communicate it to others. We need a way of evangelizing that helps us deal with questions we can't answer, without being embarrassed or afraid. We especially need to be sure that the results of our evangelizing don't depend on us, but on the Holy Spirit's work in others' lives.

8. Assuming People Don't Want to Hear the Gospel

A final reason why Christians don't evangelize is that they assume others aren't interested in hearing about Jesus. This is only half true. No one is interested in hearing about God when it means being manipulated, embarrassed, or used. Many people, however, are interested when they hear about Jesus in a caring, accepting relationship that allows them to feel valuable and worthwhile to God and to the caring evangelist.

Five Common Reasons People Don't Want to Be Evangelized

After looking at problems with evangelism from the evangelist's point of view, let's consider the point of view of the people being evangelized. There are at least five major reasons why people don't respond to the Gospel—reasons that our evangelism needs to take into account.

1. People Don't See the Good News as Relevant to Their Daily Lives

Many people misunderstand the Christian message as something that applies only to some otherworldly "spiritual" part of life—not to "real" life, here and now. They think, "God only cares about saving my soul. But my soul isn't a problem for me right now. The *real* problems in my life are:

- "I don't have enough money,"
- "My kids won't listen to me,"
- "No matter how much I accomplish, I never feel happy," or
- "Someone I love just died and I don't know if I can keep on living."

This list of real problems could go on and on. We need a way of evangelizing that will address these immediate needs—a way of sharing the Gospel that touches people right where they're hurting. Our evangelism must communicate God's love for others as whole persons—not just "souls."

2. The Church People See Is One They Don't Want to Join

What is the public's perception of the Christian Church? It could be better. Very often non-Christians see only the negative in the Church.

People may point to the history of the Church with the Inquisition, and atrocities during the Crusades. And what about more recent history? Dr. Elton Trueblood points out the irony of a television evangelist of the 1980s who made $1.6 million a year while claiming to serve Jesus, the Savior who once said he didn't even have a place to sleep![1] Stories of fallen televangelists and other scandals in the Church are hot news when they happen, and bad news for the reputation of the Christian Church.

It's important to admit that much of this bad reputation is deserved. Christians have done many things that dishonor the Lord they claim to follow. But this shouldn't be the end of the story for evangelism.

We need a way of evangelizing that gives people a different vision of the Church. Our evangelism needs to show people what Christian community was designed to be—a group of people who care for each other, nurture each other's growth, and challenge each other to serve Jesus in every area of life.

3. People Reject Christianity Because of Past Bad Experiences

Sometimes people react defensively to the claims of Christianity because a Christian church or person has hurt them in the past. They may carry bad memories from childhood of being forced to attend church, or to follow certain rules on pain of hellfire. They may have been embarrassed, ridiculed, or betrayed by Christians they trusted. It is no wonder that these people react so negatively to evangelism.

We need a way of evangelizing that enables us to understand the hurt these people have experienced, and that allows them to express their feelings of anger and pain. Our evangelism needs to be a healing, caring experience—one that doesn't reopen old wounds, but rather brings healing, and helps people to move beyond the pain of past bad experiences with Christianity to see that God is caring and loving.

4. People Don't Think They Can (or Want to) Fit the Christian Image

"I couldn't ever be a Christian." Have you ever heard a statement like that? Sometimes what the person is really saying is, "I don't think I can fit into the Christian mold. I'm too different, and I like being the way I am."

One of the misconceptions people hold about Christians is that they're all alike. Here are some common stereotypes about Christians:

- Christians always carry around a ten-pound black leather Bible from which they quote at every opportunity.

- Christians dress in clothes that are 20 years out-of-date.

- Christians are anti-intellectual—they reject any knowledge that doesn't fit certain narrow beliefs.

- Christians are narrow-minded fanatics.

- Christians are behind the times scientifically and socially.

- Christians don't know how to have fun.
- Christians are saintly—they have no struggles, problems, or sin like other people do.
- Christians are judgmental.

With such a list of stereotypes, small wonder if non-Christians are afraid to think about becoming Christians! They know they don't fit these images, and they don't want to. They enjoy their individuality, whether they express themselves through race car driving, political action, playing darts in the local pub, or studying nuclear physics. They fear becoming a Christian will smother them. They don't want to be forced into a mold.

We need a way of evangelizing that respects the individuality that God created in everyone. Our evangelism cannot be a memorized, one-size-fits-all presentation. Instead we need to communicate the Good News about Jesus Christ, crucified and resurrected, to each person in a way that fits his or her life.

5. People Don't See Their Own Need for a Savior

Some people may question their need for the Gospel. They may say, "I know I'm not perfect, but I'm not any worse than anyone else. I've lived as good a life as anyone else. God has no right to demand more than that." For such people the Good News seems like bad news. They can't receive God's love until they admit that they need a Savior—and they don't want to do that.

In a "do-it-yourself" culture that glorifies independence, it is very difficult for people to admit that they need help, that they need a Savior to die and rise for them. People would rather think of themselves as totally self-sufficient, able to make it on their own. Admitting they need a Savior is a little death for them, because it means giving up their illusion of self-sufficiency.

It is frightening and painful for people to face their need. Our evangelism must aim at creating a relationship in which this will be possible. Caring for others with accepting love can help them find the courage to face their deep needs and admit they need God. Then we can gently direct them to the God who has already met their needs in Jesus.

A New Way of Evangelizing

For all these reasons, we need a new way of evangelizing.

We need a way that will meet our own needs as Christians, allowing us to share the wonderful love we have received without worrying about rejection, looking fanatical, or having to be perfect. Those around us also need a new way of being evangelized—one that strives to understand them, respect them, and put them in touch with the God they so desperately need and long for.

This kind of evangelism is possible. Even for those of us who never though we could be evangelists, there's good news. We can! Caring Evangelism is sharing God's Good News in ways that fit who we are, while at the same time understanding and respecting others.

What Is Caring Evangelism?

Here's a definition of Caring Evangelism:

Caring Evangelism is communicating, through word and deed, the Good News about Jesus Christ to Christians and non-Christians in a process-oriented, other-centered way so that others discover their need for a Savior, receive the forgiveness and new life that God gives in Jesus, and respond to God's love faithfully.

This definition makes several key points about our role as caring evangelists:

- In Caring Evangelism, we communicate the Good News about Jesus in many different ways—through what we say *and* what we do. We don't limit our evangelism just to words, or just to actions. We balance both words and actions in order to tell and show the love of God.

- As caring evangelists we share God's Good News in ways guided by what others need, not by our own compulsions to witness or convert them. Instead of forcing our ideas on others, we try to understand what they think, believe, and feel.

- Instead of just telling people they need God whether they know it or not, we listen and witness in order to help them discover for themselves their need for a Savior.

- Others are then free to respond to the message of God's love with the faith God gives them. We don't need to convince, argue, or bully people into the Kingdom of God. Instead, we remember that the Holy Spirit is the one who convinces people of their need, creates faith, and brings about change.

The Caring Evangelism Adventure

All of us are called to be witnesses, to go out and make disciples. And it is possible for all of us to do so! There's an old hymn that says, "If you cannot speak like angels, if you cannot preach like Paul, you can tell the love of Jesus, you can say He died for all."[2] We don't have to preach in front of thousands of people in meeting halls, sell the Gospel to people we've never met, or become religious fanatics. Caring Evangelism is a way for each Christian to discover the ways God has uniquely called and gifted him or her to evangelize others. Discovering, developing, and using our God-given gifts as caring evangelists is an exciting adventure that lasts a lifetime.

[1]*Encourage One Another.* A videotape featuring Dr. Elton Trueblood. (St. Louis: Stephen Ministries, 1991).

[2]Daniel March, "Hark! the Voice of Jesus Crying," in *The Lutheran Hymnal* (St. Louis: Concordia Publishing House, 1941), 496.

Chapter 2

Evangelizing the Evangelists

Do you ever have one of those times in your life when God seems to arrange things so that one experience builds on another, when it seems like God is trying to tell you something? That's what started happening to me after I talked to Margaret that evening. God's message to me seemed to be, "Andy, I love you just as you are, but I'm not finished making you into the person I want you to be."

My first visit with Margaret was on a Saturday. Later that evening I was thinking a lot about her, and about what I said to Sarah about never being an evangelist. I knew I didn't want to be a pushy, obnoxious "religious fanatic," but that wasn't the only reason I didn't want to witness to her. I knew there had to be other ways to evangelize people. My reason sounded more like a rationalization. There was something else going on in me, some way that I wasn't telling myself the truth.

The next morning I went to church and listened as Pastor Ed preached about the Sermon on the Mount. The part I remember vividly was when he talked about seeking the Kingdom of God first. I remember that morning after the worship service, I felt irritated and wasn't very nice to Sarah and my daughter Erica after church. I reacted the way I usually do when I'm challenged and I don't want to admit I'm wrong.

Monday I went to work and ate lunch with Jim Hayashi. It was an unusually nice early spring day, and we both went outside and sat at a picnic table and ate and talked. Jim is the kind of Christian I really respect. He's sort of quiet. He seems to live his faith a lot more than he talks about it, but when he talks about God it seems like the most natural thing in the world—to him and to the people he's talking to.

There are two things I notice about Jim when I see him; one is his eyes and the other is how calm he is. When you're talking, Jim looks straight at you, and you just know he's listening to you. His dark eyes communicate attention and care. Then there's the calmness in this man. I've never seen anyone sit as still as he sits. I fidget and shift and drum my fingers all the time, especially when I'm sitting on a rock hard picnic table bench. Jim just sits there, really relaxed, and it shows.

So Jim and I were eating lunch at the picnic table. Jim was listening to the birds and I was fidgeting, thinking about the things I had to do that afternoon. Then, out of the blue, Jim said, "Would you like to come to a retreat this weekend?"

It took me a moment to shift mental gears and think about what he had said. "What kind of retreat?" I asked.

"Our church is having a retreat and I'm leading it. We're going to talk about living as followers of Jesus." Jim rested his hands on his knees and waited for me to think about the invitation.

"Thanks for asking. But I'm curious. Why me?"

"It just came to me. I was thinking about the retreat, and you and I have talked about God before, and I thought you might like to be a part of it."

I asked for more information, mostly as a way to put off having to make a decision. Jim told me when and where the retreat was happening. Then he said, "Don't decide right now. Let me know by Thursday morning. If you'd like to come, you'll be welcome; if not, that's fine too."

At first I didn't think I could make it. We had made plans with some friends for Saturday night, but then they called and canceled. When Sarah got off the phone, she said, "Since they're not coming, why don't you go to that retreat Jim mentioned? It'll be good for you to get away for a weekend." I tried to get out of it by saying that there were a lot of things I needed to get done at home, but Sarah told me not to worry about them this weekend.

So I decided to go. I still had this feeling that there was something going on inside me that I didn't understand—something I needed to find out about. On Thursday morning, I told Jim I'd like to come on the retreat. He said, "Great. See you there."

The retreat started out wonderfully, with lots of nice people having fun together. I got to know the people in my small group very quickly. Then, Saturday afternoon, everyone gathered and Jim began to teach. He said, "One of the reasons we're here is because we want to learn to follow Jesus more faithfully. I've been wrestling for many years with how to do that. What I'd like to do this afternoon is tell you about my journey with God and some of the things I've learned on the way. Then I'd love to hear your stories."

Jim leaned back in his chair and said, "I've been converted five or six times. That doesn't mean I stopped being a Christian and then came back. It means I changed . . . I grew. Each time I have learned to trust God more and follow Jesus better.

"I first met Jesus when I was a teenager. I'd been sort of wild for a couple of years, but I got a big shock when I was caught vandalizing a grade school and had to spend a night in jail. I decided I didn't like the consequences of that kind of lifestyle and I'd better find something different.

"Soon after that I went to a weekend youth retreat with some kids from my parents' church. God really grabbed hold of me that weekend. I left that retreat and went home and told my parents I was going to be a different person. And it really happened. God turned me around. I got serious about school, I stopped fighting with my brothers, I made different friends, and I actually got to know my parents as real people."

Jim described other times in his life when he had grown in his relationship with God. He told us about his experience with a Christian fellowship group in college. He was deeply involved in ministry to inner city children during his first two years of college, and that experience taught him a lot about his faith.

But then he started to worry about his future, about whether or not he'd get a job once he graduated. He drifted away from the Christian fellowship group and started studying morning, noon, and night. After he graduated he kept up the same kind of work schedule in his first job. Finally he burned out. Jim wound up feeling depressed and empty.

"I didn't know what to do," Jim continued. "I had tried as hard as I could to make my life come out right, but it didn't work. Something was still missing. So I went looking for a church. I started attending this very large congregation with three services and thousands of members. I didn't really meet many people or get really involved, but the worship services filled that empty place in me. I started thinking about God again and not just about work. I finally realized that my work couldn't give me everything I needed. I began to spend time with God every day, praying and reading the Bible, trying to find some meaning, some balance in my life."

Jim sat back and closed his eyes for a moment, and the

tall-ceilinged room at the retreat center was quiet except for the crackling sound of the fire. Then he leaned forward and said, "I could tell you many more stories; about when I married Linda and how her faith helped me know God better, about how lonely I was when she died and how God became so real to me as I was grieving, about how hard it has been to give up my compulsive work habits and to learn to spend time with God. But I don't want to take up all the time talking about me.

"Let me just wrap up my story by saying this. In my life with God, I keep getting to know Jesus over and over again. Every time I reach a plateau in my life with God, something happens—sometimes wonderful things and sometimes things that really hurt—but something happens to show me I need God even more than I thought I did before. Somehow God breaks through and loves me in ways I couldn't have imagined before. I want to share this idea with you because I think the same thing is true for all of us. God keeps finding ways to reach us more and more deeply. We never stand still in our journey of faith."

Jim invited others to share their stories and some did, but I didn't really listen. I was thinking about myself and wondering if God was trying to reach me. I also thought about Margaret. I wondered how she was feeling and if she knew that God loved her. And I thought about what I'd said to Sarah about sharing God's love with Margaret. I realized that I had come up with all sorts of self-righteous reasons for not talking to her about God, but the simple truth was, I was scared.

I might have been angry at myself all night for that, but we closed the evening with a communion service. I listened to the pastor describe how Jesus had sacrificed himself for me and I remembered that Jesus understood what it was like to be scared. I went to bed that night less fidgety. I felt in me some of the peacefulness I'd seen in Jim.

Evangelizing Is Also for Christians

The title of this chapter may have surprised you. Many people think of evangelism as only something Christians do to non-Christians. Many think that evangelization only takes place for a limited time, and ends when people come to believe in Jesus or start going to church.

But this is only part of the story. Evangelization continues and helps people grow in faith in Jesus Christ. In chapter 1 you learned that the purpose of Caring Evangelism is, ". . . so that others discover their need for a Savior, receive the forgiveness and new life that God gives in Jesus, and respond to God's love faithfully." Christians don't outgrow the need to discover, receive, and respond in these ways. Evangelizing the evangelists is how we help each other mature in faith.

A Closer Look at the Word *Evangelism*

Some may say, "That certainly isn't what I've been told evangelism is. I've always thought it meant helping those who aren't Christians to believe in Jesus." Let's look at the Bible to understand more of what evangelism means.

Actually, the word *evangelism* is never used in the Bible. The closest word is *evangelist,* which is only used three times (Acts 21:8, Eph. 4:11, 2 Tim. 4:5). In the Ephesians passage, the Bible describes the work of an evangelist:

> The gifts he gave were that some would be apostles, some prophets, *some evangelists,* some pastors and teachers, *to equip the saints for the work of ministry, for building up the body of Christ,* until all of us come to the unity of the faith and of the knowledge of the Son of God, to maturity, to the measure of the full stature of Christ. (Eph. 4:11-13)

This passage doesn't limit the work of evangelists to non-Christians. It says that evangelists help "equip the *saints*" (emphasis added). Saints are people who are already Christians. Evangelists help build up Christians by equipping them to do "the work of ministry," to agree about their faith, to know Jesus, to mature as disciples, and to become more like Jesus.

The Process Is the Same

Christian growth begins when the Holy Spirit first brings a person to faith in Jesus. This is what most people think of as evangelism.

How do we help others begin to believe in Jesus? Working in partnership with the Holy Spirit, we help them see their need for a Savior and we tell them about Jesus, the Savior God has provided. The Spirit uses our relating, our care, and our words about Jesus to create faith in the other person.

But becoming a Christian is not an end; it is the beginning of life lived with Jesus in the Kingdom of God. How do we help our fellow Christians mature in their faith, trust, and discipleship? We use the same evangelizing process by which people first come to faith. We help them see their need for Jesus at deeper levels; we remind them of all Jesus has done and encourage them to trust Jesus more completely. The Holy Spirit uses our evangelizing to deepen faith and create Christian maturity.

All Christians evangelize and are evangelized. It is a central part of God's plan for all God's people.

Like Parenting

Evangelizing the evangelists is a lot like parenting. Being a parent begins before the baby's birth—but it doesn't stop when the baby is born. Good parents continue to nurture, teach, challenge, and encourage their child to grow.

Parenting means providing a safe and caring environment for a child. Parents give their child food, clothing, shelter, and all the other things the child needs to survive and thrive. Parenting means loving and encouraging the child, building his or her self-esteem.

What would you think of a parent who never expected his or her child to change and grow? If the child didn't want to learn to use the toilet, the parent would simply keep changing diapers. If the child decided he or she didn't want to go to school, the parent would allow him or her to drop out.

Most people would call this neglect. One of the main reasons parents provide a safe and caring environment for their children is so that the children can feel secure enough to take risks, try new things, and grow up. Parents also challenge their children by setting standards for them and teaching them to take on new responsibilities. A combination of nurture and challenge helps children become mature, happy, and independent adults.

Evangelizing Includes Nurture and Challenge

This same process of nurture and challenge should take place when Christians evangelize the evangelists. People need nurturing—they need to be cared for, taught, and continually reminded of God's wonderful love. They also need to be challenged to grow, challenged to "work out your own salvation with fear and trembling" as the Spirit makes them into the kind of strong, mature Christians God plans (Phil. 2:12).

What happens if the evangelists aren't prepared, aren't challenged in the church? Then they remain immature Christians, babies in the faith. They certainly never evangelize others because they have never matured enough to do so.

The book of Ephesians gives a vision of a Christian congregation where all God's people are continually evangelized:

The gifts he gave were that some would be apostles, some

prophets, some evangelists, some pastors and teachers, to equip the saints for the work of ministry, for building up the body of Christ, until all of us come to the unity of the faith and the knowledge of the Son of God, to maturity, to the measure of the full stature of Christ . . . we must grow up in every way into him who is the head, into Christ, from whom the whole body, joined and knit together by every ligament with which it is equipped, as each part is working properly, promotes the body's growth in building itself up in love. (Eph. 4:11-13, 15b-16)

As members of the body of Christ, we have this kind of responsible, loving, cooperative growth as our goal. Evangelizing the evangelists is part of how it happens.

Who Evangelizes the Evangelists?

The Ultimate Evangelist

God the Holy Spirit is at work in all evangelism, bringing people to faith in Jesus. When we evangelize people outside the church, it is the Holy Spirit who helps them see their need for a Savior, believe in Jesus, and grow in their relationship with God. When we evangelize each other within the church, the Holy Spirit continues this same work, helping people mature in faith.

Evangelizing Each Other in Christian Community

When we gather together as the church we evangelize the evangelists. But we don't do this on our own. The Holy Spirit works through all we say and do.

The Holy Spirit is at work when we gather for worship. When we gather to hear the Word of God read and preached, the Spirit helps us to see our need and comforts us with the Good News that God has met our needs in Jesus. The Holy Spirit also evangelizes us through baptism and the Lord's Supper, through confession and forgiveness, and through the faith stories of our sisters and brothers in Christ.

The Holy Spirit is at work when we meet informally with Christian friends. In informal Christian community we tell each other about our joys and struggles in our life of faith, we sing together, we read the Bible together, we pray, and we love each other as sisters and brothers in Jesus. God evangelizes us through each other when, "speaking the truth in love," we gently challenge each other to take next steps in our growing relationship with God. In all these ways the Spirit works through Christian community to bring us closer and closer to Jesus.

Evangelizing Yourself

The Holy Spirit is at work when we find ways to put ourselves in touch with God. In a sense, whenever we deliberately seek God, we evangelize ourselves.

Richard Foster shows how Christians can use the classical spiritual disciplines of Christianity to evangelize themselves. The disciplines he discusses are meditation, prayer, fasting, study, simplicity, solitude, submission, service, confession, worship, guidance, and celebration. Foster writes:

> A farmer is helpless to grow grain; all he can do is provide the right conditions for the growing of grain . . . This is the way it is with the Spiritual Disciplines—they are a way of sowing to the Spirit. The Disciplines are God's way of getting us into the ground; they put us where he can work within us and transform us. By themselves the Spiritual Disciplines can do nothing; they can only get us to the place where something can be done. . . . God has ordained the Disciplines of the spiritual life as the means by which we place ourselves where he can bless us.[1]

We begin as caring evangelists by first of all evangelizing ourselves. The faith God creates as we do so will overflow out of us as we live and share the love of Jesus Christ with others.

Why Evangelize the Evangelists?

You've already learned the most important answer to this question. We evangelize the evangelists because that is how Christians continue to grow as faithful disciples of Jesus. The church isn't like a club you join and then attend to enjoy the benefits. Christianity is an all-encompassing way of life. In Philippians, after Paul recounts the sacrifice of Jesus, he says:

> Therefore, my beloved, just as you have always obeyed me, not only in my presence, but much more now in my absence, work out your own salvation with fear and trembling; for it is God who is at work in you, enabling you both to will and to work for his good pleasure. (Phil. 2:12-13)

God is at work in us, transforming us into the image of Jesus Christ. The Holy Spirit works through us as we evangelize others in Christian community.

Growth Keeps Faith Fresh

Another good reason to evangelize the evangelists is to keep our faith fresh. Have you ever put a weak battery into a flashlight? The light is pretty dim—if you get any at all. But if you recharge the battery, you'll have plenty of light to see your way.

It's the same way with faith. When it has been a long time since we have spent time with God in worship, Bible study, or Christian fellowship, our faith life shows it. Our light grows weak and dim. But when the Spirit evangelizes us, our faith picks up power. Now there's plenty of light—for us and for the people with whom we share God's love.

We Are Motivated to Evangelize

Experiencing God's love motivates us to evangelize others. C. S. Lewis writes:

All enjoyment spontaneously overflows into praise. . . . The world rings with praise . . . readers [praising] their favorite poet, walkers praising the countryside, players praising their favorite game—praise of weather, wines, dishes, actors, motors, horses, colleges, countries, historical personages, children, flowers, mountains, rare stamps, rare beetles, even sometimes politicians or scholars. . . . I think we delight to praise what we enjoy because the praise not merely expresses but completes the enjoyment; it is its appointed consummation.[2]

It's only natural to praise what you love and enjoy, to tell others about it with enthusiasm. It's only natural that, when you find something wonderful, you want to tell others about it.

Expressing praise begins with experiencing the praiseworthy thing. Before we want to tell others—before we *can* tell others—*we* need to be in touch with God. As we are evangelized, we will find it easier, even a pleasure, to share that joy with someone else.

We Relate More Compassionately to Others with Needs

Being evangelized is a process of facing our own need for God, over and over again. If we're being evangelized, we can't ignore our difficulties, or pretend that, as Christians we have it all together.

Staying in touch with our own need for God makes us better able to relate to others with needs. We will avoid talking about God in ways that make people feel inferior (while building ourselves up at their expense). Instead we can share, as honestly as possible, our own continuing need for God, and how God rescues us again and again.

Amazingly enough, this is part of what makes Caring Evangelism so effective. People can see that we are also struggling, that we share their frustration and confusion as we try to make sense out of living in this world of hurt. If we struggle just like they do, and have found hope in Christ, it is easier for them to believe Jesus might help them also.

We Better Understand the Process of Growing in Faith

Some people are reluctant to share God's Good News with others because they don't know what they would do if the other person answered, "Yes, I'm interested. What do I do now?" They are uncertain about how to help someone else grow in God.

When we are continually growing spiritually, we understand more of the process of growing in faith. We become better able to walk along that path with others, helping them know what might come next in their walk with God and giving them the information and support they need at each step. We know, because we've been there before.

Take this example. Someone says to you, "Everything was so wonderful right after my conversion. Now all the excitement has died down. Sometimes I don't even feel like praying, and this scares me. Does it mean I'm not really a Christian?"

If you've been through a similar experience of doubt and growth, you will be able to help. You can assure the person that low periods are a normal part of Christian life, and that you've been through them also. You can listen caringly while the other person talks about his or her feelings. Then you can share with him or her the things that have helped you—talking with a Christian friend, joining a Bible study to learn more about God, or pouring out feelings to God in prayer.

Evangelization Never Ends

God's loving actions for us don't end when we become Christians. That is only the beginning. God wants us to live lives that are full of Jesus' love and that imitate Jesus' life of service to God and others. God is at work in us every time we repent and turn to God for forgiveness and new life, every time we are filled with the joy of knowing how much God loves us, every time we make the hard choices involved in dying to ourselves and living for others. God works through our fellow Christians. Together we are the body of Christ. God blesses us with growth, renewed faith, and more abundant life as we constantly work to evangelize each other.

In the next chapter this evangelization process is presented in more detail. This will help you better understand how you can grow in God's love and then walk with others along the path of coming to faith in Jesus.

[1]Richard Foster, *Celebration of Discipline, Revised Edition* (San Francisco: Harper & Row, 1978, 1988), p. 7.

[2]C. S. Lewis, *Reflections on the Psalms* (New York: Harcourt, Brace & World, Inc., 1958), pp. 94-95.

Chapter 3

Growing in God

"The stuff you talked about on the retreat really got through to me," I told Jim while we ate lunch at the picnic table the Monday after the retreat. "But you left me with a problem I don't know how to solve."

Jim smiled and said, "Good." When he saw my surprised reaction he said, "Often, when we work on problems we don't know how to solve, that's God helping us grow. Tell me about what you've been thinking."

"My neighbor across the street just lost her husband," I said. "I took some supper last week and talked to her for a while. I think she's really lonely. I can't stop thinking about her. I really feel bad for her. I feel like I should do something, and I'm not sure I want to."

"What do you mean?" Jim asked.

"Well, when I went over to visit Margaret—that's my neighbor's name—I left with the feeling that she's going through this really tough time and she doesn't even have God to rely on to help her."

Jim asked, "What makes you think that?"

"I'm just putting together some clues." I told Jim about my visit with Margaret, the conversations Sarah and I had about evangelism, and the things I realized on the retreat. Then I said, "I don't know how much sense all this makes, but I've decided I'm not going to let being scared keep me from helping her—that is, if she even needs my help. But that's where I get stuck. How do I know if she's a Christian or if she even wants to be? And what if she is interested in God? What would I do then? I don't know how to lead someone to Jesus, or whatever it is you're supposed to do. I don't even know where to start."

Jim was silent for a moment. Then he asked, "Where did you start?"

"What do you mean? Where did I start what?"

"With God. Where did you start to know God?"

"That was so long ago."

"Well, what about right now? You're getting to know God better right now. What you've been telling me is the beginning of another chapter in your story with God. So where did you start out?"

"I don't know. Two weeks ago I didn't even know that I needed another chapter in my story with God. What are you getting at?"

"I think there's a process we go through as we grow up as Christians. One way to learn how you can help another person get to know God better is to understand how that happened for you."

"What kind of process? Tell me more."

Many Christians ask the same questions Andy did. How do people discover where others are in their spiritual lives? What happens as people grow in God?

The purpose of this chapter is to answer these questions.

The Caring Evangelization Cycle

The Caring Evangelization Cycle is one way of understanding how people grow in their faith in Jesus. The Caring Evangelization Cycle is a process people can go through as they come to see their need for a Savior, appreciate that Savior's love, and respond with faith to the relationship God offers in Jesus.

The symbol at the center of the cycle is a *Chi Rho,* a symbol for Christ. It reminds us of the truth that our evangelizing and our growth in God takes place always and only because of Jesus. Even though the cycle talks about things we do, we know that these steps are only possible because the Holy Spirit makes them possible.

Let's consider each of the steps in the Caring Evangelization Cycle. We'll see how Saul the persecutor, who later became the Apostle Paul, moved through these steps in his own conversion experience (Acts 9:1-19; Gal. 1:11-24).

1. God Reaches Out to Us, So That . . .

For all of us, our journey around the Caring Evangelization Cycle starts with God reaching out to us in love. From Genesis 1:31 ("God saw everything that he had made, and indeed, it was very good") to John 3:16 ("For God so loved the world that he gave his only Son, so that everyone who believes in him may not perish but may have eternal life"), to name only two examples, the Bible tells us over and over about God's constant and unchanging love for us. God never stops reaching out with love for us, as the Psalmist says: "For the Lord is good; his steadfast love endures forever, and his faithfulness to all generations." (Ps. 100:5)

God's Initiative

The Apostle Paul said, "For while we were still weak, at the right time Christ died for the ungodly. Indeed, rarely will anyone die for a righteous person—though perhaps for a good person someone might actually dare to die. But God proves his love for us in that while we still were sinners Christ died for us." (Rom. 5:6-8) Paul shows that it is necessary for God to take the initiative. Without the Spirit empowering us, we aren't even able to know about our need for God or ask for God's help.

God Reached Out to Paul

God reached out to Paul in many ways. From his childhood Paul had studied the Scriptures, and he knew them extremely well. Undoubtedly even then God was reaching out to Paul through Scripture to show him the truth about the Messiah. God also reached out to Paul through Christians. Acts 7 tells us that Paul was there listening when Stephen witnessed to Christ and was killed for it. Then Paul himself began persecuting Christians, going to house after house in Jerusalem, "dragging off both men and women, he committed them to prison." (Acts 8:3) During that time Paul must have heard many Christians witness to Jesus.

Finally, God reached out to Paul in a very dramatic way, while he was traveling to the city of Damascus in order to arrest Christians there.

> Now as he was going along and approaching Damascus, suddenly a light from heaven flashed around him. He fell to the ground and heard a voice saying to him, "Saul, Saul, why do you persecute me?" He asked, "Who are you, Lord?" The reply came, "I am Jesus, whom you are persecuting." (Acts 9:3-5)

As a result of God's initiating love, Saul the persecutor became Paul the Christian, the evangelist, and finally the martyr.

God's Goal

Step 1, God reaching out to us, is what makes steps 2-6 possible. God keeps working in our lives to help us see our need for Jesus to forgive us our sin, to give us the faith we need to trust Jesus for everything, and through Christian community to make us into people who are more and more like Jesus. None of these steps can happen without the Spirit's power and direction.

2. We Experience the Failure of Our False Gods

Jesus told a story about one person who built a house on sand and another who built the house on a solid foundation of rock.

> Everyone then who hears these words of mine and acts on them will be like a wise man who built his house on rock. The rain fell, the floods came, and the winds blew and beat on that house, but it did not fall, because it had been founded on rock. And everyone who hears these words of mine and does not act on them will be like a foolish man who built his house on sand. The rain fell, and the floods came, and the winds blew and beat against that house, and it fell—and great was its fall! (Matt. 7:24-27)

Everyone experiences crises that expose the ways in which our lives are built on sand instead of rock. So often we build our security and happiness on things—money, work, relationships, even alcohol or other drugs. When something very difficult, or maybe even something very wonderful, happens, we feel our foundations crumble. Our old ways of maintaining our security and happiness no longer work. Our lives seem to be falling apart and we don't know how to make things better.

Ideally, when such a crisis occurs we would turn immediately to God for help. Usually, however, this is not the case. Instead we keep trying to make our old ways of doing things work. Or we try to find a different stop-gap solution to solve our problems, or at least to take away our pain. But nothing helps.

In this kind of a crisis situation we experience the failure of our false gods. We realize that instead of placing all our trust and hope in the one true God, we have kept certain parts of our lives under our own control. We have been counting on things or human relationships to provide the happiness, security, and hope that only God can provide. But all these false gods have something in common—they always fail. They simply can't deliver what we need from them.

Paul Experiences the Failure of His False Gods

The experience on the road to Damascus was a crisis for Paul. The Christians turned out to be right—Jesus *was* the Savior God sent. And Paul, who had considered himself a servant of God, had been persecuting the Christians—and, therefore, God. Paul had counted on his own knowledge of God and his religious zeal to make God love him. These false gods were now exposed.

When Paul got up he was blind (Acts 9:8-9). Paul's blindness was a physical change that mirrored his spiritual state. Both literally and figuratively, Paul didn't know where he was going anymore. The men with him led him into the city, and Paul spent three days there fasting and praying.

3. We Admit Our Powerlessness, Our Need for a Savior

As our false gods fall away we see ourselves more clearly. We see that we have important needs, such as hope, security, and happiness, that go right to the core of who we are—but we are unable to meet those needs on our own. We see that we need someone stronger, wiser, and more loving than we to help us solve our most serious problems. Without that help we are doomed to helplessness and unhappiness.

This realization can be terrifying. If we have always prided ourselves on self-sufficiency, it can be very difficult to learn that we have no choice but to rely on another.

It's only by God's grace that we can face this truth about ourselves—and we will probably only see small parts of our basic powerlessness at any one time. But the Holy Spirit can help us see that we cannot make our lives what we want them to be on our own—we need a Savior. This is the third step in the cycle.

Paul Faced the Truth

During those dark days in Damascus, Paul faced the truth about himself. He had been wrong—completely, absolutely wrong. He had done great harm to the people of the very God he thought he was serving. And now he had to start over, from the very beginning. His old way of thinking and living had to change. It no longer fit the truth he knew. The entire life Paul had built for himself lay in ruins around him. Paul needed a Savior.

4. We Receive and Believe in Jesus

During this time of helplessness, God comes to us. Like the prodigal son who saw his father running down the road to meet him (Luke 15:11-32), we look up and see Jesus Christ rescuing us, providing for our every need, and making us God's own children. All of this is a free gift from God, who loves us.

All the good gifts that Almighty God gives us are ours for the asking. When we think we can earn or deserve them, the deal's off. We know that Jesus has already been good enough, obedient enough, religious enough for all of us for the rest of eternity. All God's treasures are opened to us. We are the beloved children of the God who rules the universe. There is nothing we need that God will refuse us.

Paul Was Baptized

While Paul was praying and fasting in Damascus, God was already caring for him. God told another Christian in the city, a man named Ananias, to go visit Paul and heal him. Ananias laid his hands on Paul and said, "'Brother Saul, the Lord Jesus, who appeared to you on your way here, has sent me so that you may regain your sight and be filled with the Holy Spirit.' And immediately something like scales fell from his eyes, and his sight was restored. Then he got up and was baptized." (Acts 9:17-18) The Holy Spirit replaced Paul's doubt and self-accusation with faith and trust in God. Paul became a member of God's family.

5. We Grow in Christian Community

The fifth step in the cycle is growing in Christian community. Christianity is not a solitary lifestyle—it was never intended to be. God knows that we need each other, and so God provides us with Christian brothers and sisters in Christ to encourage and support us. Jesus promises to be with us in special ways when we gather together with other Christians (Matt. 18:20). We have already seen in chapter 2 how the Holy Spirit evangelizes us through the Gospel message that is communicated in many different ways in Christian community.

God Gave Paul Christian Community

God did this with Paul also. God sent Ananias to visit Paul and to touch him at a time when Paul may have felt untouchable. Then Ananias called Paul "brother." What a wonderful gift of encouragement and love!

Later Paul became active in the church at Damascus. When he traveled to Jerusalem, a Christian brother named Barnabas (whose name means "Encourager") welcomed him and smoothed his way in the church. In his letters to various churches, Paul very often spoke of the wonderful support and love his sisters and brothers in Christ showed him that made his ministry possible.

6. We Serve God and People

As we grow and mature in Christ's love, it is only natural for us to respond to the Holy Spirit's call to serve (John 13:12-17, 34; John 15:12; Phil. 2:5-8). Christian service is the natural result of knowing God's love. This is the sixth step in the cycle.

The Holy Spirit gives every Christian the ability to serve. Whether we pray, teach, visit, listen, evangelize, or take care of the physical needs of others, we are serving God and building up the body of Christ, his Church. All of us are necessary for God's work, and it can be exciting to discover the special gifts God has given each of us for service!

Jesus said service is necessary for every Christian. The last time he and his disciples were together before Jesus was crucified he washed their feet. Here's what happened next.

> After he had washed their feet, had put on his robe, and had returned to the table, he said to them, "Do you know what I have done to you? You call me Teacher and Lord—and you are right, for that is what I am. So if I, your Lord and Teacher, have washed your feet, you also ought to wash one another's feet. For I have set you an example, that you also should do as I have done to you. Very truly, I tell you, servants are not greater than their master, nor are messengers greater than the one who sent them. If you know these things, you are blessed if you do them." (John 13:12-17)

Paul Served

According to the book of Acts, Paul began almost immediately to serve God by telling people in Damascus about Jesus.

Supported by the church at Antioch, he made several trips as a missionary, encouraging churches and starting new congregations. In loving concern for these Christians, he wrote them letters that became many of the books in the New Testament. His aim was to serve the Lord who had loved him so completely.

How We Move through the Cycle

The steps in the Caring Evangelization Cycle don't always happen in this order. Sometimes a person will skip back and forth in the cycle, perhaps trying to serve God (step 6) only to discover he or she needs to become better grounded in faith first (steps 1-4). He or she might then turn to Christian community for help (step 5). However, the sequence given above is a common one.

The Caring Evangelization Cycle is in the form of a circle because all of us need to continue growing as faithful disciples of Jesus. Evangelism doesn't stop at conversion. The Caring Evangelization Cycle not only describes how a person might come to believe in Jesus for the first time, but it also shows the steps we take again and again as we keep growing in God.

God Is at Work

Paul wrote to the Philippian church:

I thank my God every time I remember you, constantly praying with joy in every one of my prayers for all of you, because of your sharing in the gospel from the first day until now. I am confident of this, that the one who began a good work among you will bring it to completion by the day of Jesus Christ. (Phil. 1:3-6)

Just as the Philippians did, we continue to grow, to mature, to be transformed more and more into the image of Jesus. Even as we "work out our own salvation," or help others to do so, we know that God is the one who is really at work. It's impossible for us to manufacture our own spiritual growth. It is all a gift from our gracious God.

How We Help Others Move through the Cycle

The Caring Evangelization Cycle is a useful tool for us as caring evangelists because it helps us understand what is happening in the spiritual journey of a person we are evangelizing. But how can we help others move through the steps of the

Caring Evangelization Cycle? The outer layer of the Caring Evangelization Cycle helps us answer this question.

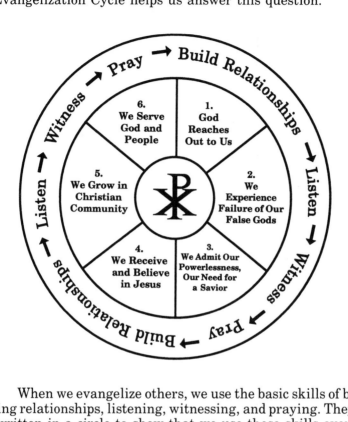

When we evangelize others, we use the basic skills of building relationships, listening, witnessing, and praying. They are written in a circle to show that we use these skills over and over again through the process of evangelizing others. The rest of this book will show how to develop and use these skills.

Chapter 4

Process-Oriented Evangelism

After supper that evening, Sarah and I sat in the living room and talked for a while. The weather had turned cold so we had a fire in the fireplace and we sat and watched it while we talked.

"Tell me about your retreat," she said.

I described the various retreat activities and then told her about Jim's talk on Saturday night.

Then I said, "You know how sometimes you say something and you're absolutely sure you're right and then you start thinking about it and you start having all these doubts and you find yourself wishing you hadn't been so . . . I don't know . . . emphatic or positive or something when you were talking?"

She stared at the ceiling and tried to make sense out of that paragraph of a sentence. Finally she said, "In other words, you stuck your foot in your mouth."

"I suppose you could put it that way . . ."

She chimed in, "But you were trying to avoid actually coming out and saying you put your foot in your mouth."

I saw she was ready to laugh so I gave in and admitted she was right.

"Okay," I continued, "so that's the way I've been feeling ever since we talked about Margaret last weekend. I said that there was no way I would ever talk to her about church or God, but then I thought about all the reasons I had given and they all sounded pretty weak to me.

"Then while I was thinking about what Jim said at the retreat it came to me that the real reason I didn't want to talk to Margaret about God is that I'm scared to."

Sarah said, "Noooooo," with mock seriousness. Then she saw that I was really serious so she said, "I'm sorry for kidding around. This is important to you. Go ahead."

"So I talked to Jim over lunch today and he helped me understand more about talking to people about God. He said I can understand what it's like for other people by looking at how I've grown in my own relationship with God. Probably other people won't have exactly the same experience, but their experience will be similar."

Sarah thought about that for a moment and then said, "Okay, that makes sense."

"Anyway, I can't stop thinking about this and I really feel like I should do something, so I'm going to go over there and invite her to come to church with us next Sunday. Then we can introduce her to Pastor Ed. I'm sure she'll like him. Then I thought we could take her out for brunch—you know, treat her like a guest. Besides, maybe the brunch offer will convince her to come to church. Or— here's a good idea—we could see if Pastor Ed and Susan want to come to brunch with Margaret and us. That'd be great. Then we can just start taking her to church with us every week until she gets used to it, makes some friends. Then maybe she can start driving herself. What do you think?"

"I think you need to ask Margaret what she thinks before you make all these plans."

I felt a little hurt. "What are you trying to say? I'm really feeling enthusiastic about this, like it's the right thing to do. Are you trying to throw a wet blanket on all my plans?"

Sarah took a deep breath, folded her hands in her lap, and looked me straight in the eyes. "No, I don't want to dampen your enthusiasm. I think it's wonderful. But I do think you ought to find out what Margaret wants before you spring all these plans on her."

"Okay, you're probably right. But I really think I'm on to something here. I got to know God at church, especially when Pastor Ed came and I started learning from him. I'm sure it'll work for her too. So I'm going to go over there right now and see if she's home."

"All right," Sarah said, "but just remember what she's been through."

When Margaret opened the door she looked happy to see me.

"Oh, Andy, please come in."

She took my coat and hung it in the hall closet. Then she ushered me into the living room, where she had a fire going. There was a photograph album open on the coffee table with a half-empty cup of tea beside it.

Margaret motioned for me to sit down on the sofa and said, "I was just having some tea. Would you like some?"

"No, thanks. Keeps me awake. Thanks, though."

Margaret walked into the kitchen and called back over her shoulder, "I've got your casserole dish here to give back to you. I've been meaning to bring it over . . ."

She handed the dish to me and I set it on the floor by the sofa and said, "Thanks."

Margaret sat on the other end of the sofa, by the photograph album. "I was just looking at some old pictures," she said. "The neighborhood really looked different twenty years ago."

I looked at the pictures. "The trees are a lot bigger now."

"Uh huh."

I saw an old picture with a man standing in front of Margaret's house. I pointed and asked, "Is that Roy?"

"Yes." She took a sip of tea and brushed a strand of hair back from her face. "I've been looking at old pictures . . . remembering."

I saw a box of tissues on the floor and thought, *She's been crying.* I said, "You must have a lot of memories in this house."

She nodded and turned the page of the photo album. There was a picture of her daughter, Emily. There were photographs of people at a barbecue in the backyard of some former neighbors, Francisco and Lupe Gomez, who always had the best parties every year.

I really enjoyed chatting with Margaret, talking about our families, and looking at pictures for about a half hour, but then I remembered why I had come over in the first place.

"Where is your son now?" Margaret asked. I had to ask her to repeat the question because I hadn't been listening, I'd been trying to figure out how I was going to bring up the subject of church. Margaret repeated her question, but I saw that she was sitting a little straighter, less relaxed.

I answered her question, but then the conversation started to drag. Margaret yawned behind her hand and then closed the photograph album. I started to feel panic because I knew I'd have to leave soon and I hadn't said anything about church. I started to feel angry at God for bringing the whole thing up in the first place.

Finally, when I saw Margaret look at her watch, I blurted out, "Don't you think you should go to church?"

She didn't say anything or even look at me. I felt furious with myself for saying it that way. The silence seemed to last forever. I felt my face get very warm and I started to sweat.

I tried to repair the damage. "I didn't say that right at all." She looked up at me. She was sitting stiffly and formally, her hands folded in her lap. "What I mean is that Sarah and I have been talking about you." She raised an eyebrow.

I felt like swearing. I spoke deliberately, "We have been thinking that you're all alone and that it's probably pretty . . . I don't know . . . lonely, I guess, being here . . . all by yourself, I mean . . . now that Roy is dead . . . I mean gone. And we thought that if you got to know God . . . or our pastor . . . or, I don't know, somebody at church . . . it might help."

I stopped, hoping she'd say something. Instead she looked at her watch again.

"We'll take you out to brunch . . ."

"I'm sure that's a very kind offer, Mr. Simons. Thank you very much, but I'm afraid I need to turn in, so if there's nothing else?"

I wondered if I should try to argue with her, convince her that she should come to church with me. Then I decided against it, got up, mumbled a good-bye, and beat a hasty retreat.

As soon as I was out the door she turned the porch light off. I smacked myself on the side of the head in frustration. It was a long, long walk across the street.

When I reached my front door, I just stood there. I didn't want to have to go in and tell Sarah what had happened, so I stood out there for a couple of minutes. As I finally reached for the door knob I realized I'd left the casserole dish on the floor by Margaret's sofa.

Two Conversations

Consider the following two conversations. As you read them, ask yourself the following questions:

- Which of these ways of witnessing would be more comfortable for me?

- Which would be more comfortable for the person being evangelized?

- Which would be more likely to begin a relationship in which the evangelist could more effectively share the love and care of Jesus?

The First Conversation

Frank: "Hi, I'm Frank. I'll be working in the same department as you. This is your first day here, isn't it?"

Carl: "Hi, Frank. I'm Carl. I guess you can tell I'm new here by the confused look on my face."

Frank: "Oh, don't worry, it'll get better soon. Are you new in the city also?"

Carl: "Yeah, we just moved in last week. We're still trying to find our way around."

Frank: "Have you found a church yet?"

Carl: "Well, no. My family and I just aren't really churchgoers, I guess."

Frank: "Oh, don't say that! Everyone needs God in their lives. You know that, don't you?"

Carl: "Well, I guess . . . but we just don't have time on Sundays."

Frank: "That's just an excuse. If you set your priorities right, you can always get in some time for God. Tell you what, this Sunday we're having a special evangelism service at my church. I'll pick you up and take you."

Carl: "But I can't. I've got to watch the kids while my wife's at work."

Frank: "So bring the kids! We have a special program just for them. They'll love it. Besides, you *do* want your kids to have all the blessings God can give them, don't you?"

Carl: "Well, yes, I guess."

Frank: "Then it's settled. Believe me, you won't regret this. Now, let me have your address . . ."

A Different Conversation

Frank: "Hi, I'm Frank. I'll be working in the same department as you. This is your first day here, isn't it?"

Carl: "Yes, it is. My name is Carl. I guess you can tell I'm new. I feel pretty confused."

Frank: "Yeah, the first day can be tough. Are you new in the city also?"

Carl: "Uh huh, we just moved in last week. We're still trying to find our way around."

Frank: "I remember. I had to take a map almost everywhere I went for the entire first year. Do you know anybody here yet?"

Carl: "Well, not really. I've been introduced to a lot of people at work, but I keep forgetting their names."

Frank: "That can be embarrassing."

Carl: *(smiles)* "This morning I pretended to remember some-one I hadn't even met."

Frank: *(laughs)* "Have you met any of your neighbors at home?"

Carl: "Yeah . . . they seem okay, but I don't know . . . people here just don't seem as friendly as they are where I came from."

Frank: "It sounds like you miss your old friends."

Carl: "I do . . . and the kids do, too. They don't know anyone at school yet. I think they wish they had some friends to talk to and do things with."

Frank: "How old are they?"

Carl: "They're both in junior high right now. That's a hard age to lose friends. I wish they could meet some new people."

Frank: "I know what you mean. I have three teenagers and they had the same problem when we moved here last year."

Carl: "What did you do?"

Frank: "The thing that really helped was we'd been going to this church for a few weeks and they had a picnic. My kids met some friends there and from then on things were okay."

Carl: "If kids can find at least one friend, that seems to make the difference."

Frank: "Yeah, you're right. *(Thinks for a moment)* You know, that picnic's coming up again. Do you think your family might be interested in coming with us?"

Carl: "Well, I'm not sure. We haven't been to church in a long time. Let me think about it."

Frank: "Okay, sure. Just let me know. Did anyone show you where the lunch room is, yet?"

Results Orientation vs. Process Orientation

These imaginary conversations illustrate two very different ways of relating and evangelizing.

In the first conversation the evangelist is very controlling. Frank has an answer to every objection, and he's not going to give up until he argues, shames, or bullies Carl into saying he will bring his family to church. This is an example of evangeliz-ing with a *results orientation*. A results orientation is a style of relating in which people care more about getting their own way and controlling others than they do about the needs, feelings, or well-being of others.

The second conversation illustrates evangelizing with a *process orientation.* In process-oriented evangelism the emphasis is on caring for others and sharing Christ's love with them. The results are left up to God. In this second example, Frank does his best to care for Carl, listen to him, understand his needs, and share how his church might be able to meet one of those needs. Frank doesn't consider it his duty to force Carl to accept his invitation.

Caring Evangelism is always process-oriented evangelism. Let's consider the differences between results- and process-oriented evangelism.

Results-Oriented Evangelism

It can be very easy to slip into a results orientation in evangelism. Results-oriented evangelists often use any tactics they can think of to get the other person to come to church or make a decision for Jesus as quickly as possible—even bullying, manipulating, and making people feel guilty. They might make comments like these:

- *"Of course* you can find time for church on Sunday. You can always find time if it's important enough. You just have to get your priorities straight."

- "I'm sure God would be glad to see you in Bible class more often."

- "I'm sorry to hear the bad news, but maybe this crisis wouldn't have happened if you'd been more faithful in your Christian life."

- "Don't you think your kids should have the benefit of a Christian education? I wouldn't let *my* kids miss out."

These comments come from good motives—in each case, the speaker is honestly concerned about the other person's relationship with God. There's nothing wrong with that. But there *is* a problem when concern for the spiritual life of another person makes an evangelist lose sight of the other's feelings and needs right now. Too often this leaves the other person feeling battered, bewildered, and angry.

Process-Oriented Evangelism

Process-oriented evangelism is very different. Here the emphasis is on the relationship rather than on the desired results. As process-oriented evangelists we don't try to control people or force them to change; instead we concentrate on caring for people by listening to them, trying to understand them, relating to them in a nonjudgmental way, and witnessing to them at the right time. The results are up to them and God.

Process-oriented evangelizing happens when:

- Jane listens to her friend Andrea talk about the problems of being a single parent. Instead of immediately saying, "Jesus can solve all your problems," Jane accepts Andrea, problems and all. Jane listens, tries to understand, and gently witnesses when Andrea seems to be open to hearing about God's love.

- Sam, a Christian for many years, models God's love by caring for Roger who is grieving for the death of his wife. Sam shows God's care by helping Roger with shopping, cooking, and cleaning. He prays for Roger daily, and Roger knows this. Sam spends a lot of time listening to Roger sort out his feelings, even when it means that Sam misses out on activities he enjoys. Roger finally becomes curious about the God who inspires this kind of love.

- Al, a police officer, gently witnesses to his partner, Cristina, over a period of years. When Cristina argues or criticizes Christianity, Al tries hard to understand what she thinks and believes. When Cristina asks questions, Al answers honestly and authentically out of his own experience. Finally Cristina indicates an interest in going to church, and Al invites her to come with him the following Sunday.

As process-oriented evangelists, we care for people "over the long haul." We don't expect that others' problems will go away quickly or that they will change overnight. We care out of love and obedience to Jesus, even when that is difficult.

Of course we hope that people we care for will develop a relationship with Jesus. But we don't force people to go along with our plans for this. We care for people as they are, and we allow the Spirit to work out God's plan.

Comparing Results- and Process-Oriented Evangelism

The following table compares results and process orientations from five different perspectives, in order to give a clearer idea of how they differ. Following the table each of the comparisons is discussed in greater detail.

Results-Oriented Evangelists...	Process-Oriented Evangelists...
1. try to do for others what only God can do.	1. concentrate on what they themselves can do and leave the rest to God.
2. try to solve others' problems and impose "cures" on them.	2. concentrate on caring for others.
3. try to make decisions for others and decide what is best for them, which fosters dependency.	3. help others see their own needs and find their own solutions, which helps people relate to God independently of the evangelist's control.
4. use evangelizing to satisfy their own needs to feel successful, important, justified, or in control, which is self-centered.	4. focus their evangelizing on understanding and meeting the needs of others, which is other-centered.
5. try to control the behavior of others.	5. try to control their own behavior.

1. Doing What You Can vs. Doing What Only God Can

Occasionally you may hear evangelists talk about how many souls they have saved. This kind of talk can be very misleading. Jesus Christ is the only one who saves. Sometimes Jesus uses individuals as instruments to reach other people, but we need to remember that it is God and God alone who brings people to faith.

What Only God Can Do

As evangelists, it is important for us to remember the distinction between what only God can do and what we are able to do. Only God can:

- convince people of their sin and their need for a Savior (John 16:8-9);
- give people faith (John 1:12-13; Eph. 2:8-9);
- defeat death and give eternal life (John 10:27-29; John 11:25; 1 Cor. 15:51-57);
- forgive sin and free people from guilt (Ps. 51:7; Isa. 1:18; Ps. 130:7; Ps. 32:5; 1 John 1:9);

- bring people to conversion and repentance (John 16:7-11; John 14:6; Acts 11:17-18; 2 Tim. 2:25);
- give people real peace (Ps. 4:8; Isa. 9:6, 26:3; John 14:27, 16:33; Rom. 5:1-2; Phil. 4:6-7); and
- give people lasting hope (Rom. 15:13; 2 Thess. 2:16-17; 1 Pet. 1:3).

What We Can Do

As evangelists, *we* can:

- listen with accepting love;
- build a trusting, caring relationship;
- model Christ's love by helping others who are sad, lonely, depressed, or who have other needs;
- try to understand the feelings, needs, beliefs, ideas, and hopes of others;
- pray for others;
- witness assertively when others seem open to hearing; and
- invite others to attend church or to begin a relationship with Jesus when they are ready for such an invitation.

Realizing this can be very freeing. God doesn't hold us responsible for the results of our witness! It is our job to care, to witness, and to live the love of Christ for others as much as we can. It is God's job, not ours, to bring these people into a relationship with Jesus. What a relief to leave this responsibility in God's hands!

2. Care vs. Cure

Another good way to think about the difference between results-oriented and process-oriented evangelism is to think of them in terms of *care* vs. *cure*. When people are sick we care for them by giving them special food and drink, making sure they rest, giving them medicine, and seeing that they receive needed professional medical care. But no one, not even a physician, can make them get well. Only God can do that. We do all our caring so that God can do the curing.

When people evangelize others in a results-oriented way, *they* take the responsibility for changing the beliefs and behaviors of others. They believe they have the right, the ability, and the duty to change others "for their own good."

But most of the time these cures don't work. Then they may become very discouraged about their witnessing. They may also blame others, saying that they didn't try hard enough, have enough faith, or follow directions well enough. The others end up even more alienated from God and the evangelists end up feeling either guilty or self-righteous.

In process-oriented evangelism, we don't try to cure others. Instead, we concentrate on what we *can* do: caring for others, sharing our own experiences, or, if necessary, even sacrificing our own immediate needs for the sake of others. God takes care of the cure in God's own way and time.

3. Creating Dependence vs. Facilitating Independence

With a results orientation, evangelists make decisions for others and decide what is best for them—whether this means going to church more often, stopping a bad habit, or beginning a relationship with Jesus. This tends to make others dependent on evangelists. Here's an example of how this can happen.

Creating Dependence

Janet was very concerned about the spiritual well-being of Katherine, a co-worker. Janet decided that Katherine needed to start going to church, and she nagged her about it until Katherine finally gave in and promised to find a church near her home. But Janet said, "Oh, no! I want you to come to church with me. I need to be sure you go to the right kind of church. I'll pick you up Sunday morning."

Even though Katherine lived 30 minutes away from Janet's church, Janet gave her a ride every Sunday morning for three months. Katherine never offered to drive herself or to help pay for the gasoline. She only attended church because Janet pushed her. Finally Janet became frustrated with Katherine. When Janet stopped providing transportation, Katherine stopped attending. When people at Janet's church asked her where Katherine was, Janet said, "I guess Katherine's conversion wasn't real. She just isn't as committed to Jesus as she needs to be."

Real, lasting change only comes from within a person; it cannot be imposed from the outside. If an evangelist tries to force others to change, they will stay changed only as long as the pressure is on. This leaves them dependent on the evangelist, and that's not healthy.

Facilitating Independence

On the other hand, evangelizing with a process orientation works to make others independent of us and healthily dependent on God. We don't spend our time policing the actions of others; instead, we let them take responsibility for their own spiritual growth with the Holy Spirit's help and guidance.

This means that the spiritual growth that happens is real and lasting. We haven't forced it on others—it comes from God's grace and their own choices and decisions. That makes their growth in God much more permanent. We can rest assured that, even when we are no longer in touch with these people, they will be able to continue growing in their relationships with God.

Consider what might have happened if Janet had been process-oriented in her evangelism.

Instead of nagging Katherine to go to church, Janet developed a friendship with Katherine. As they got to know each other, Janet began to understand what it was like for Katherine to be alone in a new city with few friends.

Janet remembered how lonely she had felt when she first moved into the area, and how she had found friends at her new church. Gently she asked Katherine if she would like to meet some of her friends at their Christian small group meeting. When Katherine looked uncomfortable, Janet dropped the subject and suggested they go out for lunch.

As the weeks went by, Janet continued to model the love of Christ in her relationship with Katherine. She kept listening, praying, and simply being there for her. Katherine noticed this, and one day she asked, "Most of the people around here are okay, but they don't really have time to listen or really talk. But you've always been there for me. Why are you different?"

Janet told Katherine very briefly and gently about the difference Christ made for her. When Katherine seemed interested, Janet said, "There's a new group starting at my church just to talk about subjects like this. Would you like to go with me?" Katherine agreed.

Katherine finally decided she wanted to join a church, but they both agreed that Janet's church was too far away. Katherine asked Janet to visit several nearby churches with her. They found a church where Katherine felt welcome. Janet attended with Katherine for several months until Katherine became comfortable at her new church. Finally Katherine joined that church, while Janet returned to her own congregation.

Since Janet gave Katherine the care and respect that come with a process orientation, Katherine was able to make her own choices about church and begin a strong relationship with God and with a congregation.

4. Self-Centered vs. Other-Centered

Still another way of looking at results vs. process is to say that evangelizing with a results orientation is *self-centered,* and a process orientation is *other-centered.* A results orientation is often selfish because the evangelist is trying to meet his or her own needs, instead of the needs of the other person.

Examples of Self-Centered Evangelism

How do people use evangelism to meet their own needs? One way is by evangelizing in order to get rid of guilt feelings. Rebecca Manley Pippert describes the way she used evangelism to do this:

> There was a part of me that secretly felt evangelism was something you shouldn't do to your dog, let alone a friend . . . And because it was so hard to do I thought such evangelism had to be spiritual. The result was that I would put off witnessing as long as possible. Whenever the guilt became too great to bear, I overpowered the nearest non-Christian with a nonstop running monologue and then dashed away thinking, "Whew! Well, I did it. It's spring of '74 and hopefully the guilt won't overcome me again till winter of '75." (And my non-Christian friends hoped the same!)[1]

For what other self-centered reasons might people use evangelism? Let's listen to some imaginary "true confessions." Most of these are not confessions you would ever hear people make, but if some evangelists were to tell the real truth, here's what they might say.

- "I feel powerless in the rest of my life, but when I evangelize, I can have power over others. This makes me feel worthwhile and important."

- "I have some doubts about my Christian faith, but I'm afraid to admit them. Maybe if I prove my beliefs are right to others, I'll feel better about them myself."

- "I always have to be right. I evangelize because I want others to admit I'm right and believe the way I do. If they don't, I feel threatened."

- "I'm out to 'win souls' so that God and the rest of my church will think I'm a good evangelist. I want others to believe I'm spiritually mature."

- "Our church is losing members and having trouble meeting the budget. The church leaders told us that the church will close unless we get more members, so I'm trying to get as many people as possible to join our church."

A process orientation is different because it is other-centered, not self-centered. Instead of trying to meet our own needs, we try to meet the needs of the person we are evangelizing. We listen and care, and then we witness when the person is ready to hear it—*not* when we feel a personal need to speak. We go at the other person's pace.

No evangelist's motives are 100% pure, of course. Everyone has a mixture of self-centered and other-centered reasons for whatever he or she does. People often don't even realize all the reasons why they do what they do. Nevertheless, as caring evangelists we can strive to be as other-centered as possible.

An Example of Other-Centered Evangelism

As other-centered evangelists, we try to forget ourselves and focus on the other. We use every caring and sharing skill we have in order to learn about the other person's needs and to help him or her discover how God can meet those needs.

Jesus practiced this other-centered, process-oriented evangelism. Remember the story of Zacchaeus the tax collector, who climbed up a tree so he could see Jesus when he passed by? Jesus evangelized him by paying attention to Zacchaeus's needs instead of his own.

What needs did Zacchaeus have, and how did Jesus meet them? First of all, Zacchaeus had a need to see Jesus and get as close as possible to him. That was why Zacchaeus climbed the tree—he wasn't tall enough to see over the crowd. Jesus recognized this need in Zacchaeus. Not only did he stop so that Zacchaeus could get a good look at him, but he called Zacchaeus to come down out of the tree, and then invited himself over to Zacchaeus's house for dinner!

Jesus also saw that Zacchaeus had another need—a need for love and acceptance. As a hated tax collector, Zacchaeus wasn't accepted in society. By inviting himself to Zacchaeus's house, Jesus showed him the love and acceptance he needed so greatly.

What about Jesus' own needs? Was there anything self-centered about his evangelism? The grumbling of the crowd gives the answer. "He has gone to be the guest of one who is a sinner." (Luke 19:7) Having dinner with a tax collector was social suicide, and religiously it meant that Jesus was considered ritually unclean. If Jesus had been focusing on his own needs, it would have been better for him not even to speak to Zacchaeus, let alone go home with him! But Jesus' love for

Zacchaeus was so great that he met Zacchaeus's needs instead of his own. Jesus' evangelism was other-centered.

And it worked! Jesus' love gave Zacchaeus the strength and courage to stand before Jesus and say, "Look, half of my possessions, Lord, I will give to the poor; and if I have defrauded anyone of anything, I will pay back four times as much." Then Jesus said to him, "Today salvation has come to this house. . . . For the Son of Man came to seek out and to save the lost." (Luke 19:8-10)

5. Controlling Others vs. Controlling Ourselves

A final way to look at the two orientations is in terms of control. With a results orientation, evangelists try to control the actions and beliefs of others. Evangelists tell themselves they're doing it "for their own good."

This can be very frustrating, though. Others don't like being controlled, and will often resist by doing the opposite of what the results-oriented evangelist thinks they should do. This can leave the evangelist with a feeling of failure, and it can leave others feeling angry and frustrated. They may even end up farther from God.

Why Not Control Others?

But why not control others if it's for their own good? We can find at least a partial answer in the story of God's relationship with Adam and Eve.

When God put people in the Garden of Eden, God gave them one command—"Of the tree of the knowledge of good and evil you shall not eat, for in the day that you eat of it you shall die." (Gen. 2:17) Then God left the choice up to them, whether to obey or disobey. God deliberately chose to create people free, free even to sin, rather than making us robots. God does not control us, although God could. God leaves us free.

In evangelism, we can do no better than to follow God's example. We too must leave others free—free of our control, free to respond to the Holy Spirit's leading as God enables them, and free even to make mistakes if that happens. We can pray for them and care for them, but we may not control them.

Controlling Ourselves

With process orientation, we leave others free. Instead of trying to control them, we focus on controlling *ourselves*—our own actions and reactions in the evangelizing relationship. This is really all we have the right or the power to control, anyway!

Self-control is certainly enough to keep any of us busy.

Caring for others is not always easy. Just paying attention can be extremely difficult at times. It can also be difficult to keep from taking over relationships by offering advice or solutions to others' problems. Living a consistent, Christ-centered witness takes a great deal of concentration, self-discipline, and energy. We can't do it without God's help. But with God's help, we can grow in our ability to live and relate in a self-controlled, process-oriented way.

The Advantages of Process-Oriented Evangelism

Guaranteed Success

When we focus on controlling ourselves instead of the other person, we set ourselves up for success. With God's help we can listen, try to understand others, and respond with accepting love. We can pray. All of these acts are within our control.

This means that we can be successful evangelists—100% of the time! We can measure success in self-control, listening, and care. If the results in the other person's life aren't what we had hoped for, that doesn't mean we're failures. We leave the results to God.

The Surprise of a Process Orientation

"All this is fine," you may be thinking, "but does a process orientation *work*?" The answer is yes!

As a caring evangelist, what kind of results do you want to see? You want to see:

- people coming into a lasting faith relationship with Jesus;
- Christians experiencing greater depth in their relationship with God;
- churches growing, both in numbers and in maturity;
- churches experiencing greater fellowship, joy, and awareness of God's love; and
- Jesus being honored as Lord and Savior by more and more people.

When evangelists try to force this kind of growth, they only get in God's way. They leave others angry and turned off to the message of God's love. But when evangelists trustingly place the results of their evangelizing in God's hands and concentrate instead on caring and communicating God's Good News, they leave the Holy Spirit free to work. And very often, God chooses to work through their caring.

God tells us in Isaiah, "For as the rain and the snow come down from heaven, and do not return there until they have watered the earth, making it bring forth and sprout . . . so shall my word be that goes out from my mouth; it shall not return to me empty, but it shall accomplish that which I purpose, and succeed in the thing for which I sent it." (Isa. 55:10-11) When we evangelize in a process-oriented way we can rest assured that God will take care of the results.

Advantages of a Process Orientation for Others

The advantages of a process orientation for others are clear. They learn about God's love from a person who treats them with respect and care. They actually see the love of God as it is modeled for them by the caring evangelist. This can draw them to Jesus.

Perhaps most important, others don't have to work through the emotional roadblocks of feeling manipulated or forced into religion. They don't have to wonder about ulterior motives in our care for them. With the Spirit's help, people can move past previous bad experiences with the church or evangelism and become free to respond to God's love.

Advantages of a Process Orientation for the Caring Evangelist

When we care in a process-oriented way, we can relax. We leave the results to God.

We don't have to feel pushed, burdened, or coerced into witnessing in ways that are uncomfortable. We can care and share in natural ways, instead of feeling under pressure to use strong-arm tactics that abuse others.

With a process orientation, we can also stop worrying about time. There is no pressure to produce visible results quickly. Remember that the Spirit does God's own work in God's own time. Whether our friends take two weeks or two decades to begin a faith relationship with Jesus, we can relax, knowing that it is in God's hands—not ours.

When we evangelize with a process orientation we are not working alone. We are partners with God, and the Holy Spirit is in charge. Even if we don't have the chance to evangelize people all the way until they come to a new or renewed faith, we can trust the Spirit to complete God's work in their lives.

When you feel free to be natural in your evangelism, and when the pressure for results is taken away, something wonderful can happen. Evangelism can become something to enjoy and look forward to, not something to dread. You may even find that evangelism, the part of Christian life you used to dread most, becomes the part you enjoy most!

[1]Rebecca Manley Pippert, *Out of the Saltshaker & into the World: Evangelism as a Way of Life* (Downers Grove, IL: InterVarsity Press, 1979), p. 16.

Chapter 5

Building an Evangelizing Relationship

When I walked in my front door after the disaster with Margaret, Sarah was on the phone with her sister. I breathed a sigh of relief and went to bed. When Sarah came in later I pretended to be asleep so I wouldn't have to tell her what happened. Actually I hardly slept at all. I just kept replaying the conversation with Margaret over and over again.

The next morning I stopped by Jim's office and asked if he wanted to have lunch together. I breathed a sigh of relief when he said, "Sure."

At lunch I told Jim about the conversation at Margaret's house the night before. When I got to the part about inviting her to brunch he hid his face in his hands and groaned.

"You're a lot of support," I said.

He grinned and said, "Sorry. It's just that I've been there and I know what it feels like."

"You mean I'm not the only one to pull a bonehead stunt like this?"

Jim said, "Of course not. Can I tell you a story?"

I said, "Sure."

"Well, it happened in my first year of college. The day I arrived there were all these information booths set up by various organizations on campus—you know, fraternities, sororities, and service clubs and that kind of thing. I was looking for a Christian organization to belong to and I found a booth for one and signed up.

"A couple of weeks later someone called me and set up a meeting. When I met with him, we chatted for about five minutes and then he pulled out this little booklet and asked if he could share it with me. I said, 'Sure,' and so he proceeded to read the basic facts about Christianity to me out of this booklet. Then he asked me if I wanted to accept Jesus.

"I didn't know what to say. I was already a Christian. I thought he knew that. But I prayed his prayer with him anyway and he gave me this booklet and showed me a place where I could write my name and the date and put it on my refrigerator door or somewhere to remind myself that I was a Christian.

"After that I was in the organization and I became a part of a 'team' with three or four other students. We went to Bible studies once a week, which were pretty good. I learned a lot about God and the Bible. It was also good being with other Christian people. The team would also pray together and memorize Bible passages. All this helped me grow as a young Christian.

"The other thing the team did was to witness. I didn't like that part nearly as well. We would meet at noon at the big, grassy quadrangle area where students would sit in the sun and eat their lunches and study. We would scout around to find someone who was sitting alone and walk up to him and ask if we could join him. If he said yes, we'd find a way to read our booklet to him and try and convince him to be a Christian.

"Sometimes the people we witnessed to would argue with us and tell us that Christianity was just a crutch for emotional weaklings. Other times people would make up an excuse to leave. One time my partner and I witnessed to a student and he said, 'Yes!' He prayed the prayer and took the booklet and said he wanted to be a Christian. We were so shocked that we didn't even find out his address and phone number. We never saw him again. I felt guilty for years after that. Here was this person who had trusted us without even knowing who we were and we just dumped him. I have no clue what happened to him.

"The last time I ever witnessed in this way it was a sort of cloudy, windy day. There weren't very many students sitting on the grass and we were about to give up when we saw a really tall, husky man sitting with his back to a tree about 30 feet from us. This guy was huge. He looked like a lineman on the football team. My partner and I looked at each other and shrugged and walked over to him.

"He was one of the most polite people we'd ever approached. He welcomed us, even offered us some of his lunch. He'd been reading some real thick philosophy book by someone I'd never heard of. We talked for a while and found out his name. I can still remember it. It was James. Not Jim like me . . . James. After a few minutes of small talk my partner pulled his booklet out of his shirt pocket and asked James if he could share the booklet with him.

"James said, 'Sure, I'll take it with me and read it.'

"My partner said he didn't want to do that, he wanted to read the booklet to James, but James could look at it while he was reading it. That was the way we were told to witness, but it didn't sit too well with James.

"James said, 'I'd be happy to take your booklet and read it, but I'm really not interested in listening to you read it to me.'

"My partner was insistent. I started to get very uncomfortable. James stopped smiling and folded his arms across his chest.

"'What's the booklet about?' James asked.

"My partner said, 'It's about Jesus.'

"James just looked at my partner with this expression of disbelief on his face. Finally he asked, 'What do you know about me?'

"My partner started to look worried. 'What do you mean?' he asked.

"James said, 'It's a simple question. Tell me what you know about me.'

"My partner sort of stuttered for a minute. He looked at me and I looked away quickly. Then my partner said, 'Ah . . . your name is James . . . ummm . . . you're taking philosophy—'

"James broke in, 'How do you know I'm taking philosophy? Did I tell you that, or did you just assume it because of the book?'

"My partner shook his head.

"Then James said, 'What is my last name?'

"We couldn't answer.

"James asked, 'Am I already a Christian?' He glared at us, and I felt my face get red. 'Or am I Jewish? Moslem? Buddhist?'

"When neither of us could answer, James continued. 'Before you start reading something to me, don't you think you ought to know who I am? What if someone who claimed to be a Christian just got my sister pregnant and then left her to deal with it on her own? If that were true, don't you think you ought to know that—take it into account? Am I sad because my mother died last week or am I happy because we're celebrating her birthday tonight? Did I just win a scholarship or did I just flunk a class? Do I know nothing about the Bible or do I know enough to make you look like a fool? Do I preach in a church every Sunday or do I debate Bible-toters and eat them for lunch? Well?'

"My partner shrugged his shoulders and said, 'I don't know.'

"James said, 'Then you can leave your booklet or you can take it with you, but you're not going to read a thing to me.' Then James picked up his philosophy book again and started reading it like we weren't even there.

"I got up and left. I assume my partner did too. I don't know. I didn't even look back."

Jim stopped and took a bite of his apple and looked at a cardinal that had landed in a nearby tree. Then he said, "Sometimes I thank God for James. He taught me such an important lesson. I can honestly say that there hasn't been a time in my life since that day when I told another human being about Jesus without first getting to know that person."

I breathed a deep sigh. Jim noticed and said, "It's a hard lesson to learn for some of us."

I nodded. "I wish I'd heard your story before last night."

Jim said, "The way I think about it now is that I earn the right to tell someone about Jesus by first learning what it's like to be that person. Then I can tell if the person is really ready to hear what I have to say.

"There've been times when I knew a person really well, but I didn't say anything about God to the person for a long time. I don't mean that I tried to hide the fact that I was a Christian, because I didn't. But I never found a time when it felt right to talk to that person about God.

"But later on things changed with some of those people. They reached times when their lives fell apart and they were trying to figure out what to do. They knew they could trust me, so they told me how they were hurting and pretty much asked me to tell them about God.

"So I had a chance to tell them, and things worked out really well. But if I'd said anything sooner it would have been a mistake, and I never would have had the chance when the time was right."

We were both quiet for a couple of minutes. Then I asked, "So what do you think I can do about Margaret?"

Jim thought for a moment. Then he said, "You know, Andy, you really got off to a pretty good start with Margaret before you put both feet in your mouth last night."

I winced, but kept listening.

Jim smiled and reached over to squeeze my arm. "Maybe you'll thank God for Margaret some day like I do for James. Meanwhile, I think you were doing a good job caring for Margaret, and I believe God still wants you to.

"What I'd suggest is that you go back over to her house, tell her that you know that you blew it yesterday, apologize, and see if she'll accept your apology. I think you're right that she needs someone to be her friend now. Just work on being her friend. Leave the church stuff alone for now. You can talk about that later, if and when you get to know Margaret well enough to know that she's ready to hear more about God."

I nodded and said, "Thanks." Then I picked up my empty lunch bag and went back to the office.

Caring Evangelism Always Takes Place in Relationships

From the beginning God has wanted a relationship with people. The book of Genesis pictures God talking with Adam and Eve while the three of them walked together in the Garden of Eden in the cool of the day. Later, when God wanted to create a special nation, God began by developing a relationship with Abraham—a relationship that was so close that Abraham was called the "friend of God" (James 2:23). Finally Jesus came to heal the break in our relationship with God and to restore us to God's family. Then, on the day of Pentecost, the Holy Spirit came to be with us forever.

It's clear that relationship is at the very heart of life with God. It makes sense, then, for evangelism, also, to take place in relationships.

What Is an Evangelizing Relationship?

What are evangelizing relationships like? Evangelizing relationships are characterized by genuine care and concern for the other person. An evangelist focuses on learning about the person and trying to bring Jesus' love to him or her in any way possible. Sometimes that might mean bringing over a meal, or helping a person mow a lawn. Other times it will mean praying for a person or witnessing.

An evangelizing relationship is also process-oriented. As evangelists we are not trying to get another person to do something or to change in some way. We are simply loving the other person as Jesus has taught us to love. We trust that the Holy Spirit will use our relating to effectively communicate the Good News of God's love to others.

Obviously, an evangelizing relationship takes a great deal of energy. It takes effort to keep the focus on the other person, instead of on ourselves. It's difficult to listen when you'd rather talk. And it can be tough to hold yourself back when you have the urge to "fix" the other person's life.

In *The Road Less Traveled,* M. Scott Peck defines love as "the will to extend one's self for the purpose of nurturing one's own or another's spiritual growth."[1] He says that such love is hard work, and it requires courage.

Building an evangelizing relationship takes this kind of love. It makes us stretch ourselves—do things we never thought we could do—for the sake of others. But it's worth the effort because God can use this kind of relationship to help the other person really hear and respond to the Good News of God's love—maybe for the very first time. Here are some reasons why.

Why Evangelize in Relationships?

Trust Grows in Relationships

Would you discuss embarrassing financial problems with a complete stranger? What about family problems with a person you've known only a few days? Most of us would say no. People usually only feel comfortable talking about intensely personal issues to people they trust.

That's one reason for evangelizing in relationships. Questions like, "Is there a God? Am I valuable to God? Can God forgive what I've done?" are all highly personal. A close, continuing relationship allows a level of trust to develop that makes people more comfortable talking about spiritual concerns.

Talking about your relationship with God is also a risky thing for *you* to do. Sometimes Christians don't evangelize because they are afraid it would reveal a great deal about their own needs, struggles and beliefs, and they're not sure if they can trust others with such personal knowledge.

In order to talk about such sensitive matters with someone else, we need to be able to trust him or her. We need to be sure the other person will not use our vulnerability to hurt us. We need to know that the other person will keep our secrets safe and not use them as weapons against us.

How can we gain the trust that will make it possible for us and someone else to risk talking about God? Only through relationships in which we become acquainted and begin to trust each other.

As we consistently care, putting others' needs ahead of our wants, others can begin to trust us. They recognize that we have their best interests at heart. Then, when they reach a difficult time in their lives and they need someone they can trust to listen and care, we will be there for them.

We Earn the Right to Evangelize

Another reason to evangelize in relationships is that we *earn* the right to talk about God by first caring for people with no strings attached. Our care shows others that we are concerned for them as individuals, not just as potential converts. That way, when we finally have the opportunity to tell them about Jesus, they know that our witness comes out of our love for them as individuals. People are much more likely to trust our words about God's love when they have already seen us live that love in a relationship.

How *Not* to Build Evangelizing Relationships

How can you build evangelizing relationships with others? First of all you need to know how *not* to do it. Following are several pitfalls to avoid.

Don't Expect Evangelizing Relationships to Just Happen

Many Christians think that they don't need to do anything actively to create evangelizing relationships. They may think, "I'm a Christian, and I live my faith. If anyone asks me about Christ, I'm willing to answer. This means that all my relationships are evangelizing relationships!"

That's not quite true. It *is* true that God will work through you as you try to live your faith day to day. God will give you chances to witness that you don't expect. But you can also *deliberately* develop deeper, evangelizing relationships with a few people. These are relationships in which you consistently pray for the person. You make time for him or her, listen and try to understand his or her feelings, look for concrete ways of helping in order to communicate God's love, and gently witness—day after day. You develop these evangelizing relationships deliberately and purposefully—not by just "falling into" them with no effort on your part.

Don't Be Results-Oriented

Being results-oriented is another big roadblock to evangelizing relationships. Evangelists are results-oriented whenever they start relationships with a hidden agenda. They may be determined to convert the other person no matter what, and decide that appearing friendly and caring is the best way to get him or her to accept what they're pushing.

When cultists do this, it's called "love bombing." They

shower a person with incredible amounts of love and acceptance, but really all they want to do is to get the person into the cult. If the person refuses to join, the "care" is quickly withdrawn.

Even if the person joins the cult, he or she quickly experiences an unpleasant surprise. Within a very short time the intensive loving and caring stop. Suddenly no one is taking the time anymore to listen, to care, to offer acceptance and love. The cult members have gotten what they wanted—a convert—and now they move on to someone new.

As a caring evangelist, you should steer clear of this kind of behavior. If you "love-bomb," even with the best of intentions, such as wanting the other person to become a Christian, you are still trying to manipulate the other person. This doesn't work. The other person will eventually sense that your care is false, and possibly wind up even farther from God.

Love-bombing can have bad effects on you as an evangelist too. Manipulating people is not consistent with Christian love. It may well leave you angry at yourself and frustrated about the effects you see in others.

A truly evangelizing relationship is one in which both people are free. The caring evangelist is free to care, to listen, and to gently share God's love when the other person is open to hear. Those you evangelize are free to be themselves, responding to God's love as the Spirit enables them, instead of feeling that they have to live up to someone else's requirements.

Don't Stereotype

Stereotyping is a surefire way to sabotage the evangelizing relationship before it even gets off the ground. Evangelists can make this mistake if they assume they already know what the other person is like instead of working to understand the real person. If evangelists say to themselves, "Thomas has a college education, so he must be anti-Christian," or "LeeAnne hasn't been to church for a while, so she must be slipping away from God," they are setting themselves up for failure in the relationship. Because of preconceptions about others, they may try to meet needs that don't exist and fail to see the real needs that do. The other people will be able to tell that the evangelists haven't taken the time to find out anything real about them, and they will resent this.

Here's an example.

Robin had just begun to make friends with Patricia, one of the other waitresses at her work. Often during breaks they talked about their personal lives or parties they'd been to recently. Robin hoped that, over time, Patricia would be open to hearing about Christ.

One day as they were talking Robin discovered that Patricia was going to graduate school during the day, working toward a Ph.D. in psychology. Robin didn't know what to say. She was afraid that her own ideas and understandings would seem simplistic to Patricia. She worried that if she started talking about God, Patricia would psychoanalyze her, or tell her that religion was a psychological crutch. So she deliberately kept the conversation light, steering clear of anything remotely religious.

One day she arrived at work to find Patricia in tears in the break room. Patricia's brother had been in a terrible car accident, and no one knew if he would live. Patricia told Robin, "I don't know what to do. I feel so helpless."

Robin began to see Patricia as another human being who was hurting and in need of care. Instead of feeling threatened by Patricia, Robin listened, gently witnessed, and prayed for Patricia's brother. Patricia accepted and appreciated all that Robin said and did. Later Robin wondered why she had been so afraid to talk about God to Patricia.

The best way to avoid the mistake of stereotyping is a simple one: listen. When you concentrate on listening, you may learn things you never dreamed about people. They may tell you about their problems, concerns, and worries, or share their hopes and joys. As you get to know the real person, you will begin to see ways of communicating God's love to him or her.

Don't Be Judgmental

Yet another guaranteed way to stop an evangelizing relationship from developing is to judge the other person. When you develop deeply caring relationships with others, very often they will trust you enough to tell you about aspects of their lives they are not proud of. For example, they may tell you about dependence on alcohol or drugs, about promiscuity, or about problems in relationships where it's clear that they have caused the problem.

If evangelists haven't come to terms with their own continuing sin and brokenness, they may be afraid to face such deep need—in themselves or in others. Such fear may lead them to respond to others with judgment instead of care. Their words, tone of voice, or actions (withdrawing from the relationship) say that they're willing to accept the good, but not the bad in the other person. How ironic—since the evangelizing message is that we have a Savior who accepts us as we are.

Being judgmental can hurt relationships deeply. If others trust enough to share very personal issues and receive judgment in return, it may be very difficult for them to trust again.

Love is patient. Love cares and accepts—even when it hears about actions it can't agree with.

If you maintain a calm, caring attitude, others will know that you still value them, even though you may not agree with what they are doing. Eventually, patient, accepting love can help people get to the point where they are open to hearing about God's love.

Accepting others doesn't mean you have to give up your own values. It doesn't mean, for example, that you should agree that adultery or stealing are right. That would be betraying your own beliefs. It would also be unfaithful to God's call to live as a follower of Jesus.

What accepting a person does mean is exactly that: accepting the *person,* not the sin. You can continue to make your love and acceptance of the person clear, while not going along with what he or she is doing.

There are times, however, when you must judge and take action. Failing to do so in a situation where a person is endangering the physical safety of others or him- or herself is a failure of your responsibility as a Christian and a human being. Instances of spouse abuse, elder abuse, child abuse, and suicidal behavior are all occasions demanding action on your part. In such a case, stopping the destructive behavior is even more important than preserving the relationship. These are the times you should say clearly, "This is wrong, and you need to get help to stop it." For example, if a parent tells you that he or she is abusing a child on a continuing basis, you need to take action. Fortunately most situations are not so drastic.

Don't Treat the Other Person as an Inferior

Because Christians have something to share—the priceless message of forgiveness and acceptance in Christ—they may be tempted to treat the other person as an unconverted "heathen," someone who is languishing in darkness until they arrive with the light. (Drum roll, please!) Or if the person they are caring for is already a Christian, they might be tempted to see him or her as immature and in need of their superior spiritual wisdom.

In one sense this is right. People without Christ *are* in darkness; immature Christians can benefit from the advice of others. However, this is just as true for evangelists as it is for others. We too were in darkness before God gave us light in

Christ; we too are immature in many ways and need care. Paul says, "For by the grace given to me I say to everyone among you not to think of yourself more highly than you ought to think, but to think with sober judgment, each according to the measure of faith that God has assigned." (Rom. 12:3) Faith is a gift. It is not a reason to treat others as inferiors. Jesus died for all people, whether or not they have claimed the redemption God gives. All are of ultimate worth to God. As a caring evangelist, you must communicate in all you do and say how valuable others are to God.

Don't Break Confidentiality

You may learn very personal things about others as you get to know them better. Be sure to keep what they tell you confidential. Breaking the trust of confidentiality is a sure way to do a lot of damage to a relationship.

The Right Way to Build Evangelizing Relationships

There are several very practical ways to create and maintain evangelizing relationships.

Beginning the Relationship

Focus Your Caring

Evangelizing relationships take hard work. That's a good reason why you shouldn't feel obligated to develop one-on-one evangelizing relationships with everyone you meet. No one has the time or the energy to do it, and God doesn't expect it.

Even Jesus focused his caring. While he cared for the crowds who followed him by preaching and healing, he spent the greater part of his time and energy building relationships with his twelve disciples.

Instead of trying to create evangelizing relationships with everyone you know, you can look for special opportunities to relate with one or two people. Obviously you'll continue to use your listening, caring, and witnessing skills when appropriate with those you meet in your daily life. Jesus did this also. But when you focus your intensive, continuing care on just a few relationships, you will make effective use of your time and effort.

Allow Enough Time

How long does an evangelizing relationship last? Many

evangelizing relationships last for months and even years, but shorter ones are possible. What counts in a relationship isn't length of time—it's the level of trust and authenticity that develops. Sometimes God may give you the opportunity to go from being complete strangers to intimate friends with someone in only a matter of days, or even hours. More often it takes weeks, months, or years. However long it takes, you can use caring, listening, and witnessing skills to build the relationship, step by step.

Ask God

How do you find the person with whom you develop an evangelizing relationship? Ask God to show you the person God wants you to evangelize. Sometimes the answer will be obvious. You will focus on a parent, a child, a neighbor, or a friend for whom you have been concerned for a very long time.

When it's not so obvious, keep praying. Ask God to point out a person with whom you can share Christ's love. Then keep your eyes open. Keep praying about it as you make a decision and begin developing the relationship.

Building the Relationship

As you build an evangelizing relationship, here are two very helpful principles to follow.

Be Yourself

First of all, be yourself. Being genuine, without trying to impress someone else, is a key part of establishing a trusting relationship.

In evangelizing relationships you may sometimes be tempted to put on a false front, to give the other person the impression that as a Christian you have it all together, and that you don't have any more problems or sin to deal with in your life. You might even think that you have to put on a mask of Christian perfection, or others won't have anything to do with you—or with God.

But this is a mistake. When Christians pretend they no longer struggle with sin or doubt, others will quickly see that they are not as perfect as they pretend to be, and their witness to Christ will probably seem false. Or others might say, "I could never be as perfect as so-and-so, so Christianity must not be for me." Either way, falseness drives people away from God.

Amazingly, people react much more positively when you reveal yourself just as you are—good points, weaknesses, struggles, and all. When others see that you have the same kind of problems they do, yet you find strength and hope in Jesus, this allows them to believe that God might help them too.

Trust God

The Apostle Paul talked about the way of relating that is required for building evangelizing relationships. He said:

> Do nothing from selfish ambition or conceit, but in humility regard others as better than yourselves. Let each of you look not to your own interests, but to the interests of others. Let the same mind be in you that was in Christ Jesus, who, though he was in the form of God, did not regard equality with God as something to be exploited, but emptied himself, taking the form of a slave, being born in human likeness. And being found in human form, he humbled himself and became obedient to the point of death—even death on a cross. (Phil. 2:3-8)

Sometimes, in order to build an evangelizing relationship we need to die to our own needs, our own comfort, our own pride, and our own schedule, so that we can really care for the other person. But how can we ever find it within ourselves to give in this way? Only by relying on God to make it happen in our life. Paul says the fruit of the Spirit is "love, joy, peace, patience, kindness, generosity, faithfulness, gentleness, and self-control." (Gal. 5:22-23) God is the only one who can make us into Christlike, caring people. And God is doing that as the old, selfish person dies and the new, Christlike self comes more and more to life.

Remember that "dying to ourselves" doesn't mean creating relationships in which we give of ourselves as a way to control others, expecting them to do what we want since we've given so much to them. The love Jesus modeled is one in which we give without expecting in return.

The Foundation for Caring Evangelism

There is a saying, "People don't care what you know until they know that you care." A caring, trusting relationship is the foundation for Caring Evangelism. Until evangelists demonstrate their respect and care for others, they should not expect others to care about what they have to say.

[1]M. Scott Peck, M.D., *The Road Less Traveled: A New Psychology of Love, Traditional Values and Spiritual Growth* (New York: Simon and Schuster, 1978), p. 81.

Chapter 6

Listening: The Most Important Evangelizing Skill

When I got home from work I went right over to Margaret's house. I was dreading the visit and I knew I'd better not put it off. I knew I'd feel even worse if I didn't at least try to clear things up with her.

When Margaret didn't answer her doorbell, I walked around the side of her house to see if she was working in the backyard. That's where I found her, kneeling beside a flower bed.

I cleared my throat and she looked over her shoulder and saw me. She stood up, took off her gardening gloves, and wiped her forehead with the back of her wrist. Then she looked at me and said, "I suppose you've come for your casserole dish."

I cleared my throat again and said, "Ah . . . actually I've come to apologize."

Margaret folded her arms across her chest and waited.

"This is really difficult for me," I said. "I've felt terrible ever since last night . . . I don't know what to say . . . except that I'm sorry."

Margaret sighed. She thought for a moment, and then said, "I have thought quite a bit about yesterday evening also, Mr. Simons. I invited you into my home and shared some very important memories with you. I was surprised at myself at the time. I am usually a private person.

"Then you abruptly changed the subject and began to speak about me as if I were some kind of project you and your wife had been discussing. It seemed you didn't mean the kindness you had shown to me—as if all you really wanted was to convert me to your religion."

I waited for a moment and then said, "I know. I feel terrible. I'm really sorry." There were a few moments of quiet. I finally broke the silence. "You have a right to be angry with me."

"I felt more betrayed than angry."

"Yeah," I said, "I can see how you would."

Margaret looked at her watch and said, "Let me get your casserole dish. Just a moment."

She went into her kitchen, and I looked around the backyard. It was terraced with five or six raised flower beds. Two large maples were just beginning to bud. I could see that it took a lot of work to keep the yard up.

Margaret came back outside.

"You have a beautiful yard," I said.

"I work hard at it. Thank you."

"I can tell."

Margaret held out the dish. I took it and said, "Thank you."

I thought for a moment and then said, "I want you to know that last night was just a mistake. It wasn't premeditated. I haven't been trying to set you up. Actually, I felt embarrassed. I didn't know what to say, and those words just came out as my clumsy way of trying to help. I hope you'll accept my apology."

Margaret began to put her gloves back on. "Yes. Well. Good day, Mr. Simons."

The following Saturday morning, while I was picking up the newspaper, I saw Margaret pull into her driveway in her old station wagon. She got out and walked to the back and opened the rear door. I wanted to talk to her, just to see if she was still angry at me, but I couldn't think of a good reason to go over. I waved and I felt relieved when she saw me and waved back.

She had several big bags of fertilizer or something in the back of her car. When she started struggling to lift one out I went over to help her.

"Can I get that for you?"

She hesitated, then sighed deeply. Then she said, "Yes, please. Thank you, Andy."

As I lifted the bag, she said, "Roy always did this kind of thing. It is very frustrating to learn I am not as self-sufficient as I thought I was."

I heaved a 40-pound bag of peat moss out of the back of the car and grunted, "Where would you like this?"

"Actually, I need it in the backyard, if you don't mind." She looked a bit embarrassed at having to ask.

After I had lugged three bags to the backyard, I asked Margaret what she was going to do with them.

"Oh, I'm putting in some new flower beds."

I looked around for a moment, then said, "You must really enjoy gardening and flowers. I guess you'd have to enjoy it to do all this work every year."

Margaret nodded and hesitated a moment, as if she were making a decision. Then she said, "Would you like a guided tour?"

I said, "That'd be great," and spent the next half hour listening to Margaret talk about the trees and flowers in her yard. She told me about when things were planted and what part of the world they came from. I asked questions and tried to understand the intricacies of gardening; but mostly I just listened, fascinated by Margaret's love for her trees and flowers.

By now it probably doesn't come as a surprise that listening is just as important as speaking in evangelism! So often people think of talking as the main way to share the Good News. But listening—real, caring listening—is also essential to communicating God's Good News.

Basic Considerations for Effective Listening

What Is Good Listening?

In their book *Communication Skills for Ministry,* John W. Lawyer and Neil H. Katz define listening as "following the thoughts and feelings of another and understanding what the other is saying and meaning from his or her frame of reference."[1] Real listening involves getting into another's skin, seeing the world through his or her eyes.

Choosing the Environment

You take the first step toward caring listening when you choose a good setting for the conversation. A good listening environment is one that is private enough for the other person to feel comfortable talking about deep personal feelings. As much as possible, it should be free of distractions like telephone calls, loud music, conversations, or interruptions by other people.

Paying Attention

When you listen, focus completely on the other person, and

don't let yourself be distracted by what's going on around you, or by your own inner dialogue. The one you are listening to should be so important to you that you pay attention to nothing else.

In *The Road Less Traveled*, M. Scott Peck describes the activities that are part of loving. The first one he lists is paying attention. Dr. Peck says, "The principal form that the work of love takes is attention. When we love another we give him or her our attention; we attend to that person's growth. . . . When we attend to someone we are caring for that person. The act of attending requires that we make the effort to set aside our existing preoccupations. . . . Attention is an act of will. . . . By far the most common and important way in which we can exercise our attention is by listening."[2]

Sometimes it is very hard work to pay attention to others. When we do so, we are loving them. When we listen with concentrated attention, we show others the love God has given to us and offers to them.

"Hearing" Nonverbal Communications

Often people say more through their facial expressions, their posture, or what they are doing with their hands than they do with the words they say. Caring listening means paying attention to the nonverbal communications. Listen with your eyes as well as with your ears.

For example, a person may say everything is fine and be wringing her hands at the same time. Or, a person might not say anything about his child, but when the child is mentioned you notice a look of pain on the person's face. Part of listening is paying attention and trying to understand what that facial expression means.

Listening for Understanding

Listening for understanding is a way of trying to understand accurately what others say and mean, and giving them the chance to talk more, and more deeply, about issues that concern them. This requires you to learn and practice the specific skills of asking questions and reflecting. These skills do not come automatically. Expect to get better at listening for understanding as you practice.

Asking Questions

One good way to better understand others is by asking

questions. But it's important to know that some kinds of questions are more useful than others.

Open- and Closed-Ended Questions

The most helpful questions are those that encourage others to say a lot when they answer. These are called open-ended questions. Open-ended questions encourage a fairly lengthy answer. They're the kind of questions that invite an "essay-type" response. Closed-ended questions, on the other hand, can be answered with only a few words, or even one word.

Here's an example. Instead of asking the closed-ended question, "Were you very angry with your father when he did that?" you could ask, "How did you feel when your father did that?" The first question expects a simple yes or no answer, which can be a conversational dead end. The second prompts much more—the person is free to make many different responses, instead of being limited to a yes or no answer to your question about anger. With an open-ended question he or she will probably talk more and longer, opening up new memories and feelings. Here are some more examples:

Closed: "Did you think your supervisor was being unfair to you?"

Open: "How did you feel about your supervisor's action?"

Closed: "Did your family enjoy the church service?"

Open: "How did your family enjoy the church service?"

Closed: "Was that very painful for you?"

Open: "How did you feel when you heard the news?"

Clarifying Questions

Clarifying questions are also useful because they help you find out more exactly what others mean. If a person says, "Last Tuesday was a really bad day," you might ask, "What made it so bad for you?" You may find out that the speaker lost his or her job that day; or "bad" could simply refer to the weather. Asking a clarifying question can keep you from misunderstanding.

When you use clarifying questions, be sure to phrase them gently. Phrases like "Could you tell me exactly what you meant by . . . ? I didn't quite catch it," can make your question less blunt. Sometimes more aggressive phrases, such as, "I want to know why you did that," may break the bond of trust and cause others to withdraw.

Reflecting

Reflecting means trying to understand what others say, and then responding by rephrasing or summarizing what they have said. The dialogue below between a person named Bernice and a caring evangelist contains an example of responding this way.

Bernice: "My new boss is so critical. No matter how hard I try, it's not good enough. All she does is complain."

Caring Evangelist: "It seems to you like you just can't please your new boss."

The caring evangelist has simply rephrased what he or she thinks Bernice just said.

What Happens When You Reflect?

What might happen in the conversation after you reflect what you have understood? If you have the message correct, the person might say, "Yes, that's right. I've tried and tried to figure out what she wants . . ." Then you know that you understood correctly, and the conversation goes on without a break. The person knows that you are paying attention, as well as understanding, and this encourages him or her to talk more.

What would happen if you misunderstood what the person was saying in the first place? Then you might get a response such as, "No, that's not really what I meant." This kind of correction is also a valuable part of the listening process. It helps you understand the other person more clearly. It also lets him or her know that you care enough about what he or she is saying to try to get it straight.

How to Phrase Reflecting Responses

Many people who are learning to listen for understanding have trouble knowing how to phrase their reflecting responses. Some feel awkward at first with some of the standard ways of reflecting, such as, "It sounds like you're feeling . . . ," or, "It seems like you are having trouble with . . ." You may be concerned that such responses will sound artificial or that they will quickly wear out if you use them over and over again in a conversation.

Those with a lot of experience at this kind of caring listening say that even though it sounds awkward at first, it really works. On paper, reflective responses often *do* sound artificial. That is because these responses aren't meant to be read; they work when they flow naturally out of a conversation in which you are so focused on the other person that your sincerity adds meaning and care to the words.

Following is a list of ways caring evangelists might say their reflecting responses. Don't just memorize this list and then use these statements in unnatural or stilted ways. Instead, become familiar with the responses in the list and practice using some of them. See which ones sound natural to you in various situations, and think of more. You will grow more and more comfortable with reflecting as you practice it.

Possible Reflecting Responses

- "You're wondering if . . ."
- "It sounds like you're feeling . . ."
- "I get the idea that . . ."
- "When you say that, it sounds like you mean . . ."
- "As I understand it, then, your plan is to . . ."
- "This is what you have decided to do and the reasons are . . ."
- "If I were to say that . . . would I be on target?"
- "If I understand you correctly, you're feeling . . ."
- "Would it be accurate to say that you thought . . .?"
- "As you saw it, the situation was . . ."
- "Were you feeling . . . right then?"
- "At that point you were feeling . . ."
- "So your assessment of the situation is . . ."
- "As you see it, it all boils down to . . ."
- "From all that you've said, you seem the most concerned about . . ."

Reflecting Is Not Just Parroting

Remember that listening for understanding is supposed to be a way of caring for others. It is easy to repeat back what the other person is saying without really understanding or caring. There are even computer programs that can do this! But this kind of parroting is not beneficial, either to the speaker or the listener. It is mechanical, and sooner or later the other person will realize that there's no real caring involved. Real, caring listening must involve the heart and mind as well as the ears and mouth.

Reflecting Content, Feelings, and Spiritual Concerns

There are three kinds of information you might reflect as

you listen for understanding: content, feelings, and spiritual concerns.

What Is Content?

Content is the who, what, why, where, when, and how of communication. It is usually the first thing people think about when someone asks, "What did Bill (or Jane) say?" Content includes such matters as:

- thoughts
- ideas
- opinions
- hopes
- beliefs
- attitudes
- expectations
- values
- plans
- dreams
- judgments
- wishes
- evaluations

Reflecting Content

Once you think you understand some of the content of what someone is saying, you rephrase it and say it back to the other person. Here's part of a conversation in which the caring evangelist reflects content:

Sam: "My supervisor just told me I'm being promoted. It's a great opportunity, but they're transferring me across the country."

Caring Evangelist: "It sounds like this is a really big change."

Sam: "Yes, and that's going to be a hassle. Pat's going to have to find another job, and the kids don't want to change schools."

Caring Evangelist: "So your family's going to have to make some major adjustments?"

Sam: "Right, and they're not happy about it. But they know how important this move is to me, and for all of us, so they're not saying too much."

Caring Evangelist: "I get the impression you think they're avoiding the subject?"

Sam: "I guess you could say that. I think I need to bring it up myself and clear the air."

Caring Evangelist: "It sounds like you want to give them a chance to talk about it openly."

You can see that the statements in this dialogue are very short. They are purposely kept short here in order to give you several examples of listening for understanding of content. While you may sometimes have "rapid-fire" conversations like this, usually as a caring evangelist you will listen to the other person for a much longer time before saying anything.

What Are Feelings?

Feelings are the internal reactions generated by our own interpretation of people, events and life experiences. The list of words below describes some of the many feelings people experience.

- sad
- angry
- afraid
- happy
- glad
- secure
- pleased
- amazed
- relaxed
- nervous
- excited
- joyful
- anxious
- furious
- frustrated

Reflecting Feelings

When you believe you have identified some feelings the other person is expressing, you summarize them and reflect them back. Here is how this might happen in conversation:

Annie: "Well, it's finally happening. Sally's leaving for college tomorrow. I miss her already."

Caring Evangelist: "You're feeling lonely about Sally leaving."

Annie: "Yes, I suppose I'm sad . . . but I don't think I should be. I remember my college days. They were a lot of fun. I'm sure she's going to have the time of her life."

Caring Evangelist: "So you're also feeling excited for her."

Annie: "Yes, I'm happy for her, but sad for me. It makes me feel so selfish, but I really wish she wasn't going away."

Caring Evangelist: "This really hurts."

Annie: "Yes, it does. It's hard to let go of your children."

By reflecting feelings in this dialogue, the caring evangelist gave Annie permission to talk about feelings that aren't always easy to discuss. That was a very caring thing to do. Having someone to listen to painful feelings can help a person come to terms with a difficult transition in life.

What Are Spiritual Concerns?

After you listen and build a relationship for a long time you may reach a level of trust where the two of you are able to talk about spiritual concerns. You can invite others to talk about their need for God's love by reflecting back to them these "spiritual concerns"—things they say that may be related to a deeper need for a Savior. This special kind of listening for understanding will be covered in chapter 10, where you'll learn much more about the process of helping others see their need for God's love.

Five Traps to Avoid While Listening

Here are five traps to avoid in order to keep your listening other-centered and caring.

1. Don't "Send Solutions"

Sending solutions means ordering, threatening, moralizing, advising, or trying in any other way to solve problems for others. It's much better to keep your listening process-oriented. Concentrate on helping others find their own solutions.

Examples of Avoiding Sending Solutions

When someone says: "I just don't know what to do. He's lied to me again and again, and talking to him about it doesn't help."

Don't say: "You should really read this book . . ."

Do say: "Right now it seems that you're feeling helpless, like this situation is out of control."

When someone says: "I'm having a really hard time dealing with my roommate. Dale never does the dishes, never takes out the trash, and I'm getting sick of it."

Don't say: "What you need to do is get tough. Tell your roommate . . ."

Do say: "You're feeling frustrated . . ."

2. Don't Evaluate

Evaluating is another way of derailing the listening process. You evaluate by judging, praising, labeling, or trying to diagnose others' problems. If the evaluation is negative, the other person may feel hurt and withdraw from the relationship. Even if the evaluation is positive—a form of praise—it can effectively end the conversation right there, leaving the other person frustrated because he or she didn't have a chance to talk out feelings and difficulties.

Examples of Avoiding Evaluation

When someone says: "It's really tough trying to raise two children on my own. I don't like having to put them in daycare so much, but what can I do?"

Don't Say: "It's too bad you got a divorce. Now it's really hurting your kids."

Do say: "It seems you're really worried about the effect this might have on your kids."

When someone says: "Ever since my father went blind, I've been going to see him once a week. I try to cheer him up, but he just seems to get more depressed."

Don't say: "Your father is so lucky to have a son like you."

Do say: "Tell me more about what happens when you visit your father."

3. Don't Withdraw

Perhaps the least obvious trap you can fall into in your listening is withdrawing. It is possible to withdraw by being too passive and silent, or by not responding at all. Listeners may withdraw in order to avoid the pain, discomfort, or hard work of true listening. Others feel the listeners' lack of response and conclude that they aren't really interested.

4. Avoid Resolution That's Too Early or Too Easy

Another common way to shut down the listening process is to give easy reassurance to troubled people. Telling others not to worry because it'll be all right can seem like a good idea, but if you do so before others have a chance to fully express their concerns and struggles, they may conclude that you don't want to listen. And if you listen for a while and then tell them not to worry, they may decide you don't really understand how important or difficult their problems are. They may even think you are telling them to stop feeling the way they do. This can be very damaging to the relationship.

Examples of Avoiding Easy Resolutions

When someone says: "I just can't believe he's gone. I keep thinking I'll wake up and find him next to me . . ."

Don't say: "You'll be fine. Just keep your chin up, and remember time heals all wounds."

Do say: "It sounds like you miss him very much . . ." *(and encourage the person to continue expressing her feelings).*

When someone says: "We lost everything when the fire hit our house. Jill's baby pictures, my grandfather's watch . . ."

Don't say: "Oh, I'm really sorry to hear that. But don't worry—the insurance will take care of most of it. Speaking of insurance, did I ever tell you . . ."

Do say: "What a terrible loss. I'm really sorry."

5. Avoid Wild Analysis

When you reflect what another person is saying, avoid wild analysis. Wild analysis means jumping to conclusions about another person's deepest thoughts and feelings on the basis of just a few statements. It means reading your own ideas into what another person says.

An Example of Avoiding Wild Analysis

When someone says: "Sometimes I wonder whether my life will ever really add up to anything."

Avoid wild analysis, such as: "I can tell you're struggling with self-esteem issues. Your childhood must have been really tough."

[or]

"Since you're sitting so stiffly, with your legs crossed and your arms folded, I know you're feeling very defensive right now."

Wild analysis can be very threatening to the other person. He or she may decide that it's better to stop talking completely than run the risk of being so completely misunderstood. It's much better not to analyze—that is, to try to discover hidden meanings in what people say or do. Instead listen carefully, reflect what you hear others saying, and wait for them to reach their own new insights about their feelings or actions with God's help.

Benefits of Good Listening

Real listening is one of the most precious gifts you can give others. It benefits them because being listened to gives them a warm sense of welcome and acceptance. When you listen you create an atmosphere of trust that enables others to focus on themselves, to see their needs and hurts more clearly, and to find their own solutions, with God's help.

Real listening also brings benefits to you as a caring evangelist. Listening is good spiritual exercise. When you truly listen to others, you are getting out of yourself, forgetting yourself, and serving others. That's the kind of love Jesus gives us. This kind of love leads to personal spiritual growth, as the Bible tells us: "If we love one another, God lives in us, and his love is perfected in us." (1 John 4:12)

Finally, because listening protects trust, it helps build the kind of relationship in which it is natural and comfortable to talk about your relationship with God. You'll learn more about this in later chapters.

[1]John W. Lawyer and Neil H. Katz, *Communication Skills for Ministry* (Dubuque, IA: Kendall/Hunt Publishing Company, 1987), p. 19.

[2]M. Scott Peck, *The Road Less Traveled: A New Psychology of Love, Traditional Values and Spiritual Growth* (New York: Simon and Schuster, 1978), pp. 120-121.

Chapter 7

Empathic Evangelism

The afternoon after my tour of Margaret's garden I went to watch Erica's softball team play. When we got back, Sarah called from the kitchen. I walked in while she was getting some chicken ready for the grill. She looked up and said, "I saw you talking with Margaret this morning and it gave me the idea to invite her over for supper. I'd been thinking about it all week and this seemed like a good opportunity."

I felt my stomach tighten. I hadn't told Sarah much about what had happened when Margaret and I talked. I was still embarrassed, and it had stung when Margaret said she didn't like being "discussed."

"What did she say?" I asked.

"Oh, she'll be over about 4:30. I hope this is okay with you."

"Yeah. Great. It's great." I smiled at Sarah and gave her a hug. I was happy and relieved that Margaret had agreed, and I found myself looking forward to spending time with her.

After supper Erica went out with some friends, while Margaret, Sarah, and I sat on the patio and enjoyed the warm evening. We chatted and drank coffee as the sky grew darker.

There was a time of silence while we all watched the moon, and then Margaret looked at me and said, "Andy, I've been thinking more about our conversation last Monday night, and I would like to tell you a little about myself that might help explain the way I reacted when you suggested that I attend church with your family."

I said, "You don't have to."

Margaret was insistent. "I know that, but I want to tell you this so you'll understand my feelings about the matter.''

I said, "Okay," and leaned forward in my chair to listen.

"When I was a child," Margaret said, "my father became a member of a small, very strict church. My father had always been kind and tolerant up to that time. I remember adoring him as a young girl, and I always looked forward to our time together.

"But at the time of his conversion he changed quite a bit. He became unreasonable and demanding toward my mother and me. He made us attend his church two or three times a week. He forbade me to associate with my friends who were not members of the church. He became a cruel person.

"Every evening that we weren't at church we had to sit through my father's evening devotion. He would read to us out of the Bible for 20 minutes and then spend an equal amount of time criticizing others who didn't live according to his standards. Often his targets were relatives and others about whom I cared deeply.''

Margaret paused and Sarah reached over, squeezed Margaret's hand, and said, "I'm so sorry."

Margaret took a deep breath and then continued. "At first I remember feeling hurt and confused. I would cry myself to sleep at night. My mother would come into my room and hold me, but when I said anything about my father she would say, 'He's your father, so just do as you're told.'

"Then as I grew older and started high school I began to deeply resent my father. He had taken all the joy from our family and made my life miserable. He did all this in the name of his God, and it seemed to me that God was even crueler and more of a killjoy than my father.

"Since that time I have had a deep distrust of churches and religions. Roy and I had nothing to do with any religion in all the time we were married.''

Margaret fell silent. I felt very sad, and I also felt angry at her father.

"So," Margaret continued, "when you brought up the subject of church, Andy, all those old feelings returned. But after I told you about how I felt and you apologized, I began to think about how my reaction must have seemed to you. I wanted you to know that there was more behind my reaction than simply your awkward invitation. I thought it might help you feel less angry at yourself.''

I closed my eyes and felt the breeze against my face. Then I looked at Margaret and said, "Thank you. I still feel terrible about treating you that way. Your understanding helps, though.''

Margaret said, "Good," and sipped her coffee.

Empathy is one of the foundational caring skills in evangelism. Empathy is the skill of accurately knowing what others are feeling. This is an important skill for us as caring evangelists for several reasons. Empathy is vital to building relationships. It is an irreplaceable part of good care. Empathy is also a must if we want to help others discover their own need for a Savior.

What Is Empathy?

According to Dr. Carl Rogers, empathy means: "to sense the [other person's] private world as if it were your own, but without ever losing the 'as if' quality. . . . To sense the [other's] anger, fear, or confusion as if it were your own, yet without your own anger, fear, or confusion getting bound up in it."[1]

Relearning How to Empathize

Think of a baby. Unable to communicate through language, nevertheless the child has little problem making his or her needs known. Babies communicate on the level of feelings. When they cry, laugh, smile, or make happy sounds they are telling how they feel.

Babies and young children also pick up on the feelings of others. They are very good at sensing when someone near is angry, worried, or frightened. They can also sense warmth, love, and acceptance.

People are born with the skill of empathy. But as people grow up, they tend to lose this ability. Our culture teaches not to show or admit to feelings in public. As children, we hear "Big boys (and girls) don't cry;" we learn that showing anger or affection in public is something to be embarrassed about. We learn to "keep a stiff upper lip"—even at the funerals of those we love most. When others see that we aren't crying, they make their approval clear with comments like, "Isn't he taking it well?" or, "She's so brave." And more and more, our feelings shrivel up inside of us.

We need to relearn what we once knew as children. If we're ever to care for others effectively, we need to get back in touch with our own feelings. We need to learn once more how to sense the feelings of others.

All Feelings Are Important—Even Difficult Ones

Some feelings are wonderful. People want to feel happy, at peace, and hopeful, for example. Other feelings really hurt. Feelings like anger, sadness, frustration, and anxiety are difficult to have. People want to get rid of them as soon as possible.

Sometimes people try to deal with difficult feelings by ignoring them or condemning them. One of the customary responses to difficult feelings—rage, jealousy, or loneliness, for example—is to just pretend that they aren't really there. Other times individuals might say that such feelings are bad and that those who feel them are bad also.

But trying to make such feelings go away without admitting to them is one of the least helpful things a person can do. All feelings are important. All feelings need to be acknowledged and expressed. If they aren't people can pay a large price.

All Feelings Need to Be Acknowledged and Expressed

The best response to feelings is to admit they are there, learn from them, and find appropriate ways to express them. When people take ownership for their feelings they can find constructive ways to let those feelings out. It's when people deny their feelings and try to suppress them that those feelings are most likely to come out in hurting or destructive ways.

There can be times when people find it difficult to let others know about even their happiest feelings. They may be embarrassed or wonder if others will share their feelings. But when people express their feelings of love, pleasure, joy, and satisfaction, they give their relationships the chance to flourish. If they hide those feelings they rob others of the chance to know them and enjoy relating with them.

Difficult feelings can be even harder to express. To let others know about feelings of anger, guilt, envy, impatience, or hurt can lead to arguments or hurt feelings. But when they aren't expressed the consequences can be much more difficult.

When people don't own their feelings and take responsibility for them, the feelings can fester, build up, and spill out in destructive ways. One of the fastest ways to spoil relationships is to suppress your feelings about the other person, no matter if they are happy feelings or difficult ones. Physicians have known for years that many diseases get started, or get worse, because a person is stifling difficult feelings. Unexpressed difficult feelings can build up to the point where they explode in ways that make little sense and are very hurtful to others.

Caring for People's Feelings

As caring evangelists we can live Christ's love with people in a very concrete way by helping them understand, own, and express their feelings. We can "Bear one another's burdens, and in this way . . . fulfill the law of Christ." (Gal. 6:2) Since feelings can be so difficult, we can extend ourselves in love by bearing the burden of others' feelings together with them. We can help people avoid the consequences of suppressing their feelings by listening to them, reflecting their feelings, and inviting them to say more. Sometimes it might hurt us to share others' feelings of hurt or sadness. We can show people the kind of love Jesus gives by willingly experiencing their pain with them. Can there be a more Christ-like way to relate with others?

Cautions When Reflecting Feelings

As you talk about feelings, there are several cautions to keep in mind.

Don't Judge

First, don't judge people for having certain feelings. That's the quickest way to make the other person feel rejected and stop discussing personal matters.

Don't Discount

Also avoid putting down, invalidating, or discounting the feelings of others. For example, if someone is grieving for a stillborn baby, it would be terrible to say, "At least you can have other children." In effect, a statement like that is really saying, "You have no right to feel sad about this baby's death. Stop hurting and pull yourself together."

Of course, people who make comments like that don't mean to hurt the grieving person. They are trying to make him or her feel better. But grieving people need time to mourn. They can't get over it quickly. Instead of discounting someone else's feelings, or subtly telling him or her that such feelings are not acceptable, simply listen with accepting care. That's really all they want.

Don't Try to Fix Difficult Feelings

Do not think you are obliged to fix the bad feelings of others. If someone is sad or unhappy, you shouldn't try to cheer them up or fix their problems. Their feelings belong to them—not to you. No one has the right to barge in and fix someone else's feelings. But loving, accepting listening is always welcome and greatly appreciated.

Empathy in Caring Evangelism

Empathy is vital in Caring Evangelism. It is quintessential care. Empathy is being willing to journey with people though their pain. Empathy doesn't fix anything—it is completely process-oriented care. But empathy is a gift of love that can soften the hardest hearts. Often people who are angry at God or at the church need to get those feelings out before they can hear about God's love and the church's concern for them. The only way we can enable that is by our empathic listening.

[1]Carl R. Rogers, "The Necessary and Sufficient Conditions of Therapeutic Personality Change," *Journal of Consulting Psychology,* vol. 21, no. 2 (1957): p. 99.

Chapter 8

Holistic Evangelism

That evening when Margaret first came over for supper was the beginning of a strong friendship among the three of us. Over the weeks and months that followed we got into the habit of having supper together about once a week. Sarah and Margaret would talk on the phone, and Margaret and I would chat out in the front yard regularly. She became an important part of our lives.

One day I was standing at the kitchen sink peeling potatoes while Sarah cooked dinner, and she said, "I enjoy talking to Margaret so much, but she still seems so sad. Sometimes she talks about Roy and she starts to cry."

I asked, "Does that make you feel uncomfortable?"

"Sometimes. But I try not to think about that. Mostly I just want to try to help her when she hurts like that. I know it's not much but I think just being there helps some . . . because she doesn't have to feel that way all alone."

I thought for a minute and then said, "Sometimes when Margaret has come over for supper she's talked a lot about the past and seemed pretty depressed. A couple of times I tried to cheer her up, but it never really worked. Then I decided to just let her be herself and feel however she wants to feel. I want her to feel comfortable here . . . not like she has to be in a good mood every time she visits."

"I think that's a good thing to do," Sarah said. "I don't know if she has anyone else to talk to when she's feeling down."

Several times I had a chance to help Margaret with tasks she wasn't used to handling. I remember going over to see her one day about a week before taxes were due. She came to the door with eyes red from crying. When I asked her what was wrong, she led me into the kitchen where there were papers and receipts and tax forms spread all over the table. She pointed and said, "That."

I said, "You've never done these before, have you?"

"Not since I was married."

I looked at the overflowing table and said, "Umm."

Margaret said, "There's no reason why a reasonably intelligent person shouldn't be able to figure all this out. But I keep finding things that make me remember Roy, things we did together . . . and I can't concentrate. Then I get angry at myself and I lose my concentration even more. I read the same instructions over five times and still can't make sense of them. I'm starting to panic. Taxes are due in a week and I don't know if I can get them done." Margaret slapped the tax code book down on the table and said, "Do you know how to do this?"

"I've done ours for years," I said. "Can I help?"

She sighed deeply and said, "Thank you. I think I really need some help."

We started looking through her papers and discovered that many necessary records were missing. While Margaret looked for various receipts and documents, I tried to make sense out of previous years' returns.

After an hour I called Sarah and told her what I was doing. She brought over some sandwiches and helped sort papers. We went until about midnight that night and the next, but we got the work done, and Sarah also set up a system Margaret could use to save the information she'd need the following year.

When we finally finished we were so tired we were silly. We opened a bottle of diet soda and, in the spirit of loving your enemies, toasted the Internal Revenue Service.

That June there was a thunderstorm that blew a big branch off the old oak in Margaret's front yard. I went over with my chain saw and cut it up for her. I also started mowing the lawn for her, because her lawnmower was too heavy and hard for her to control.

Later that summer her clothes dryer stopped working. She told Sarah she was going to call a repairman and Sarah asked her to let me try to fix it first. I'd never fixed a clothes dryer before in my life, but I bought the repair manual and tried this and that until I finally figured out what was wrong and actually fixed it!

That evening Margaret came over for supper. I kept talking about my great accomplishment of fixing the dryer and Sarah kept making fun of how proud I was.

Margaret said, "It would have cost me a lot to have someone come out and repair that machine. Let me at least pay for the book you bought."

I shook my head and Sarah said, "Of course not."

Margaret said, "I'm not sure I can return the favor."

Sarah said, "Just forget about that. We care for you. We want to help."

I said, "You're our friend. That's what friends do for each other."

Margaret smiled and said, "Thank you."

Which of the following activities can be parts of evangelism?

- Picking up groceries for a shut-in neighbor
- Telling another person about your own experiences with God
- Watching a friend's children while she visits her father in the hospital
- Bringing a friend to church
- Cooking a meal for a family with a new baby
- Listening to a lonely person
- Doing yard work for an older person

The answer may surprise you. All of these actions can be ways to communicate God's love to others. They can be vital parts of holistic evangelism!

God's Whole Love for Whole People

God created us as whole people—that is, people who are physical, emotional, social, intellectual, and spiritual all at the same time. This simple truth is obvious when you take the time to think about it. Unfortunately, it is one that people often overlook.

There have been times, for example, when the medical profession treated people's physical problems and ignored the rest of their lives. But emotional stress, loneliness, ignorance about health care, and despair and depression can all be just as dangerous to a person's well-being as injuries or germs. Every part of our life is important. We are whole people. We can't separate one aspect of life and "treat" it as though the other parts don't matter.

Similarly, there have been times when Christians thought that evangelism should only be concerned with people's souls—

that is, with their spiritual dimension. But such evangelism ignores the simple truth that God created us as whole people. God loves us completely, as whole people. Christian evangelism also must be holistic, bringing God's love to people at every level. You can see this clearly in the ministry of Jesus.

How Jesus Evangelized

Jesus was a holistic evangelist. How did he evangelize? Jesus described his whole evangelistic ministry once by reading a short passage from Isaiah: "The Spirit of the Lord is upon me, because he has anointed me to bring good news to the poor. He has sent me to proclaim release to the captives and recovery of sight to the blind, to let the oppressed go free, to proclaim the year of the Lord's favor." (Luke 4:18-19)

Jesus healed the sick, fed the hungry, comforted the bereaved, freed the captives, and raised the dead. While communicating the Gospel message Jesus demonstrated his care for the needs of the people, whether they were physical, intellectual, emotional, social or spiritual needs. (See Matt. 14:14-20, Mark 2:2, John 9, Luke 19:5-7, John 11:20-26, Mark 6:34.) He communicated the Good News of the Kingdom of God through both words and deeds.

The Need to Stay Balanced

There are two traps we can fall into when we evangelize.

Caring Must Include Sharing

The first trap is to care generally for the other person, but then, when he or she is ready to hear the Good News, not telling the person about Jesus' life, death, and resurrection. This may be valuable caring ministry, but it's not evangelism. Telling about Jesus is an integral part of Christian evangelism. If we don't tell the Good News of sins forgiven for Christ's sake at the right time, our evangelism is incomplete.

Sharing Must Include Caring

The second trap we can fall into with evangelism is the trap of speaking but not acting. It can be easy to think that if we've only said the right words about God, our evangelism is complete and we can stop right there. But a words-only witness is incomplete. A complete witness involves caring actions, as well as words.

Preparing the Way for Speaking the Gospel

When you know that evangelizing includes both words and actions, it often makes sense to begin with acts of care and save the words for a little later. Acts of care can prepare the way for you to speak the Gospel. This happens in several ways.

Acts of Care Make Your Witness Credible

Concrete, caring actions show that your witness is not just empty words. You are "putting your money where your mouth is"—and not only your money, but your time, patience, and effort. When people see that you practice what you preach, they are much more likely to trust your message.

Acts of care can even open up opportunities to witness to people who don't trust easily. Here's an example of this.

A young couple began visiting and caring for a family of refugees. The couple helped them find furniture, fill out an apartment lease, and talk with their landlord. They also occasionally provided transportation to the doctor's office.

After three months, the woman asked, "Why are you doing this for me and my family? We cannot pay you. Everyone else wants something from us. Why are you different?" To answer her question, the couple gently told her about how God loved her, and that God's love was what motivated them to care for her. The woman continued to listen as they talked about God's love.

A few weeks later, the woman's elderly mother who lived with her asked, "What have you done to my daughter? She never used to trust anyone. She has had too many bad experiences. But now she trusts you." Later the woman became active in the local church. Acts of care had made the Gospel seem credible to her.

Acts of Care Make Your Witness Relevant

Acts of care can also make your message about God relevant to others. When people who aren't Christians hear the Gospel message that Jesus loves them and forgives them, they may think, "This is wonderful, but what does this have to do with me and my life?"

How do you make the Gospel relevant for a single parent with two children and a full-time job who never has a chance to relax? How about someone who is facing retirement from a much-loved occupation and wondering, "What is going to motivate me to get up in the morning?"

Martin Luther once said that as Christians, we "are Christs

one to another and do to our neighbors as Christ does to us.''[1]
Paul says that *we* are the body of Christ (1 Cor. 12:27). Others
can't see God with their eyes, but they can see us, and God's
love shining through us. When we care in concrete ways for
others, we make it much easier for them to believe in a God
who cares about *them.*

Acts of Care Make Your Witness Hearable

It may sound strange, but sometimes people just can't hear
you when you share the Gospel. A growling stomach or a scream-
ing baby can be very effective in drowning out the Gospel! To
put it another way, when people have other, very important
concerns on their minds, this can easily block out the message
you're trying to share.

Abraham Maslow, the well-known psychologist, explains
why this happens in terms of a hierarchy of needs.[2] He explains
that everyone has certain needs—physical, intellectual, emotional, social, and spiritual—and some of these are more basic
than others.

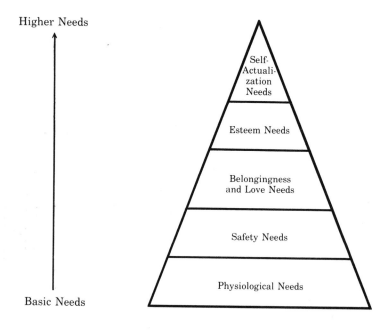

Higher Needs

Self-Actualization Needs

Esteem Needs

Belongingness and Love Needs

Safety Needs

Physiological Needs

Basic Needs

Maslow points out that if a person has two or more needs at
the same time, he or she will normally concentrate on the more
basic one first. Only when the more basic need is met will the

person move on to deal with the higher need. In Maslow's system, religion—that is, issues of meaning, eternity, and relationship with God—is one of the higher needs, and usually gets attention only after the basic needs for food, shelter, security, and affection are met.

This clearly applies to evangelism. Imagine a homeless person named Milt. Milt has several needs. On a physical level, he needs shelter, good food, and possibly medical treatment. On the social level, he needs to feel that others see him as a worthwhile person. On the spiritual level, Milt needs to learn about Jesus and receive God's gift of faith.

Since physical needs—food, shelter, and health—are most basic, those will be the needs that Milt spends his time and energy on. He probably won't even think about his higher needs until he finds a place to stay and something to eat. He's too busy worrying about the basic needs.

Holistic evangelism means bringing God's love to Milt to meet all his needs, from the most basic to the highest. Maslow's hierarchy shows you that your holistic evangelism needs to begin with the most basic needs in order to effectively meet all Milt's needs. If you deal only with the needs that are labeled as spiritual, your evangelism will not only be incomplete, it will be ineffective.

As you grow as a caring evangelist, cultivate an awareness of more than just the spiritual needs of others. Become sensitive to physical, emotional, mental, social, and spiritual needs. Then you can share God's whole love with whole people. Your acts of care and your words of hope will show others a God who loves them completely and is concerned with every aspect of their lives.

[1]Martin Luther, *The Freedom of a Christian*, Luther's Works, vol. 31, ed. Harold J. Grimm (Philadelphia: Fortress Press, 1957), p. 368.

[2]Abraham Maslow, *Motivation and Personality* (New York: Harper & Row, 1954).

Chapter 9

Evangelizing in Crisis

About six months after Roy died Margaret went through an especially tough time. Though we didn't know it then, it became a turning point in her relationship with God.

We were getting ready to go out of town on a week's vacation. I was packing the car, and Sarah called Margaret.

When Sarah got off the phone, she looked worried. "I asked Margaret to pick up the mail and the paper for us, and she said she would."

"Good," I said. "How is she doing?"

"I don't really know. She said something about a meeting at the school where she works—budget cuts or something like that. I hope it's nothing serious."

"Oh, I'm sure she'll be all right. We can check in with her when we get back."

When we got back home the next week, there were several newspapers lying in our driveway. Sarah and I looked at each other. "Maybe I ought to go over and check to see if Margaret's okay," she said.

I unpacked the suitcases and was throwing clothes in the washer when I heard Sarah come in the house. When I walked out of the laundry room I saw Sarah sitting at the kitchen table, her chin resting on her hand, with an upset look on her face. This was so unlike Sarah that I stood and stared for a moment.

She saw me and said, "I'm pretty sure she's home, but she wouldn't answer the door."

I went to the phone and said, "I'm going to call her. Maybe she's hurt or something."

Her phone rang about 15 times. I was about ready to hang up and call the police when Margaret answered.

"Hello." She sounded tired.

"Hi. This is Andy." She didn't say anything so I went on, "We just got back and wanted to call and say hi."

"Oh. Hi."

There were about ten seconds of silence. Then I said, "Are you okay?"

"Yes. I'm fine."

I held my hand over the mouthpiece of the phone and whispered to Sarah, "Should I invite her over tonight?"

Sarah nodded yes. I said to Margaret, "Listen, we're going to cook out tonight. Sort of bring the vacation to an end. We'd love it if you'd come over and join us."

Margaret was quiet for a moment, then she said, "Well . . . I don't . . ."

I cut in. "Oh, come on over. We've missed you."

"All right . . . I suppose."

"Great. We'll probably eat in about an hour."

I hung up and said to Sarah, "She doesn't sound very happy at all. I wonder what's going on."

Margaret showed up an hour and a half later. Her clothes looked all wrinkled and disorganized. She had always worn very plain clothing, never any bright colors, but her clothes always looked crisp and clean. Now she looked like she had worn the same skirt and blouse for a couple of days in a row.

We had supper ready and sat down to eat as soon as she arrived. Sarah and I told Margaret about our trip and she listened without saying much.

After a while the conversation waned and we ate in silence. Finally I said, "Margaret, is something wrong? You don't seem yourself."

She took a deep breath and said, "It's nothing really. I'm doing fine."

Sarah got some coffee and we drank it quietly until Sarah said, "Margaret, it really seems like there's something wrong. If it's none of our business, just say so and we'll honor your privacy. But if you don't mind, we'd like to know how you've been . . . what's been going on the past week or two. And frankly, I'm concerned about you. You seem . . . I don't know . . . sad or something."

Margaret looked at Sarah for a moment and then smiled a feeble smile. She said, "I've been fine . . . I suppose all the things going on at work have had me preoccupied."

We waited for a moment and she continued, "They're talking about budget cuts in the school district if a tax increase doesn't get passed this fall. We'll probably lose five or six teachers from our school."

Sarah said, "Oh, no."

"I don't think I'll lose my job," Margaret said, "I've been there so many years . . . but I'm sure one or more of my friends in the English department will go."

We talked a bit longer, but Margaret didn't seem in the mood to visit. She went home soon after we finished our coffee.

When I got home from work the next evening I looked over at Margaret's yard. The grass had gotten really high since I mowed it last, before vacation. I decided to go over after dinner and mow it for her.

When I knocked on her door she didn't answer. After waiting for a few minutes I decided to go get my mower and just do it without bothering her. After I had cut the grass for a minute or two I looked up and saw Margaret standing on her front porch. She looked furious.

I stopped the mower and walked over to her. "I knocked, but when you didn't answer, I thought no one was home. So I brought over my own mower. I hope you don't mind."

She stood for a moment with her fists clenched. Then she said, "I do mind. I don't need you to mow my lawn anymore. I am completely capable of taking care of myself." Then she turned and went back in the house.

I pushed my mower back across the street and went inside. I was feeling angry. I told Sarah what had happened.

"You're upset," she said.

"Yes, I am. I don't think I deserve to be treated that way. I have half a mind to go over there and tell her so."

Sarah steepled her fingers and pursed her lips. That's how I knew she didn't agree.

"Okay, then, what do you think I should do?"

She thought for a moment. "Just let it rest. Be patient. Margaret's going through a tough time, and I think it has to do with more than just her job."

"All right. I really didn't want to go over there and yell at her anyway." I pushed my chair back and put my feet up on another chair. "But I want to do something. It's frustrating to just sit here when there's something wrong."

Sarah shrugged.

I looked out the open window. It was almost dark. "Maybe we could pray for her."

"Now that's a good idea," Sarah said. "I think the thing she needs most right now is God's help."

She sat down at the table. As I started to pray I heard Margaret's lawn mower start up across the street.

All of us have times of crisis, times when our normal ways of living and coping suddenly no longer work. Often these are painful times that cause us to question the assumptions we have based our lives on.

Times of crisis can be times of spiritual growth, as the experiences of Jacob, David, Job, and Peter illustrate (Gen. 27:41-33:20; 2 Sam. 11:1-12:25; Job; John 18:10-11, 15-27, John 21). As a caring evangelist, you have a special opportunity to care, to listen, to live Christ's love for others in crisis.

You will be much better able to care for others if you have some understanding of what happens to people in crisis. This chapter will explain the crisis process and describe how you can help people in crisis receive the love and hope that God offers in Jesus.

What Is a Crisis?

What is a crisis? How do you know when a person you care about is experiencing a crisis?

According to Karl Slaikeu, "A crisis is a temporary state of upset and disorganization, characterized chiefly by an individual's inability to cope with a particular situation using customary methods of problem solving, and by the potential for a radically positive or negative outcome."[1]

Kinds of Crisis

There are two types of crises: accidental and developmental. Accidental crises are set off by an unexpected event. A car accident, a sudden death of a loved one, the loss of a job—these are all events that could touch off an accidental crisis. Developmental crises arise from predictable life events. Going away to college can be a crisis for many people; so can be watching the last child leave home. Marriage or the birth of a child can be crises. These are all predictable life changes that can spark a crisis, even when a person thinks he or she is prepared for them.

A Time of Change

A crisis is a time of rapid change in a person's life. Suddenly the stable, reliable world has been turned upside down, causing the individual to feel lost, out of control, or unable to cope.

Sometimes changes in a person can bring on a crisis. Changes in appearance or health can do this. Becoming disabled can certainly lead to crisis. Adolescents may face crisis as their bodies change and grow.

Nonphysical changes in an individual can also bring on crisis. A good example of this is conversion. For some people, the changes that come with beginning a relationship with God are so sweeping and unsettling that they constitute a crisis.

Crises can also involve changes in relationships. Leaving home, marriage or divorce, a death in the family, becoming a parent—all of these involve great changes in relationships that can bring on a crisis.

Changes in one's environment can also bring on a crisis. Moving can be very stressful, as individuals try to adjust to a new place, a new climate, and new people. Changes in the emotional environment can also cause crises. One example of this might be the stress caused by the divorce of a parent or child.

A Time When Old Ways of Coping Don't Work Anymore

Another way to describe a crisis is as a time when the old ways of coping just don't work anymore. Over time people develop certain ways of dealing with stress that work well. But then they're faced with a completely changed situation, and suddenly the old ways just don't work anymore.

This can be very frightening. They may feel overwhelmed and out of control. They experience a crisis.

The Time Frame of a Crisis

The average length of a crisis is four to six weeks. By the end of that time, most people will have found a way to resolve the crisis, whether the way is positive or negative.

Recognizing Signs of Crisis

How can you tell if someone you care for is experiencing a crisis? There are several warning signs that can tip you off. Knowing the signs can help you identify and care for these people better.

Social Signs of Crisis

People in crisis often feel overwhelmed and desperate, and this can affect their relationships with other people. They may withdraw from social activities and relationships. They may stop attending club meetings or church. They may stop visiting friends, withdrawing into a private world instead.

Crises can also affect their performance at work, school, or in the home. People in crisis feel overwhelmed, and the ordinary responsibilities of work and home life may suddenly be too much for them. They may be absent or late more frequently; assignments and projects may not be finished on time.

Physical Signs of Crisis

Going through a crisis can also affect a person's health. Some common problems are headaches, ulcers, upset stomach, or constantly feeling tired. People in crisis may begin sleeping much more or less than they normally do. Occasionally they will also misuse food, alcohol, or drugs.

Mental and Emotional Signs of Crisis

Another sign of crisis is an inability to cu..centrate. People may seem preoccupied or become easily confused. They may be anxious or worried about something, and this interferes with their ability to think well and organize their ideas.

Emotionally, they may seem depressed or withdrawn. They may be very touchy, overreacting to events or circumstances that are actually not important.

Spiritual Signs of Crisis

In the spiritual realm, a person in crisis may express anger, doubt, or rejection toward the God who has allowed the crisis to take place. These are normal reactions. Alternately, the person may show a much stronger dependence on God for support to get through the crisis.

Crisis: Opportunity or Danger

A crisis often becomes a turning point in life. Sometimes people discover very constructive ways to resolve their crises. Other times people choose very destructive solutions.

Growing through Crisis

Dealing effectively with a crisis can help people gain greater maturity. The crisis forces them to develop more effective ways of dealing with the world, with others, and with themselves.

Through crises people can also gain new knowledge about themselves. They discover new strengths and new weaknesses. They may develop a deeper relationship with God based on honesty about their own needs and increased reliance on God's strength.

Negative Resolutions to a Crisis

Unfortunately, it is also possible for a crisis to have a negative outcome. When people fail to deal with a crisis in an effective and healthy way, it can be very costly. They may destroy relationships that could have been saved. They may try to deny their problems and lock themselves into a prison of lies and self-deception. They may even turn to substance abuse or suicide. Worst of all, they may choose to reject God, slamming the door in God's face.

An Unstable Triangle

During ordinary times people's lives are pretty firmly anchored, just like the base of the triangle on the line below. They are not very likely to experience any changes that tip their lives to either side.

During a crisis, all that changes. A crisis is a very delicate point, when people are poised between a healthy and unhealthy resolution. Even a small force can knock them over, one way or the other.

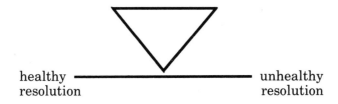

healthy resolution ————————— unhealthy resolution

Just like the upside-down triangle, when people are in crisis their lives are unstable. They can end up with either a healthy or unhealthy resolution.

The Value of Care for Those in Crisis

What determines whether people choose a healthy or unhealthy resolution to a crisis? While there are many factors, one of the most important is care. When you are there to listen, to encourage, to care for people in crisis, the chances become much greater that they will accept the challenge of crisis and grow, both spiritually and emotionally.

Caring for People in Crisis

So how can you care for people in crisis? What specific skills can you use to share God's love with them?

Here is some good news—it's just more of the same! Caring for people in crisis means praying, building a relationship with them, listening, helping people sort through their feelings, thinking of their everyday needs that you could help to meet, and gentle witnessing. These are all skills that you use on an everyday basis as a caring evangelist. While you may need to use these skills more intensely with a person in crisis, it's still the same kind of caring.

While the basic caring skills you use remain the same, knowing about some special needs that people in crisis experience can help you understand them and care for them better. Following are some of those special needs, and some things you can do to care for people with those needs.

Feeling under Pressure

People in crisis feel a sense of pressure. Their once stable world is falling apart, and things they've always depended on—a healthy body, a good marriage, a steady income—suddenly aren't dependable anymore. Events are happening much too fast and too dangerously in their lives, and they feel out of control.

They may also be facing important decisions that they don't feel ready or able to make. For example, a grieving person may need to make decisions about the funeral service, burial or cremation, and how to handle the cost. A person experiencing the crisis of divorce may need to find new housing, a job, and child care within a very short period of time. All of these decisions add to the sense of pressure.

Be a Source of Stability

How can you care for these people in a way that addresses their feelings of being under pressure? Start by remembering that they need a source of stability, calm, and encouragement.

They need someone who will simply be there for them. You can care for people who feel under pressure by making yourself a stable point in their chaotic world.

Withhold Judgment

People in crisis may say and do things that you don't fully agree with. If possible, you should keep your judgment to yourself. Your caring and nonjudgmental love may allow people to discover the problem themselves. Then they can change. If, however, you show that you are easily shocked or disappointed by people in crisis, they will probably avoid you simply because they don't have the energy to deal with your reactions on top of their own problems.

Encourage Them to Avoid Easy Solutions

Encourage people experiencing the pressure of a crisis to endure the crisis, instead of finding an easy and unhealthy way out. Your caring presence may give them the courage to survive the crisis without turning to an easy "fix" like abusing alcohol, denying the truth of a situation, or leaving a painful relationship prematurely.

Feeling Adrift

Another common feeling people in crisis experience is a sense of being adrift. They may feel like people in a boat adrift in a storm, desperately searching for something solid to tie on to.

This is a common feeling because of the nature of crisis itself. When the old ways of coping stop working, people often panic. They may start trying new ways—any way—just to get their lives back to normal again.

Don't Be a "Crisis Vulture"

For this reason you must be extremely careful to stay process-oriented. When you see people adrift, it can be very tempting to step in and take charge of their lives. You may want to offer advice that you *know* will work, if they will only try it. You may feel like saying, "Here. Believe in Jesus Christ and all your problems will be over."

But this is something you need to avoid. Taking advantage of a person in crisis is uncaring and opportunistic, even if it is done with the best of motives. It is being a "crisis vulture."

As a caring person, it may be difficult for you to avoid giving solutions or attempting to fix the problem. The pain of others may make you feel uncomfortable and drive you to solve the crisis to meet your own needs. But remember, God may be working in powerful ways through the pain and instability of crisis. Imposing your own solution may interfere with God's working in others' lives. It's much better to learn to live with the tension and pain in the lives of others, praying that God's will and work may be done in their lives, and then waiting—expectantly, eagerly, hopefully for God to act and for them to respond.

Feeling Guilty

People in crisis may feel guilty, either for causing the crisis, or for the way their own personal crisis is affecting others they care about. Such guilt can be either irrational or rational.

Irrational Guilt

Irrational guilt is when people feel guilty for something that is not actually their fault. It is a natural response to crisis, but it can be very harmful. Sometimes people get stuck in irrational guilt and never work through the rest of the crisis process.

How can you care for someone suffering from irrational guilt feelings? First of all, keep your evaluations to yourself. Instead of telling people, "You really shouldn't blame yourself," encourage them to talk it out. Over time they will come to this realization themselves. Meanwhile, being able to talk about their pain can help them move beyond the need for their irrational guilt.

Rational Guilt

Sometimes people in crisis feel guilty for good reason. This is rational guilt. In such cases, you can still care for the person by listening with caring acceptance. Your forgiving, accepting love can make God's forgiving love seem more real to them.

One thing that is very important is to take guilt seriously. Never ignore it or rationalize it away, or encourage people in crisis to do so. That discounts their need and doesn't solve the problem.

Instead, allow others to face their guilt at their own time in an atmosphere of caring. You can model the accepting love that fully recognizes the others' wrong and still values and accepts them. As others take responsibility for the harm they have caused or the wrong they have done, you can then gently share with them the news of God's forgiveness through Christ.

As you share, you can also be honest about your own life as a forgiven child of God. You can make it clear that you, too, are a person who needs forgiveness, and you receive it from God. This gives others hope.

Feeling Angry

Yet another common feeling that people in crisis experience is anger. They may be angry at themselves for not being able to cope, angry at others for causing the crisis, or angry at God for allowing it to happen. Anger, too, can be rational or irrational.

Anger needs expressing. A person in crisis who is feeling angry needs a safe place to talk about it. If anger is never expressed, some of the emotional results that can follow are bitterness, a tendency to get angry without cause, and depression. Unexpressed anger can lead to physical problems, including ulcers and heart problems. It can also lead to a crisis in faith.

Anger at the Caregiver

How can you care for people in crisis who are angry? First of all, listen, and realize that people in crisis will often express anger at you when you don't deserve it. You don't need to feel threatened by that—it's part of a normal reaction to crisis. Instead of being shocked, defensive, hurt, or angry, you can react calmly. This will help others move beyond their anger.

Look beneath the Anger

Often anger covers deep pain. It is a way people protect themselves from feeling hurt. If you can learn to look beneath the anger to the hurt inside, you will be able to stay calm and accepting. You will be able to love people in crisis, even when they are most unlovable.

Taking Care of Yourself

It is important to remain calm and accepting. This doesn't mean you should let yourself be hurt or abused. If an angry person is completely out of control and hurting you, the most caring thing to do may be to simply get out of the situation and wait for the person to calm down. But then, if it is possible, be there to care again. You may have to walk a tightrope, balancing your own self-care with care for the other person.

Anger at God

Sometimes people will express anger at God. This can be a special problem for caring evangelists who may feel a natural desire to defend God. They may even fear that if they allow people to express anger at God, that means those people are rejecting God forever.

In a situation like this, remember that you don't have to defend God. God is able to handle people's anger, and God continues to love them. Your role is not to defend God, but to express God's overriding love toward the others by listening.

Dealing with Deep Questions

Crises cause people to rethink their lives. They begin to ask difficult questions like "Can anyone really love me? What is important in life? How can I have better relationships with others? How can I be ready to die when the time comes?"

You can care for people while they work through these questions by listening and, when appropriate, gently sharing the truth you have found in Jesus. Even be alert for questions like these that people may have, but don't ask. If you suspect that the other person is worried about such questions, but doesn't know how to bring them up, you may wish to gently bring up the questions yourself.

Unanswerable Questions

Crisis is also a time when people who are hurting ask unanswerable questions, like "Why did God allow this to happen to me?" and "Why is there so much evil in the world?" These are questions that no one, not even theologians, can completely answer. Everyone will have to wait until heaven for the answers.

Instead of trying to answer the unanswerable, listen and share others' hurt and confusion with them. Very often people don't want spoken, logical answers at all. Instead, they are really saying, "I hurt. I'm angry. This isn't fair." As you understand the feelings behind the questions, you will be able to care for them by sharing their struggle and pain.

The Power of Prayer

God alone knows the depths of other people's need. That is why prayer is such an important part of crisis ministry. Ask the Holy Spirit to guide you in whatever you do or do not do.

Evangelizing People in Crisis

Evangelizing people in crisis gives you a special opportunity to share God's love. Your caring is in itself a form of witness. It makes God's caring more concrete to the person. As a little boy once said, it puts "skin" on God's love.

Crisis evangelism is also important because it is during crisis that people may see their own need for a Savior for the first time. Crises force people to rethink their lives, to see their own frailties and their inability to cope on their own. For this reason people are more willing to make changes, even in their relationships with God.

Because crisis is a time when people start thinking about the deep questions of life, it is a time when they are naturally interested in God. They may find a new interest in hearing the Good News at times of crisis.

As you care for people in crisis, listen especially well for indications that a person wants to talk about deep issues that may have spiritual roots. Then you can provide the opportunity to do so.

If it seems appropriate and the other person is willing to hear, you may want to tell about your own experiences of being in crisis and receiving God's care. You might also talk about what you have learned from the Bible. In all this, of course, be sure to stay process-oriented and avoid taking advantage of a painful and unsettled time in the other person's life.

[1]Karl A. Slaikeu, *Crisis Intervention: A Handbook for Practice and Research* (Boston: Allyn and Bacon, Inc., 1984), p. 13.

Chapter 10

Uncovering God-Sized Needs

Sarah and I were driving home from church on Sunday morning. I was thinking about Margaret.

"I was remembering some of the things we talked about right after Roy died, about Margaret being so alone and all. She said they'd always taken care of their own needs, and it was hard for her to depend on others."

Sarah said, "Uh huh."

"I was just thinking that maybe she's starting to realize that she can't do everything by herself anymore, and that's what's hurting her so much these days."

Sarah nodded. "You may be right. She doesn't say much about that when we talk . . . but then she wouldn't. Maybe that's part of the problem."

"I remember thinking that I wouldn't want to go through what she's going through without God's help," I said. "It's so frustrating about her and her father and the church and all. I wish she could see what God is really like. I think it could help her to know that God cares about what she's going through."

"She's struggling with something," Sarah said. "The way her life is now, it isn't working, and she's fighting against changing, against giving something up, I think. Maybe God is at work in all of this."

"I guess all we can do is keep praying," I said.

We did keep praying and doing what we could to care for Margaret. We talked to her every other day or so and had her over for dinner a couple of times. Then, about three weeks after we got back from vacation, she called and asked if she could come over.

We sat in the living room in front of the fireplace. It was a chilly, early autumn night. While I started a fire, Margaret began talking.

"Things have been very difficult for me recently. I know I've been rather rude to you, and I want to say I'm sorry. You certainly don't deserve to be treated that way. I owe you an explanation."

"You don't owe us anything," Sarah said as she put her hand on Margaret's. I pulled up a chair and sat down to listen.

"Thanks for understanding," Margaret said. "But I need to tell someone about what I'm going through. Sometimes I feel so overwhelmed I'm afraid I'm going crazy.

"This whole thing started while you were away. I had thought I was over the worst of my sadness about Roy, but it seems I was wrong.

"When the problems at work hit, I suddenly felt terribly threatened and alone. I worried constantly about what I would do if I lost my job, even though I knew that probably wouldn't happen. And then I began to feel very angry at Roy . . . for no reason except that he had died and left me alone. I wasn't sure if I could make it without him. I was mad at him for not being here to help me."

Margaret wiped her eyes and was quiet for a moment. Then she continued, "I counted on Roy, and now he's gone, and I don't want to have to count on anyone else. It hurts too much when they leave . . ." She closed her eyes, as if gathering her thoughts, and tears ran down her cheeks.

"And you can't count on anyone not to die . . ." I said.

Margaret opened her eyes and looked straight at me. "Yes, that's the problem. I can't completely count on anyone. And that started me thinking about the two of you. I know this will sound selfish, and I hope you don't take it wrong, but right when all this hit me, you were gone."

Sarah said, "Oh, Margaret . . ."

Margaret shook her head. "I'm not saying that you shouldn't have gone on vacation. I don't expect you to live your whole life around me. I'm just telling you this because I need to tell someone how afraid I am, and you've been willing to listen to me before."

I said, "But when you needed us, we were gone. It feels like you can't really rely on anyone."

Margaret said, "That's right . . . and I don't see how I can make it all by myself. That's why I got mad at you when you came over to mow my lawn. It just reminded me that I need help . . .

I need others. I didn't want to be reminded of that. It made me furious. I'm sorry, Andy. You didn't deserve to be treated that way."

"I was pretty angry at you that night," I said. "But it didn't last long."

"Thank you for that, Andy. You've been a good friend."

"You've had a tough year," I said. "Sarah and I have been trying to understand what it must be like for you . . . and we've been praying for you because we feel so helpless to do anything about the pain you're feeling."

Tears welled up again in Margaret's eyes. I couldn't think of what I could do to help, so I just sat there quietly for a while and shared Margaret's sadness. It really hurt.

After a while, I said, "Part of the reason I've been thinking about you so much is because what you're going through reminds me of when my father died . . . a long time ago, before I married Sarah."

Margaret asked, "What happened?"

"Dad had always worked seven days a week all the time I was growing up, building his business. He had finally been able to relax a little for a year or two, and then he died of a heart attack. I was at college studying business administration in order to eventually take over the family business. I ended up taking over much sooner than I expected.

"To make a long story short, within two years we were almost bankrupt and I had to sell the business for a fraction of what it had been worth. Dad had held things together with chewing gum and baling wire, and it all fell apart when he died. I was completely out of my depth. I didn't stand a chance of keeping the thing going.

"So I had failed, and my father was dead, and I hadn't even taken the time to grieve his death because I had to work so hard at the business. I felt completely alone. All my self-confidence was gone. I felt like I couldn't keep going on my own."

Margaret nodded.

"Margaret, please don't take offense at this, and if you don't want to hear it, just tell me and I'll keep it to myself."

Margaret said, "No, go on."

"What I learned about myself then was that I couldn't make it on my own . . . or maybe that I didn't want to try. That's when God really helped me. I felt God's care for me more than I ever had in my life."

I stopped, looked at Margaret, then continued, "I know you've had terrible experiences with people talking about God, and to tell you the truth, I'm scared you're going to just lump me in with all those other people who've hurt you with talk about God."

I looked at Margaret for her reaction. She said, "I'm listening."

I said, "The reason I'm telling you this is because the God whose care I experienced is very different from your father's God. God accepted me and loved me. I saw that Jesus wasn't just leaving me to suffer all this alone. He was there with me in the middle of it. And he wasn't going to die and go away like my father had. He was reliable and caring and he was there for me at my lowest time."

Everyone was quiet for a few moments. Then Margaret said, "That was a very difficult time for you."

"Yeah, it really was. I think that's part of the reason why I've been so worried about you. I remember how badly I hurt and how much I needed someone to share the pain with me."

"The two of you have done that for me," Margaret said. "I don't know if I could have made it through these last months without you."

We kept talking, the three of us. Margaret didn't say any more about what I'd said about God. She just talked about Roy and how hard it was living alone. She had a lot of hurt inside. While she told us about it, Sarah and I listened. It was early morning when we finally said good night.

"Seeing is believing." It's true that everyone has God-sized needs—needs that are so big that it takes a crucified and resurrected Savior to solve them. But in Caring Evangelism, it doesn't work to simply announce that fact to others or to argue with them in order to convince them that they need God. That is results-oriented, and it's an almost certain formula for rejection. Instead, we can help people discover their own need for God. We can care for them, listen to them, and witness to them as they begin to see for themselves that they need God's love and presence.

Why It's Difficult to Recognize God-Sized Needs

Why is it so difficult for people to see their God-sized needs? One reason is pride. People don't want to admit that they need help, that they can't make it on their own. It goes against the grain.

An even deeper reason is fear. Many are afraid to face up to their own helplessness because they aren't completely confident that God will be there to rescue them. It just seems safer not to think about such things.

When people admit their own need it can make them feel deeply sad. They are losing something very important. It might be the image they have had of themselves as completely self-sufficient. Or they might have to give up a "false god," that is, something other than God that they've been counting on to make them happy. For example, it can hurt to admit that a new job is not going to solve all the problems they faced at their last jobs.

Admitting the need for a Savior is a little bit like dying. Jesus said, "If any want to become my followers, let them deny themselves and take up their cross and follow me. For those who want to save their life will lose it, and those who lose their life for my sake will find it." (Matt. 16:24-25) The Apostle Paul said, "I have been crucified with Christ; and it is no longer I who live, but it is Christ who lives in me. And the life I now live in the flesh I live by faith in the Son of God, who loved me and gave himself for me." (Gal. 2:19b-20) Admitting they need a Savior means dying to the pride that makes them think otherwise.

How Do People Become Aware of Their God-Sized Needs?

It usually takes time and struggle for people to become aware of their God-sized needs. The Caring Evangelization Cycle you first saw in chapter 3 provides a map to show how this can happen.

Step One: God Reaches Out to Us

When the Bible says, "There is no one righteous, not even one; there is no one who has understanding, there is no one who seeks God" (Rom. 3:10-11), it tells one of the reasons why it is so important that we have a loving God who reaches out to us. The only way people can see their need for God is with God's help. Left to themselves, people will never even realize they need a Savior.

But God does not leave people on their own. Jesus identified the Holy Spirit as the one who shows people their need (John 16:7-8). The Spirit often communicates to people through circumstances. Sometimes the most loving thing God does is to allow people to live with the consequences of their choices for a while, so they can better understand and appreciate God's gift of forgiveness and new life. The Spirit also communicates through the words of Scripture. "Indeed, the word of God is living and active, sharper than any two-edged sword . . . it is able to judge the thoughts and intentions of the heart." (Heb. 4:12)

God's reaching-out love can be tough love. People would rather not know about their need for Jesus. They would prefer to remain in their self-satisfied status quo.

Step Two: We Experience the Failure of Our False Gods

But then something happens to change the status quo. Sometimes that happens when people start examining their lives and see that they simply don't measure up to what God demands. Or a crisis may shake their self-confidence. People are no longer complacent; now they feel ill-at-ease or even panicked. The crisis makes them realize that there's more to life than they thought.

Rebecca Pippert describes this stage of seeing our need for something beyond ourselves:

> It is clear we don't change unless something grabs our attention. It could be anything: a sense of inadequacy or anxiety, being fed up with feeling angry or worthless, a lack of inner peace, an empty marriage or frustration with being single, a difficult child, the pay raise that didn't bring the desired self-satisfaction, the shock of some pattern of behavior getting out of control, getting involved in destructive or unsatisfactory relationships and not knowing why. Whatever the seeds of discontent, we finally cross some critical threshold at which we get disgusted or dissatisfied enough to decide to do something about it.[1]

At this point, people may try many ways to solve their own problems, hoping to make the pain go away. But none of these solutions completely work out.

People may try changing themselves. They may go on a diet, stop smoking, change their routine, take more responsibility for their lives, read a self-help book—the list goes on and on.

They may try changing the people around them. They may decide to discipline their children differently, go to marriage counseling, get a different job, find new friends, or demand that those close to them change in some way. Again, however, these changes don't solve the deepest problems.

They may try simply to escape by using alcohol and other drugs to block the pain in their lives. People may divorce or leave home in order to escape. They may immerse themselves in their work in order to ignore problems at home. Sometimes people even go on shopping sprees in order to feel better, at least for a little while.

Many people try blaming others. Some blame their parents, children, or spouse. Others blame God. But the problem is still there.

All these solutions are false gods. They are unable to answer life's most difficult questions.

Step Three: We Admit Our Powerlessness, Our Need for a Savior

Some people finally reach the point where they clearly see the frightening truth about themselves. They see that they aren't strong enough, determined enough, smart enough, clever enough, or good enough to make their lives what they want them to be. They may see that they will never measure up to God's demands. They may even fear God's punishment. They see, more clearly than ever before, that they are going to die, and there's nothing they can do about it.

They realize that they are powerless to meet their God-sized needs. At times like this people understand that they need a Savior, someone more powerful than they who can meet the God-sized needs that they can't meet themselves.

God-Sized Needs

Here are some very specific ways people need a Savior. People need a Savior who:

- repairs the broken relationship with God;
- forgives sins;
- defeats death;

- loves them (in spite of who they are or what they've done);
- gives meaning and purpose to their lives;
- gives hope for the future;
- comforts them when they suffer;
- provides for all their needs;
- conquers evil and suffering;
- knows what it's like to experience pain, suffering, rejection, defeat, and death; and
- is a friend of sinners.

How Can You Help People See Their Deepest Need for a Savior?

Uncovering God-sized needs means building on all the Caring Evangelism skills you've been reading about up to this point. You need to build an evangelizing relationship, listen, and care for the other person's feelings and other holistic needs. If evangelists try to move right to uncovering God-sized needs without laying a caring relationship foundation, they come off as manipulative and uncaring.

Then you need to wait until people are jarred out of their comfortable self-satisfaction. With most people you won't have to wait very long for that to happen. There are others, however, who seem to always have their lives under control and who refuse to admit there's anything wrong, even when there is. With those people you still need to wait and pray and trust that God will use you when they experience the crisis that shows them that they need to change and grow.

Uncovering God-sized needs means doing three things: recognize, reflect, and witness.

Recognize

Always be on the lookout for signs that people are struggling with difficult issues. Sometimes you will see signs that others are in crisis. Other times you may realize that people are asking "God-sized" questions—questions that point to their God-sized needs, questions that can only be fully answered by a crucified and resurrected Savior.

Following is a list of God-sized questions that people might ask.

- **Identity**—Who am I? Who should I be?

- **Self-Esteem**—Am I lovable? Can I really like the person I am?

- **Meaning**—Why am I alive? Is there a reason for me to go on living?

- **Hope vs. Despair**—How can I face the future with hope and not dread?

- **Reason for Evil**—Why is there evil in the world? In my life?

- **Failure**—What if I fail? How could I live with myself?

- **Loneliness/Abandonment**—Am I really all alone in the world? What can I do about this aching loneliness I feel?

- **Addiction/Compulsions**—Is there any way to get out of this trap of addiction or compulsion I'm in? How can I stop doing things that are self-destructive?

- **Guilt**—How can I deal with the guilt I feel over what I've done?

- **Aging**—Why do I have to get old?

- **Purpose**—What am I going to do with my life?

- **Dissatisfaction**—Why doesn't my success bring me satisfaction?

- **Forgiveness**—How can I forgive people who have hurt me? How can I find forgiveness for the hurts I have caused?

- **Suffering**—Why do I, or people I love, have to suffer?

- **Broken Relationships**—Why do I fight with people I love?

- **Regrets**—Why do I do things I later regret?

- **Self-Doubt**—How can I handle the responsibilities I've been given?

- **Death**—Why do I, or people I love, have to die?

People can ask questions like these without realizing that they are, at root, religious questions. You may recognize that people are struggling with God-sized needs before they do. They may be asking about the meaning of life without knowing that God provides the answers.

When you think others are wrestling with God-sized needs, don't simply announce that to them. You can respond in two very important ways. First, pray. Thank the Holy Spirit for showing you some of the other person's needs and ask God to continue using you to care for the other person and to communicate the Good News about Jesus to him or her. Second, listen. Allow people to talk more about their problems *as they see them*, not as you interpret them.

Reflect

You can do this by reflecting the God-sized questions you hear.

As you saw in chapter 6, reflecting means saying back the concern you have heard. This gives the other person an opportunity to talk more about that concern. If he or she chooses to say more, then continue to focus on his or her feelings and questions. God works through such a ministry of listening and reflecting to help people realize their need for a Savior.

Some Cautions in Reflecting God-Sized Questions

Avoid Wild Analysis

The first caution is to avoid wild analysis. You read about this in chapter 6 on listening skills. Wild analysis means jumping to conclusions about other people on the basis of a very few words. It is exactly the opposite of long, careful listening.

This conversation between Arlene and an evangelist named Rose shows an example of theological wild analysis:

Arlene: "I feel so bad about leaving my daughter in day-care every day, but this job is important to my family."

Rose: "You feel a terrible sense of guilt and you need Jesus to forgive you and take your sins away."

You can see that Rose is way ahead of Arlene. Rose has assumed first of all that Arlene is feeling guilty, and second, that she is already interested in Jesus and the forgiveness of sin. That is only a wild guess, and there is very little evidence to support it. Wild analysis is also a good way to turn other people off, because they won't want to discuss deeply personal issues if they run the risk of being so badly misunderstood.

Instead of jumping to conclusions about the spiritual state of others, you can patiently listen for understanding. Ask questions and rephrase statements in order to make sure you really understand what the other person is concerned about. Here's how Rose might have done this:

Arlene: "I feel so bad about leaving my daughter in day-care every day, but this job is important to my family."

Rose: "It sounds like you feel a bit guilty."

Arlene: "No, not really—I know it's necessary. But I do wish
I could spend more time with her and develop our relationship."

Rose: "Being close to your daughter is important to you."

Arlene: "Yes, it is. I really want to be a good parent to her,
and that means spending time together."

Because Rose listened and tried to understand, she was able
to discover that Arlene's real concern wasn't guilt at all. It was
a concern over developing a relationship with a child, and
being a good parent to her. If Rose continues to listen, she may
discover a much deeper concern. Arlene is struggling with the
realization that she can't guarantee the child's safety and
happiness, no matter how hard she tries. Arlene may eventually
realize her need for a Savior who will also care for her child.

Avoid "Churchy" Language

There was another problem in the first conversation above—
Rose used "churchy" language. Christians often use special
words like *saved, sin,* and *redemption.* Unfortunately, these can
cause all kinds of misunderstandings for others who have not
spent much time in church. It's best to use common, everyday
language when you talk about spiritual needs. You'll learn more
about how to avoid churchy language in chapter 13.

Stay Process-Oriented

When people start to discover their own deep need for a
Savior, it can be very exciting! As a caring evangelist you may
be tempted to hurry them up, to push them faster and farther
than they are ready to go. Resist this temptation with all your
might. Getting pushy now can lead to disaster. Instead, you can
confidently and joyfully leave it in the hands of the Holy Spirit.
God will work things out in God's own time—not yours. This
allows you to relax and let others go at their own speed.

Stay in Touch with Jesus

Remember Jesus' words: "Apart from me you can do nothing."
(John 15:5) All the caring techniques in the world cannot make
people see their own God-sized needs. Only the Holy Spirit can
do that. Since you want God to use you, stay in touch with
Jesus. Listen, care, and pray silently. Ask God to give you
wisdom as you evangelize.

Witness

Witnessing is the third necessary element, besides identifying and reflecting, that the Spirit uses to help people come to see their God-sized needs.

People won't willingly face up to their need for a Savior if they don't know there's a Savior available. As a natural part of your conversations you can briefly share your own experiences of needing God and seeing those needs met. You can gently communicate that the same Savior is available to them also. Upcoming chapters will discuss witnessing in depth.

Trust God for Results

Helping people discover their need for a Savior can take a long time, but it is much better than simply telling them they need God. When others discover their own need, they are much more eager to hear about the Savior who can meet that need.

[1]Rebecca Manley Pippert, *Hope Has Its Reasons: From the Search for Self to the Surprise of Faith,* (San Francisco: Harper & Row, 1989), p. 67.

Chapter 11

Five Ways to Describe Sin

At the beginning of October we had a week of Indian summer. All I wanted was to be outside, just to enjoy the warmth and store it up for the cold months ahead.

Indian summer always reminds me of my fantasies about the way summer should be. I have always had an unrealistic expectation about summer—that it will be a lazy time for relaxation, swimming, and long afternoons of meandering conversations. In reality summer is never like that for me. It's always one of my busiest times at work.

But Indian summer is more relaxed. It makes me long for all those dream summers that never were. So on Saturday I made a big pot of iced tea, set the chaise lounge up on the back patio and sat and watched the trees and the clouds high in the rich blue sky.

Sarah and Margaret had been out looking for bargains at garage sales all morning. They came back and showed me their booty. Sarah had an old-fashioned coffee percolator, the kind with the glass knob on the lid where you could see the coffee splashing up.

"I got it just to see if the coffee would be any different," she said. "Besides, it was only two dollars."

Sarah went off to percolate some coffee and Margaret pulled up a patio chair.

"You look comfortable," she said.

I told her about my longing for imaginary summer.

She said, "I know what you mean. I have vague memories of happy summer times as a child, but whenever Indian summer comes and the leaves change color, well, . . ." She was quiet for a moment. "I have two maples in my backyard. They're just turning a glorious red now. I wish I could enjoy it more, but I know that in a month they'll be barren. Every year that happens and I feel a sense of loss and sadness. I don't know . . . I suppose it seems like it's autumn in my life also."

I thought about all Margaret's recent sadness. "You've had a lot of that recently."

She raised her eyebrows, asking what I meant.

"I mean sadness . . . loss, I guess. Sometimes trouble comes in cycles, and you seem to be in the middle of one of those times when one thing goes wrong after another."

Margaret said, "You're right." Then she leaned back in her chair, closed her eyes, and covered them from the sunlight.

I sipped my iced tea and enjoyed the warmth of the sun.

Margaret went on quietly, "In a way it reminds me of a poem that was my favorite when I was a child. I liked it at first because it had my name in it; but now it seems to apply more and more to my life."

"What was it?" I asked.

Margaret looked thoughtful. "It's called 'Spring and Fall: to a Young Child,' and it's by Hopkins. I learned it by heart. Would you like to hear it?"

"Of course," I said.

"Margaret, are you grieving
Over Goldengrove unleaving?
Leaves, like the things of man, you
With your fresh thoughts care for, can you?
Ah! as the heart grows older
It will come to such sights colder
By and by, nor spare a sigh
Though worlds of wanwood leafmeal lie;
And yet you *will* weep and know why.
Now no matter, child, the name:
Sorrow's springs are the same.
Nor mouth had, no nor mind, expressed
What heart heard of, ghost guessed:
It is the blight man was born for,
It is Margaret you mourn for."[1]

When she finished, we just sat quietly for a minute or two.

Sarah came outside and said, "I don't know how long it takes one of those things to make coffee, but it seems to be working." She looked around and took a deep breath. "What a perfect day. I love the way the air smells on days like this." She sat down and said, "So what have you two been talking about?"

"Oh, the usual somber questions of life and death and the meaning of it all," Margaret answered. Sarah looked surprised, and Margaret smiled and suppressed a laugh.

I said to Sarah, "She's half-kidding you, I think."

Margaret said, "Andy says this is an afternoon for meandering conversations. That suits me just fine, I think. We were talking about the feeling you get on days like this . . . one of longing and loss."

Sarah said, "Oh," and poured herself some iced tea.

"Lately I've thought deeply about some difficult questions," Margaret said. "I'm having to rethink my basic ideas about the world." She paused for a moment. "For many years I thought that life was there to be molded and disciplined and that we could impose order on it, if we had sufficiently strong character. Now I'm not so sure."

I thought for a moment. "I don't think I ever had the self-discipline to know if that's true or not. I've always had plans to bring my life under control, but I never can do it. Life always wins. I can keep my bad habits under control for a week or a month, but not forever. And it seems like as soon as I get one part of my life under control, about six other parts go haywire. But that's probably just me."

"I don't know," Sarah said. "It seems to me that there's just something wrong . . . at the root of things. The best people I know sometimes have the worst problems."

"I've been thinking the same thing," Margaret said. "It's like one of my favorite poems I was just reciting for Andy. It talks about the blight that seems to be part of life. But what is it about life that makes it seem so wrong?"

Sarah said, "What I've always believed is that the problem is sin."

I swallowed one of the ice cubes in my tea and almost choked. I looked over at Margaret to see if she were angry.

But she wasn't. Instead, she shuddered and said, "Ugh, what an ugly word. That word brings back so many terrible memories."

I looked at Sarah with my why-in-the-world-did-you-bring-that-up? look. She ignored me and said to Margaret, "I know. I hate it too."

Margaret said, "When I hear that word I can still see my father when he said it. His face would get all screwed up in disgust, but with a hint of a grin, as if he enjoyed being disgusted by sin. For him everything was sin, or at least everything he didn't like.''

"When I was growing up,'' I said, "I thought sex was a synonym for sin. I didn't really know what either of the words meant, but I sure knew that my parents didn't approve, and I felt the threat of hell backing up their opinions.''

"Sin wasn't just sex for my father,'' Margaret said. "It was books with ideas he didn't like, and music that didn't suit his taste, and, well . . . I suppose anything that was fun was sin for my father. He never saw his own hypocrisy. He kept reading all this stuff from the Bible about the love of God and all he did was hate.''

We were all quiet for a few minutes, lost in our thoughts.

Then Margaret said, "You said you used to think that sin was sex. What do you think it is now?''

"Oh, boy. Well, I suppose the classic definition is that sin is anything that separates us from God.''

Sarah made a sour face. "It's classic . . . and it's also dry as dust.''

"Okay,'' I said, "you do it better.''

Sarah said, "I remember a sermon our pastor preached about sin. He said he didn't agree with the whole idea of sin as breaking a long list of rules. He said sin was a much more serious problem than that.''

"What did he mean?'' Margaret asked her.

"I don't know how good I'll be at explaining this,'' Sarah said, "but I'll give it a try. Pastor Ed said sin was more like pollution. It contaminates our whole lives. But it's even worse than pollution because there's nothing we can do to get rid of it.''

"Do you mean,'' Margaret asked, "that sin isn't something *we* do? It sounds like you're talking about something out there, instead of something in here,'' she pointed toward her heart. "That *is* different from my father's idea.''

"No, that isn't exactly right either,'' I said. "I remember Ed saying that we're the ones who cause the pollution, because we do things that are so selfish . . . let me see . . . he also said that the problem got started with a break in the relationship between us and God. God wanted us to have everything perfect and we told God to get lost. We wanted to do it our own way.''

"And so God let us,'' Sarah said, "and what we see around us is the result. That's how I understand sin.''

"It certainly is different,'' Margaret said.

"It sure could explain some things,'' Sarah said.

"I suppose it could,'' Margaret agreed.

Five Ways to Describe Sin

One of the biggest challenges we face as caring evangelists is helping people understand sin. People think the concept of sin is outmoded, but actually it is as real as today's news. We need to listen to people to understand how they are experiencing sin, and we need to be able to talk about sin in ways that tie into people's day-to-day experiences.

The Problem with the Problem of Sin

Sin is a big problem—the biggest problem the human race has ever faced. It destroys relationships with God, others, and even with ourselves. The effects of sin are visible daily, in everything from addiction to abuse to acid rain. It is impossible to run away from the effects of sin.

But in spite of this, people deny the deadliness of sin, especially in their own lives. Most people never use the word sin; instead, they call it "mistakes" or "imperfection." They make excuses for sin by saying things like "I'm only human," or "I'm no worse than anyone else." They explain away other kinds of sin by saying, "After all, it's only natural," or, "If God is really loving, God will accept us the way we are." They say these things to avoid facing the seriousness of their problem. They'll do almost anything to avoid realizing the power of the sin that has a hold on them. It's too frightening to think about. It's too embarrassing.

But running away from the problem doesn't solve it, just as pretending to not have cancer doesn't cure the disease. Everyone suffers the effects of sin in the world—in war, in broken families, in the thousand petty arguments, hatreds, and rumors that can make life bitter. No one can avoid the suffering and death that come with being cut off from the Creator, the source of life.

People need to stop running. The only hope people have of finding a cure for the effects of sin is to admit that they have a serious problem with sin. When, by the Spirit's power, they admit their own powerlessness to solve their problems, they can find rescue and new life in the Savior God has provided—Jesus.

How Can We Help Others See and Deal with the Problem of Sin?

How can we help others face up to the seriousness of sin so they can turn to God for rescue? Not by lecturing. When someone is denying a problem, probably the least helpful thing we can do is to force the person to look at what he or she is denying.

People deny because of fear. They deny when they don't feel strong enough to face the truth—when they think that the reality will be too harsh to bear. If someone forces them to look at what they're avoiding, it only makes them feel more afraid, more out of control. It's like throwing a child who can't swim into deep water. The child doesn't stop being afraid of the water. The fear just gets worse.

The only way people can relax their rigid denial is for someone to show them that they don't have to face the truth alone. People can admit to sin if they are absolutely sure that someone else will be there to help, comfort, and love them. A caring, accepting, evangelizing relationship frees them to finally face the truth about themselves and about the world.

Serving as Interpreters

This means that as caring evangelists, we don't have to accuse others in order to talk about sin. Instead of being accusers, we serve as interpreters. We listen as others talk about the effects of what we know to be sin in their lives. We acknowledge the suffering that comes from living in a world alienated from God. Then we share what we believe about why the world is this way, and also what God has done about it.

This sharing and interpreting can be difficult if we don't understand sin very well. A common misconception is that sin involves a kind of cosmic demerit system, in which there's a list of things people aren't supposed to do. Every time they do one of those things it's a mark against them. If people get too many of those marks, they go to hell.

But this is actually a very simplistic way of thinking about sin. Sin is much more difficult, much more terrible than a cosmic demerit board. Sin infects and deforms everything one is and does. Worst of all, sin is absolutely inescapable, apart from Jesus.

We need to take a close look at what sin is like so that we can recognize its effects. Then we can help others to see how it affects them also, so that they can turn to Jesus for help.

Five Ways to Describe Sin

Following are five different pictures of what sin is like and how it shows itself in the world. These are not five different kinds of sin, but rather five different ways of seeing the same central reality.

1. Sin as a Broken Relationship

One helpful way of understanding sin is to see that it involves a broken relationship between us and God. Since that most important relationship is broken, all other relationships suffer also.

A Broken Relationship between Us and God

Sin is refusing God's friendship, failing to respond to the love that God offers us. Although the Holy Spirit calls us to be God's dearly loved children, we turn away, preferring to go anywhere else and be with anyone else rather than God (Psalm 53:2-3). C.S. Lewis described his own attitude toward God when he first became a Christian: "kicking, struggling, resentful, and darting [my] eyes in every direction for a chance of escape . . ."[2]

Part of the problem of sin is a lack of trust in God. Adam and Eve broke their relationship with God when they chose to believe a snake who told them they could be like God. They chose to trust the serpent's lies instead of trusting God who had made them and faithfully given them everything they needed.

We can look back and see how stupid that was, but we do the same thing today every time we knowingly go against something God has told us. We, too, trust lies instead of trusting the God who loves us. We also set our will against God's, wanting to be gods ourselves instead of trusting the real God who created us. Our relationship with God is broken, apart from Jesus.

A Broken Relationship between Us and Others

We also see the poison of sin in our relationships with others. Instead of trusting other people, we fear each other. We have good reason to be afraid, because sin has a hold on other people, just as it has on us. We *know* the evil that people are capable of doing in everyday life. This leads us to spread rumors about others, to lie to them, and to do whatever we can to get ahead of them—even if it means trampling on them. On the international scene, it means war, assassinations, and broken treaties, as well as suffering for millions of people.

Sin destroys love and the ability to put others first. When God asked Adam if he had eaten the forbidden fruit, Adam answered by blaming both Eve and the God who made her: "The woman whom *you* gave to be with me, *she* gave me fruit from the tree, and I ate" (italics added). Eve also tried to shift the blame: "The serpent tricked me, and I ate" (Gen. 3:12-13). Sin leads to a me-first, me-second, and me-third attitude, in which there's simply no room to care for others.

A Broken Relationship between Us and Nature

Sin has also broken the relationship between us and nature. This is easy to see from the way we have polluted and misused our streams, forests, and oceans. It also shows up when people mistreat animals or even kill off whole species.

But that's not all. The Bible tells us that in some mysterious way sin has contaminated the world, bending and breaking God's original plan for it (Gen. 3:17-18; Rom. 8:19-22). Now we have tornadoes, floods, earthquakes, and tidal waves—horrors that were never part of God's original plan. Diseases attack people, animals, and plants. Babies are born sick or deformed. None of this is what God wanted for us.

It's important to remember that some people can suffer from the effects of sin more than others, without being personally responsible for it. Cancer exists in this world because of sin; without sin there would be no cancer. But that doesn't mean that the person who develops cancer has sinned more or in a worse way than other people, and therefore deserves the disease. Plenty of kind, generous, moral people have developed cancer, and plenty of murderers and torturers have enjoyed perfect health. Don't assume that a sick person "deserves it." Jesus corrected his disciples when they made this mistake about a blind man (John 9:1-3).

A Broken Relationship with Ourselves

Sin even breaks our relationship with ourselves. We find ourselves doing and saying things that we hate, things we feel ashamed of later. We feel evil impulses and desires rise up within us, tempting us to do what we know is wrong. We are at war with ourselves constantly, double-minded, divided, and unable to do even a good thing with perfectly pure motives (Rom. 7:14-25).

2. Sin as Crime Deserving Punishment

Another common way—perhaps the most common way—to describe sin is to liken it to a crime, to say that sin is breaking God's law. God has given us certain commands, certain laws. They are written in the Bible, and they are also written in our hearts. Everyone has an innate sense of right and wrong—a natural understanding of God's commands. When we break these, we have sinned (Rom. 1:18-32; 2:14-15; 1 John 3:4).

This way of speaking about sin reminds us that sin deserves punishment. It can't simply be ignored or forgotten, any more than a court could ignore an act of murder or theft. Someone must pay to set things right again.

3. Sin as an Addiction That We Just Can't Break

Consider this story as an illustration of the effects of sin.

The bills were piling up, and Joe didn't know what to do. Somehow, things had gotten out of control.

He stared at the desk, thinking. How much more did he owe on the new car? And then there was the VCR he'd bought last week. And the stereo equipment.

Maybe if he paid off part of the VISA bill, they'd stop bothering him for a little while. But he wouldn't get paid until next week. Then, of course, there was the child support. He was three months behind, and his ex-wife was starting to talk about lawyers.

Joe rubbed his forehead. He honestly didn't know how it had all happened. Everything he bought had seemed like a good idea at the time. But now the money was running out. He remembered his daughter's face when he had to break his promise about buying her a dress for the prom. Joe winced.

Pushing the bills away, he stood up and stretched. Maybe a long walk would help clear his mind.

Half a block away he passed a photography shop. And it was there, in the window—the new camera he'd heard about from a friend. It had several special lenses and came with a tripod. Joe looked, hesitated . . . then walked in. He still had some credit with American Express. And he really needed the camera—to take pictures at his daughter's graduation.

A third and very timely way of understanding sin is to see it as an addiction that we just can't break.[3] Being in the power of sin is very much like addiction to alcohol or to drugs; we keep trying and trying to overcome it, but we can't. We feel frustrated and powerless.

The Bible uses an older word to describe the same reality: "slavery." We are helpless to break out of our bondage. We find ourselves doing things we never thought we'd do, things we don't want to do, but we can't help ourselves. As the Apostle Paul says,

> I do not understand my own actions. For I do not do what I want, but I do the very thing I hate . . . I can will what is right, but I cannot do it. For I do not do the good I want, but the evil I do not want is what I do. Now if I do what I do not want, it is no longer I that do it, but sin that dwells within me. (Rom. 7:15, 18b-20)

How can we overcome our addiction to sin? We can't do it on our own. Just as an alcoholic or a chemically dependent person can't free him- or herself by sheer willpower,[4] neither can we. Only God can get us out of this trap we have constructed for ourselves.

4. Sin as Disease

Yet a fourth way of thinking about sin is to see that it is like a disease we all have at birth—an infection that creeps into every area of our lives.

Just like a serious disease, sin never stays small and manageable. Without treatment, it keeps on spreading and getting worse. Rebecca Manley Pippert writes: "In *The Plague* [Camus] likens the reality of evil to bacteria that are alive, spawning disease, and always seeking to reproduce. . . ."[5] That's what sin is like in our lives. It is always looking for new ways to hurt us, and to make us hurt others. The sin sickness attacks our ability to do good, to care about anyone other than ourselves. Sometimes we are astounded at the evil other human beings can do, but if we look inside we see symptoms of the same disease inside ourselves.

The plague of sin is deadly. Allowed to flourish unchecked, it brings both physical and spiritual death. The Bible tells us that death is a direct result of sin in the world (Rom. 5:12; 6:21-23; James 1:15). Like many serious diseases, sin never gets better on its own. It needs treatment—treatment from the Great Physician, Jesus Christ himself.

5. Sin as Idolatry

A fifth way we can understand sin is in terms of idolatry. When we think of idols, we often imagine crudely carved images made of wood and stone. But there are invisible idols also, false gods that steal our hearts away from the real God we were made to love.

Today people practice a kind of invisible idolatry. There may not be any wooden statues set out for worship—no brass figurines. Instead, people worship things like money, power, success, and beauty. People put faith in these things, to get them through the hard times of life. When a crisis happens, people hope that these idols will help them put their lives back together.

All sin involves idolatry. Whenever we sin, we are choosing to serve some other god rather than the true God. We say by our actions that something else is more important than God, more trustworthy.

But we eventually find out that we are wrong. Things may seem to go smoothly for a while, but sooner or later our false gods fail us. When a crisis such as illness or the death of a loved one happens, we realize that none of our false gods can get us through. We need to turn back to the real God for help (Judges 10:6-16; 1 Sam. 12:10, 21-22).

One Central Reality

You've considered five different ways of describing what sin is like. Each image gives special emphasis to one or two characteristics of sin. But all of them point to one central fact: that without God we are ruined, destroyed, dead—and that with God, we have life, joy, and wholeness.

Whenever you talk about sin with others, choose the image that best communicates this central reality to the people you're caring for. That way your words will fit their lives. You also need to do this when you talk about God's solution—Jesus. How to do this is the subject of the next chapter.

[1]Gerard Manley Hopkins, "Spring and Fall: to a Young Child." In *The Poems of Gerard Manley Hopkins,* edited by W. H. Gardner and N. H. MacKenzie (London: Oxford University Press, 1967), pp. 88-89.

[2]C. S. Lewis, *Surprised by Joy* (New York: Harcourt, Brace and Company, 1955), p. 229.

[3]J. Keith Miller, *Sin: Overcoming the Ultimate Deadly Addiction* (San Francisco: Harper & Row, 1987).

[4]Alcoholics Anonymous recognizes this fact. In their Twelve Steps toward recovery, the first three steps call for recovering alcoholics to realize and admit their need for a "higher power" to enable them to overcome their addiction. They read:

1. We admitted we were powerless over alcohol—that our lives had become unmanageable.

2. Came to believe that a Power greater than ourselves could restore us to sanity.

3. Made a decision to turn our will and our lives over to the care of God *as we understood Him.*

Alcoholics Anonymous, Third edition (New York: Alcoholics Anonymous World Services, Inc., 1976), p. 59.

[5]Rebecca Manley Pippert, *Hope Has Its Reasons: From the Search for Self to the Surprise of Faith* (San Francisco: Harper & Row, 1989), p. 84.

Chapter 12

Eight Ways to Talk about Jesus

We were still on the patio enjoying the Indian summer day. Sarah had gone in to pour coffee and came back out saying, "Percolated coffee doesn't smell any different from the kind our coffee machine makes."

She handed out mugs and we all pretended we were coffee connoisseurs. "Here's a difference," I said as I wiped some coffee grounds from the rim of my mug.

"Sorry about that," Sarah said.

"Not to worry," I said, "especially on a day like this."

Margaret changed the subject. "I've been thinking," she said, "if sin is really the problem, like you described it, then what's the solution? It all sounds pretty hopeless to me, to tell you the truth. I don't see how people are ever going to stop being selfish and hurting each other."

"Hmmm. Even if you know what the problem is, it doesn't solve it," Sarah said.

"Exactly," said Margaret. "If the problem is that we've pushed God away, does that mean that we're just stuck with it? It seems to me that we've pushed God so far away . . . I wonder if God wants to have anything to do with us any more."

I looked at Sarah and she nodded at me. "We believe God has done something to solve the problem," I said.

Margaret said, "From all we've been talking about today it doesn't seem solved to me. But tell me, are you talking about Jesus?"

"As a matter of fact, yes, I am. And I know what you mean about the problem not seeming to be solved. I get impatient with God sometimes for all the garbage that still goes on here. But I still believe Jesus has done something that solves the problems."

"How?" Margaret asked.

"Well, you were right when you said that we've pushed God a long way away, and for a long time, too. But Jesus became a person, one of us. It's like he removed the distance we'd put between us and God. Since Jesus died and was resurrected, God is . . . I don't know . . . accessible again, I guess."

Margaret nodded slowly and said, "Ummm."

"I'm probably not doing too good a job of this." I looked at Sarah with my can-you-get-me-out-of-this? look.

Sarah said, "I don't always understand the technical explanations of all this, and frankly, I don't really care. What's important to me is that I know I'm not alone. No matter what happens to me, I know Jesus is there with me."

Sarah reached over and touched my knee. "Not that Andy isn't with me, but it's just not the same. Lots of rotten things happen in this world. But for me they'd be a lot more rotten if I had to face them alone. But since Jesus is God, and since he's promised me that he loves me, that I'll never be alone, I know I'll always be okay in the end."

"That's the other thing," I said. "If we were just stuck with all the problems we face in our lives and that was it, then I'd really hate life. But I don't believe that's the way things are."

"Are you talking about heaven?" Margaret asked. "Because if you are, I don't see what difference that makes in my life now."

"I've thought about that too," I said. "I need something that helps me deal with the evil in the world right now. I believe that when Jesus was crucified and resurrected, he fought against evil and death and he won. All the evil in the world couldn't keep him down.

"And I believe that makes a difference right now. Since Jesus defeated death and evil, they don't have power over me either. Since I don't have to be afraid of dying, I can really live. I don't have to spend all my time protecting myself and 'doing unto others before they do unto me.' I can take chances, I can really care for people, because I know that God's caring for me. God has promised me that. It's a done deal . . . a sure thing."

"It does sound attractive," Margaret said. "But it's all . . . I don't know . . . sort of abstract."

"That's exactly what I think," Sarah said. "But I also know that isn't just empty intellectual arguments. It's real."

"How do you know that?" Margaret asked.

"It's not always easy to say," Sarah replied. "The one thing that convinces me the most is what I sometimes see in the lives of Christian people. That's where I can really see the difference that Jesus makes."

"That's hard to argue when I'm around you two," Margaret smiled.

Sarah was left speechless for a second. I could see Margaret had surprised her. Then she smiled, and said, "Thank you."

Our Witness Must Be Grounded in Jesus

The last chapter explained the terrible predicament all people are in. The problem of sin distorts every area of people's lives. Without God, we are hopeless, ruined, and spiritually dead.

But that isn't the whole story. God didn't just write off the human race. God took our problem with sin seriously. God loved us enough to do something about our predicament—and that something is Jesus.

Consider briefly who Jesus is. Although he is the Son of God, Jesus was willing to become a human being just like everyone else, born into a world of suffering and evil. He grew up just like anyone else, learning, working, caring for his family.

When he was about 30 years old Jesus left his hometown to begin the ministry God had called him to. He traveled from place to place, healing the sick, raising the dead, giving sight to the blind, and welcoming the poor and outcast. Jesus' preaching made it clear what all this meant: "The kingdom of God has come near; repent, and believe in the good news." (Mark 1:15)

Jesus never lost sight of his ultimate goal—to restore our broken relationship with God—and the means to that goal, his death on the cross. When his followers had other plans for him, he rebuked them. Carefully he taught them and tried to prepare them for what was going to happen.

Finally it was time. Jesus went up to Jerusalem knowing that his enemies had arranged for his betrayal. He allowed himself to be arrested, tried, and crucified without resisting the injustice of it all. Before he died he asked God to forgive those responsible.

But that wasn't the end of the story! Three days later his dejected followers were shocked to hear that Jesus was alive again! They didn't believe it, but then Jesus came and showed himself to them. He visited them on and off for about 40 days, and gave them instructions about the future. Finally he returned to God his Father, promising to return.

Jesus' followers stayed in Jerusalem until God sent the Holy Spirit to empower them. Then they went throughout the world, telling others the story of Jesus and what God had done for all people through him (Luke 24:46-52; Acts 8:1, 4-5, 25; 14:27).[1]

Why go over this familiar story? To emphasize the fact that whenever we witness, what we say *must* be grounded in Jesus Christ, and especially in his death and resurrection. Any witness that isn't grounded in Jesus is shallow and powerless. It is like saying "God loves you," without telling a person how God made that love concrete through Jesus. It just doesn't have any staying power, though it sounds nice. When our witness is grounded in the Gospel message about Jesus Christ, however, no matter how weak and halting our words may be, we tap into the power of God.

Eight Ways to Talk about Jesus

In this chapter you'll look at eight of the many different ways the Bible gives you to talk about Jesus. These are by no means all the ways the Bible shows us Jesus. You will find more in your own study of the Scriptures. Each of these pictures of Jesus speaks to certain specific needs. One picture may speak to a lonely person; another, to someone feeling guilty.

Make these ways of talking about Jesus deeply a part of you. Study them. Practice talking about Jesus in these ways. Discover how to put them into your own words. As you caringly evangelize others, God will give you the opportunities to talk to them about Jesus. So be prepared to do so naturally and comfortably, and in ways that best fit the needs and situations of others.

1. Jesus the Healer

One important way the Bible presents Jesus is as a healer. Jesus is the one who cares for those who are sick, making them healthy again physically, emotionally, and spiritually.

Jesus healed many people. He considered this an important part of his work, as you can see from the way he described his ministry for John the Baptist: "Go and tell John what you hear and see: the blind receive their sight, the lame walk, the lepers are cleansed, the deaf hear, the dead are raised, and the poor have good news brought to them." (Matt. 11:4-5) He healed even when it got him into trouble with his enemies, as happened several times (Matt. 12:9-16; Luke 5:17-26; 13:10-17; John 12:9-11).

Not only did Jesus heal people physically, but also emotionally, socially, and spiritually. He touched lepers, he socialized with social outcasts, and he offered forgiveness to the guilty. Jesus understood people and offered the kind of healing they needed the most.

Jesus' ultimate act of healing took place through his death on the cross and his resurrection. Isaiah says about Jesus' suffering that "by his bruises we are healed." (Is. 53:5b) Jesus died and rose so that we might be healed, so that our relationship with God might be restored and every area of our lives set right again.

With whom might you share this image of Jesus? People who are hurting might find it easy to relate to this image of Jesus, whether they are suffering from physical illness or psychological pain. People who are emotionally wounded by past events or by broken relationships might also be glad to hear about Jesus, the healer (Ps. 107:19-22; Isa. 53:4-5; 57:18-19; Matt. 12:15-21; 15:30-31; 1 Pet. 2:25).

2. Jesus the Good Shepherd

The image of Jesus as a good shepherd is a familiar one to many, but it is worth exploring further. Most people don't have much firsthand contact with sheep, so it can be helpful to see some of the things that shepherds do, and that our Good Shepherd does for us.

Good shepherds love their sheep. They know each sheep by name. If one is missing, they go looking for it. Jesus loves us in this way. He knows each of us intimately, not only our names but everything about us. When we are "missing," Jesus comes after us to rescue us.

Shepherds provide for the sheep's needs; they work hard to see that their sheep have the best of everything. They may take the flock far up into the mountains to find the best pastures. Shepherds check the sheep carefully to see if any are sick or injured, and if any are, they tend them.

Jesus does this for us also. Jesus provides for everything we need in our daily lives. Jesus also watches us very carefully to see where we need help, physical or spiritual.

A shepherd's job also includes protection. Good shepherds keep a close watch on their sheep. They look out for dangerous areas and poisonous plants and lead their sheep away from them. They also protect the sheep from predators, even at the cost of the shepherd's own life.

Jesus cares for us this way, protecting us from all kinds of physical and spiritual dangers. When we got ourselves into the terrible trap of sin, Jesus chose to save us by laying down his own life for us at his crucifixion. And then he rose from death three days later, and continues to care for us and watch over us to this day. What a wonderful shepherd!

What kind of person might need to hear about Jesus in this way? This image might really speak to people who feel neglected, uncared for, and unvalued. Such people need to see the Savior who sets a very high value on them, who loves them so greatly that he laid down his life to save them.

The picture of Jesus as a good shepherd might also speak to people who are feeling frightened and insecure about the future. It's reassuring to know that Jesus, our Good Shepherd, will stay with us, protect us, and guide us through all the days of our lives (Ps. 23; Isa. 40:11; Ezek. 34:11-16; John 10:1-18).

3. Jesus the Deliverer

The image of Jesus as deliverer appears even in the meaning of his name—"The Lord saves" or "delivers." Jesus' name has an important biblical background.

When the Israelites were slaves in Egypt, God heard their cries for help. He told Moses,

> I have observed the misery of my people who are in Egypt;
> I have heard their cry on account of their taskmasters.
> Indeed, I know their sufferings, and I have come down
> to deliver them from the Egyptians, and to bring them
> up out of that land to a good and broad land, a land
> flowing with milk and honey. (Exod. 3:7-8a)

God went on to deliver the Israelites from their slavery through powerful miracles. God brought them out of Egypt and made them a new nation, a nation of people who never would have existed if it hadn't been for God's deliverance.

Jesus' name reminds us that he delivers us, like God delivered the people of Israel. Like them, we too were slaves—slaves to the power of sin. We couldn't get free, or make our lives what they were meant to be. God had to solve our problem for us— just as God did for the Israelites. It took Jesus' personal action, dying on a cross for us, to set us free.

Whom might you tell about Jesus our deliverer? This picture of Jesus might really speak to people who find themselves repeating the same destructive behavior over and over again. Oppressed people who suffer for reasons that are not their own fault might also find hope in Jesus as deliverer. Finally, all who feel out of place, who feel like they don't belong in their world, can find hope here. We know that God is bringing us home to the place we belong—with God, forever (2 Sam. 22:1-44; Ps. 18:1-19; 31:1-5; 33:16-22).

4. Lamb of God

John the Baptist called Jesus the "Lamb of God." What did he mean by it, and what does this image tell you about Jesus?

Throughout the Old Testament, lambs were used as sacrifices for sin. When a person had sinned, he or she would bring a perfect, healthy lamb to the priest for sacrifice. God would accept the lamb's death in place of the punishment the person deserved.

Jesus is like a lamb because he was the sacrifice for everyone's sin. Jesus was perfect, just like the lamb for sacrifice had to be. Jesus lived a life that was totally pleasing to God. Then he voluntarily took away the guilt of everyone by dying on the cross, and then rising again.

Jesus is special, though, because he is the Lamb *of God.* In the Old Testament people had to provide their own lambs. God provided *this* sacrifice—God's own Son Jesus (Gen. 22:8). We didn't have to pay a thing. God does everything for us. When people sacrificed lambs they had to do so every year. But when the Lamb of God was sacrificed, that was once and for all. The sacrifice never needs to be made again.

With whom might you share this image of Jesus? Sometimes people carry a heavy load of guilt for wrongs they've done. If they learn to know Jesus as the Lamb of God, they can take that guilt to Jesus. They can know that he takes their sin and guilt away; he has taken the punishment they deserve. Because of Jesus, the Lamb of God, their relationship with God is restored (Isa. 53:7; John 1:29, 35-37; 1 Pet. 1:18-19; Rev. 5:6-14).

5. Jesus the Reconciler

The Bible also presents Jesus as the reconciler, the one who restores the relationship between us and God. The Apostle Paul tells us, "God was reconciling the world to himself, not counting their trespasses against them." (2 Cor. 5:19) "For in him [Jesus] all the fullness of God was pleased to dwell, and through him God was pleased to reconcile to himself all things, whether on earth or in heaven, by making peace through the blood of his cross." (Col. 1:19-20)

Jesus also makes peace between us and other people. Some of the early Christians had a hard time getting along with each other, because some were Jews and some were Gentiles. They had grown up despising and distrusting each other. But in Christ the two kinds of people are joined as one. The book of Ephesians talks about how Jesus reconciled Jews and Gentiles:

For he is our peace; in his flesh he has made both groups

into one and has broken down the dividing wall, that is, the hostility between us. He has abolished the law with its commandments and ordinances, that he might create in himself one new humanity in place of the two, thus making peace, and might reconcile both groups to God in one body through the cross, thus putting to death that hostility through it. (Eph. 2:14-16)

Jesus still reconciles people today. As we meet and worship together as the body of Christ, we are constantly reminded that in Christ "you are all children of God through faith. As many of you as were baptized into Christ have clothed yourselves with Christ. There is no longer Jew or Greek, there is no longer slave or free, there is no longer male and female; for all of you are one in Christ Jesus." (Gal. 3:26-28) Differences such as race, color, sex, class, and educational background fall away before the reconciling love of Jesus Christ. In Christ, we form one body. Although there are many different parts, we all need each other and we all work together.

Jesus even reconciles individuals to themselves. Often people do or say things that leave them feeling angry at themselves. They may begin to hate themselves, wishing that they could escape from themselves. But since this is impossible, they fall into despair.

Jesus offers hope. Because he forgives and loves, people likewise can begin to forgive and care for themselves. They are reconciled to themselves. They don't need to keep looking at their flaws and weaknesses. Jesus forgives their sin and gives them peace.

With whom might you share the picture of Jesus as reconciler? This image could speak to a person who feels cut off from God and others—someone who feels alienated and all alone. The seventeenth century poet John Donne reminds us that "No man is an island, entire of itself; every man is a piece of the continent, a part of the main."[2] Many people feel like islands today—lonely and cut off from everyone. In Christ their relationship to God and others is restored (Rom. 5:6-9; 2 Cor. 5:18-21; Col. 1:19-23).

6. Jesus as Immanuel, God-with-Us

In the Bible Jesus is also called Immanuel, which means God-with-us. We had separated ourselves from God, so Jesus came to be one of us, to experience all that we go through in life—both the joy and the suffering. Since Jesus became one of us we know that God understands and cares about our lives.

God-with-us even traveled our road into death, although

death is something foreign to God's nature. Jesus went to the cross, making our sin his own, our suffering and death his own. Then Jesus rose again, giving us the sure hope that just as he shared our death, we will also share his resurrection.

Just before returning to heaven, Jesus promised to stay with us: "And remember, I am with you always, to the end of the age." (Matt. 28:20) We have the comfort of knowing that, whatever may happen in our lives and world, God will be right here with us, to care for us and keep us.

Who might be interested to hear about Jesus as God-with-us? A lonely person might find a great deal of hope in this picture of Jesus. Jesus is with us in our loneliness, to love us and stay with us. He is with us to help us bear it. Remembering Jesus as God-with-us is also very helpful for people who are suffering or afraid. For someone experiencing terrible pain, knowing that Jesus is with him or her in the middle of it all can be a source of strength and courage. A person facing death can take comfort in knowing that Jesus will be with him or her all the way (1 Kings 8:57; Ps. 46:7; Isa. 8:10; Matt. 1:18b-25, 28:19-20).

7. Jesus, the Friend of Sinners

Jesus' enemies sometimes referred to him as a friend of "sinners." Jesus earned this nickname by visiting people, caring for them, and treating them with respect, even if they were prostitutes or tax collectors.

Although Jesus' enemies didn't give him this name as a compliment, for us it is a wonderful description. Jesus is the one who is willing to welcome us, even when we have done or said things that leave us guilty and ashamed. Jesus is not ashamed to be called our friend.

Luke tells a story that shows how Jesus dealt with two very different kinds of sinners.

> One of the Pharisees asked Jesus to eat with him, and he went into the Pharisee's house and took his place at the table. And a woman in the city, who was a sinner, having learned that he was eating in the Pharisee's house, brought an alabaster jar of ointment. She stood behind him at his feet, weeping, and began to bathe his feet with her tears and to dry them with her hair. Then she continued kissing his feet and anointing them with the ointment.
>
> Now when the Pharisee who had invited him saw it, he said to himself, "If this man were a prophet, he would have known who and what kind of woman this is who is touching him—that she is a sinner."

Jesus spoke up and said to him, "Simon, I have something to say to you."

"Teacher," he replied, "Speak."

"A certain creditor had two debtors; one owed five hundred denarii, and the other fifty. When they could not pay, he canceled the debts for both of them. Now which of them will love him more?"

Simon answered, "I suppose the one for whom he canceled the greater debt."

And Jesus said to him, "You have judged rightly." Then turning toward the woman, he said to Simon, "Do you see this woman? I entered your house; you gave me no water for my feet, but she has bathed my feet with her tears and dried them with her hair. You gave me no kiss, but from the time I came in she has not stopped kissing my feet. You did not anoint my head with oil, but she has anointed my feet with ointment. Therefore, I tell you, her sins, which were many, have been forgiven; hence she has shown great love. But the one to whom little is forgiven, loves little."

Then he said to her, "Your sins are forgiven."

But those who were at the table with him began to say among themselves, "Who is this who even forgives sins?"

And he said to the woman, "Your faith has saved you; go in peace." (Luke 7:36-50)

In Jesus, we find a God who hates sin, but still loves sinners. When we admit that we can't justify ourselves, we can look to him for forgiving love. Jesus will not browbeat us or make us feel even worse; instead, he forgives us and takes away our guilt.

But what about the Pharisee? He, too, was undoubtedly a sinner; why did Jesus react to him with such strong words? The Pharisee wasn't willing to admit his sin; he refused to face up to the fact that he needed a Savior. Jesus always reacts to this kind of hypocrisy with strong words of warning. Jesus does this out of love for us. He doesn't want to see us deceiving and hurting ourselves.

But when the Holy Spirit helps us recognize our guilt, when we admit that we need help because we can't save ourselves—then Jesus comes to us with gentleness. He forgives us and makes us clean of the past, without reproaching us. He is truly the "friend of sinners."

Who might need to hear about Jesus as a friend of sinners? Anyone who admits to being a sinner! People who feel broken down by their own inability to be "good enough" are the ones who need to hear about Jesus as the friend of sinners.

Eight Ways to Talk about Jesus

Another group of people who will be very happy to hear about the friend of sinners are those who are considered outcasts by society. You can tell such people the Good News that there is a Savior who even promised a criminal who was being executed, "Today you will be with me in Paradise." (Luke 23:43) In the story of the woman and the Pharisee, people regarded the woman's sin as so terrible that they shunned her. There are people today who are also shunned for their sins—for example, those who commit violence against the elderly or children. While it is very important not to say that such actions are acceptable, you can tell such people the Good News that our God who hates sin is a friend of sinners (Luke 5:27-32; 7:34-50; 19:1-10; John 4:7-42).

8. Christ the Victor

Many of us are used to thinking about Christ as a victim. When we think of the cross, we remember the terrible suffering and death he endured to save us. There's nothing wrong with this picture of Christ. But to balance it, the Bible gives us another, very different picture—the picture of Christ as victor.

This picture shows us the cross as the climax of a terrible battle between God and evil. It was on the cross that Jesus decisively defeated the powers of evil, gaining the victory and rescuing us. The Apostle Paul writes that "He disarmed the rulers and authorities and made a public example of them, triumphing over them in [the cross]." (Col. 2:15)

Through Jesus' death and resurrection, he broke the power of death over us. As Paul writes,

> When this perishable body puts on imperishability, and this mortal body puts on immortality, then the saying that is written will be fulfilled: "Death has been swallowed up in victory." "Where, O death, is your victory? Where, O death, is your sting?" The sting of death is sin, and the power of sin is the law. But thanks be to God, who gives us the victory through our Lord Jesus Christ. (1 Cor. 15:54-57)

Jesus shares his victory with us, his people. Because of Christ as victor, death and sin no longer have power over us. Instead, we can entrust the future to the victorious Savior who loves us—Jesus.

How does Jesus' victory over death make a difference in people's daily lives? One answer reveals itself in what people do to deny death. So many spend large amounts of their lives and energy fearing death and trying to deny their own mortality. Some fear old age (and often reject older persons) because they fear death. Some spend money, time, and energy trying to look younger, and may become terribly depressed as they have birthdays that remind them of their unstoppable march toward death. Some leave legacies—bequests, works they have created, or even children—as a way to live on after they die, at least in people's memories.[3]

As Jesus frees people from the power of death they are able to live their lives very differently. Instead of protecting themselves from approaching old age and death, they can dedicate their lives to caring for others, to enjoying the beautiful world God has given them, and using the gifts and talents God has given them. That is the only true freedom. Until we are free from the power of death, we are not free at all.

With whom might you share the picture of Christ as victor over death and evil? Knowing Jesus, who has overcome death, can help us get through the tough time of waiting for death, either our own or that of a loved one. It can also give us hope after a loved one dies. This image of Jesus might also help people who are afraid of the future for any reason. You can help them understand that, whatever the future may bring, in the end the last word belongs to Jesus—and it is victory (Rev. 3:21; 17:14).

The Simple Answer and the Complicated Answers

What is the Gospel? This is one of the easiest and hardest questions you can try to answer. The simple answer is *Jesus Christ!* The story of Jesus, what he has done and what he promises, is the best Good News possible.

The answer becomes more complicated, however, when you start asking how God's Good News is good for people in specific circumstances. You've seen that people suffer the effects of sin in many different ways. You need to tell people about God's love in ways that speak directly to the needs they are experiencing.

Any of the eight ways of talking about Jesus in this chapter is a way for people to begin to see how God's love reaches out to them. None of these ways, however, is complete by itself. Each of them leads back to the central truth that God forgives our sins and gives us new life in the life, death, and resurrection of Jesus. As you continue growing in your faith and understanding of the biblical message about Jesus Christ, crucified and resurrected, you will learn additional and more personal ways to talk about Jesus.

[1]In addition to the very brief summary that follows of Jesus' life, you would benefit from reading one or more of the four Gospels (Matthew, Mark, Luke, or John) to get a more complete picture of Jesus. It can be especially valuable to read an entire Gospel from beginning to end, instead of reading it in small devotional segments over a period of weeks.

[2]John Donne, *Devotions Upon Emergent Occasions* (Ann Arbor, MI: University of Michigan Press, 1959), p. 108.

[3]For a complete and fascinating look at the effect that the fear of death has on individuals and on society, see Ernest Becker, *The Denial of Death* (New York: The Free Press, 1973).

Chapter 13

Guidelines for Effective Witnessing

The Saturday before Thanksgiving Jim Hayashi came over for supper. He and I had been having lunch together two or three times a week at work and I'd told him what was happening with Margaret. I'd also told Sarah about Jim and she wanted to meet him.

Sarah and I had been talking a lot about Margaret. Since we'd told her so much about God that afternoon in October we had felt a heavy sense of responsibility. I think we were torn between the witnessing and the friendship. We didn't see how the two could fit together without one getting in the way of the other. Margaret hadn't brought up the subject of religion since, but we figured she would eventually. Meanwhile, we had decided to wait for her to bring it up, but we really wanted to know what Jim thought.

So Jim came for a meal and to meet Sarah. Sarah and Jim hit it off immediately. I was the cook that night. While I was fixing supper Jim and Sarah sat in the living room and talked. Occasionally I would hear them laughing, but when I went out to see what was going on, they would clam up. Finally I listened at the door. Sarah was telling Jim about the time I thought the "2 c. garlic" in a recipe meant two cups of garlic instead of two cloves.

"We ended up going out to eat that night," she said. "And the house smelled like garlic for days."

I was just about to go in to show them I knew they were talking about me when I smelled something burning in the kitchen. Luckily it was only the butter I was melting in a frying pan. By the time I turned off the fire, the butter looked like industrial waste. I poured it out and washed the pan and started over. I decided to give my full attention to the cooking. I didn't want to have to go out to dinner that night also.

Supper turned out pretty well. While we were eating I casually said to Sarah, "I hope the pasta tastes all right. I couldn't find the pound of garlic I bought to put in it."

Jim laughed. Sarah mock-frowned and complained, "You were listening."

"You bet," I said. "If you're going to be telling stories about me I have to be able to defend myself."

"So did you hear me telling Jim about the time you bought a side of beef and a new freezer and forgot to plug in the freezer?"

"That was a long time ago . . ."

Jim and Sarah laughed.

After supper we talked to Jim about Margaret. Jim listened to us as we described what we had said to Margaret about God.

When we finished Jim said, "It sounds to me like you're doing just fine. Keep up the good work."

"But how can we know for sure?" Sarah asked.

"The more we get into this," I said, "the more worried I get about ruining it by doing something really stupid. I almost ruined my relationship with Margaret once before. I don't want to do it again."

"Actually, that's one of the reasons we wanted you to come over," Sarah said. "We both care so much for Margaret, and she's invited us over for Thanksgiving dinner. Margaret hasn't brought up the subject of God since that Saturday afternoon, but I have a feeling she will soon, and Thanksgiving seems tailor-made." Sarah sighed. "I'm new to this witnessing business. I just want to do it right, but I don't want to hurt Margaret."

"I don't either," I said.

"It's like we're being pulled in two different directions," Sarah said.

Jim listened attentively to every word we said. When we finally ran out of things to say, he smiled and said, "It sounds to me like you mostly need to relax."

Sarah looked at me and we both frowned. That wasn't the answer we'd been looking for.

Jim saw it and said, "You've been doing such a good job so far. Don't mess it up by getting all serious or religious all of a sudden. Don't you think Margaret will know something's fishy if you two suddenly start behaving differently?"

Sarah said, "She'd know it in a minute."

Guidelines for Effective Witnessing

"So just relax and use your common sense," Jim said. "There's no need to hurry. Go with the flow. Talk about things that matter to Margaret. If you do that you'll get plenty of chances to tell her what you believe about God. Keep praying for her. Trust that God's at work here. It isn't just you two.

"Be patient. You've told her some things about God, now let her think about it for a while. If she doesn't respond to what you say, let it drop. If she does, talk about it some more. Be yourselves. God will use you.

"And be prepared for when she does express interest. I've seen a lot of witnesses so surprised when someone said he or she wanted to believe, that they didn't know what to do. Think about it ahead of time. Think about what might be the right next step for Margaret. But don't impose your plan on her. Just have it in mind and see if it really does fit her ideas of what she wants to do.

"Margaret's had a lot of hurt from religion. She really needs a lot of care. I think you two are doing a wonderful job."

Jim put his hands in his lap, grinned, and looked at Sarah and me.

"Just relax . . ." I said.

"Yeah. Trust God and relax."

Caring Evangelism involves both living God's love for others and also telling them the wonderful news about what God has done through Jesus. You've already seen that without both these elements your witness is incomplete. Speaking about Jesus, at the right time, is an integral part of an evangelizing relationship.

But you might be reluctant to witness because you are unsure of the answers to many important questions. What is the right time to witness? How will you know what to say? What do you do when someone accepts, or rejects, your witness?

Here are seven guidelines to help you become a more effective witness for Jesus.

Guideline 1: Much Needs to Happen before You Share

There are several things that need to happen before you ever share God's love in words. You've encountered each of these before, but this is a good place to summarize and review.

Be Evangelized Yourself

As you read in chapter 2, you can't effectively evangelize

others until you are being evangelized yourself. If you are going to share God's love with others, you need to experience it again and again in your own life! As you continue to see your own need for God, and hear again and again the Good News of Jesus, you will be better able to share this with others.

Develop a Relationship

You have read that effective evangelism happens in relationships. As you care for others in relationships, you build a level of trust that makes sharing the Good News natural and comfortable for both you and the other person.

Listen

You listen to discover what kind of needs other people are experiencing. Many times you will have to listen for a very long time before you ever say a word about Jesus.

Listening lets you know where people are hurting. Then you can find ways of telling them about Jesus that make sense to them, that fit the problems they're experiencing. If you know that others feel unloved and unvalued, you can tell them about Jesus in ways that show how he loves and values them. If you know that others are feeling frightened and powerless, you can talk about Jesus as the Good Shepherd who watches over us to protect us.

Pray

Prayer is vital to sharing the Good News. Before you ever speak, you should be praying for the person you care for. You can ask God to make this person ready to hear about Jesus. You can ask God to send opportunities to share the Good News with the person. You will certainly want to ask God to guide you in what you say and do.

Live the Love of God

Usually before you speak about God's love you will try to communicate that love through your actions. Are there physical, social, mental, or emotional needs you could help them meet in order to communicate the love of God to them? Acting out God's love will give your words much more credibility.

Guideline 2: Know When to Witness

Once you've built a relationship, listened, prayed, and shared

Guidelines for Effective Witnessing

God's love through caring actions, how do you know when to witness?

Two Possible Mistakes

There are two opposite mistakes you can make about knowing when to talk about Jesus. You can witness too quickly, talking about God before you've listened enough and built trust. The opposite mistake is when you worry so much about moving too fast that you don't talk about Jesus even when people are practically crying out for you to speak.

How Do You Know the Right Time?

So how can you know the right time? The best way is to wait for others to tell you when they are ready. As people see Christ's love through your actions, as the Spirit helps them discover their own need for a Savior, sooner or later they will let you know they are ready to hear the Good News.

They may ask questions that make it natural for you to start talking about God and what God has done for you. For example, remember the list of God-sized questions in chapter 10—questions that show people are coming in touch with their need for a Savior. They may bring up the subject of God, church, the Bible, Jesus, or faith. They may even say they're at the end of their rope and just don't know what to do. Here is an example of how it might happen.

Lia was a caring evangelist who had been in an evangelizing relationship with Jenny for several months. Although Jenny knew that Lia was a Christian and went to church regularly, Lia hadn't said very much about Jesus. Instead, Lia listened to Jenny, and learned more about her. Gradually the relationship grew, and they developed a deeper and deeper level of trust.

Then a crisis struck. One night Jenny's husband was in a car accident. He was taken to the hospital, and his condition was extremely serious.

Jenny called up Lia in tears, and Lia came down to the hospital to be with her. They sat in a waiting room and talked for a long while. Lia mostly listened. Sometimes they just cried together.

After a few hours Jenny asked Lia, "What do you do when things like this happen to you? How do you find the strength to get through?"

With a quick silent prayer, Lia gently answered, "Whenever something really bad happens, I ask God to help me, because I know that God loves me."

"How do you know that?" Jenny asked.

Lia said, "It's because of Jesus. He loved me enough to die for me, and then he rose from death. Since Jesus did that much for me, I believe he takes care of me now also."

Jenny asked, "Believing that helps you make it through times like this?"

"That's right," Lia answered. "You remember last year, when we found out my mother had cancer. My life just fell apart. I was angry at everyone—the doctors, God, even my mother for being sick. I was really scared, and I couldn't do anything about it.

"I'm still scared whenever I think about the cancer and what's going to happen in the future. But I know that God loves me and my mother too, and I know God will stay with us during this time. Somehow knowing that I'm not alone gives me the strength to keep going."

Jenny was silent for a few minutes, thinking about Lia's words.

Notice that Lia gave Jenny time to develop trust in their relationship, before she ever started talking about the very personal subject of faith in God. Meanwhile, Lia kept praying, listening, and developing a relationship with Jenny.

Then a crisis came, and Jenny asked one of the "God-sized" questions. Essentially, she was asking, "Where can I find strength to face the future?" She was ready to hear God's answer, and Lia gave it, drawing on her own personal experience.

Guideline 3: Customize the Way You Witness

Notice that Lia didn't give a "canned" Gospel presentation. In evangelism, one size doesn't fit all. You need to customize how you present the truth about Jesus to people, making sure it fits their own very special needs.

Lia had listened, and so she knew what Jenny considered her primary need—the strength to get through the crisis. Lia spoke to that need. She didn't change the subject to something else, like guilt and forgiveness. Instead, she talked about what Jenny wanted to talk about—how God's love gives the strength to keep going during tough times.

Personal Experiences

Notice that Lia drew on some of her own personal experiences with God. This is an excellent way to tell others what Jesus is like. It allowed Jenny to see how another person had found strength in Jesus in the middle of a similar situation. If you can tell how God has made a difference for you by sharing your own experiences, do so.

Be sure your experience includes at least some of the same basic issues or feelings that the other person is experiencing. The Spirit can use such a witness to help others find hope in God during their difficult times.

When you share out of your own experience, don't imply that you know just how the other person feels. You can't, and implying that you do might make the other person angry. Just describe what happened to you. Don't expect that the other person's experience and reactions will be exactly like yours.

Also remember that you don't have to have a highly dramatic life-and-death story before you can tell it. An ordinary story of finding strength and hope for everyday life is often much more effective, simply because it is easy to identify with. And don't think your story has to have a happy ending. Paul gave a powerful witness to God's gracious love when he witnessed to the Corinthians about his "thorn in the flesh." (2 Cor. 12:7) His problem never went away, but God said, "My grace is sufficient for you, for power is made perfect in weakness." (2 Cor. 12:9) Your story about Jesus giving you the courage to bear a problem that hasn't gone away can be a powerful witness too.

Bible Stories and Promises

Another source for your sharing is the Bible. There are so many wonderful stories and verses that show what Jesus is like, and what he has done for us.

Stories are a very effective way of sharing what Jesus is like. People enjoy stories. They are easy to understand and remember. They also give people a chance to see God in action toward people.

Choose stories that fit the needs of your care receivers. For a person who feels guilty, you might talk about the story of the prodigal son; for a person who feels unloved or unvalued, you might relate the story of Zacchaeus, and the way Jesus cared for him.

You may also choose to share Bible verses that have been especially meaningful for you. If so, be sure that you explain the verse and why you have found hope in it, instead of simply "throwing" it at a person.

Centered on Jesus

When you witness you may be tempted to dwell so much on yourself that you leave out the Lord. Avoid this. Your witness must be Christ-centered. It must be grounded in the life, death, and resurrection of Jesus, as revealed in the Scriptures.

You might not tell the story of salvation in full every time you have an opportunity to witness. But as you continue to listen and share with someone in an evangelizing relationship, you will have the opportunity to share more and more—so that the person gets to know the wonderful Savior God has provided.

Guideline 4: Communicate Clearly, in an Other-Centered Manner

When it comes to sharing the Gospel, how you say it is almost as important as what you say. Your way of sharing can distort and confuse the message, or it can support and confirm it.

When you talk about Jesus, communicate clearly! You can do this best by speaking the other person's language.

Christians have a special kind of jargon that most non-Christians don't understand. Words like *save, sin,* and *redeem* mean different things to Christians and to (most) non-Christians.

Word	What Others Might Think This Word Means
save	To rescue someone, something you do with money in a bank, or a statistic for a hockey goalie
sin	Either good-tasting food ("sinfully delicious") or sex ("living in sin")
redeem	Something you do with coupons
justify	Lining up the margins on a typewritten piece of paper
faith	"Believing what you know ain't so;" forcing yourself to believe impossibilities through sheer willpower
soul	An invisible part of people that has no value except in eternity. Like an appendix, it doesn't make any difference in daily life. For some strange reason it's the only thing God cares about.

As much as possible, avoid using these terms and others like them when you're talking to someone you're not sure will understand them. Instead of saying *faith* you might start off using the more common word *trust.* Instead of saying *sinful* you may want to talk about "being separated from God" or "having a broken relationship with God." In many cases you're better off simply to explain what you're talking about in a little more detail instead of using a word like *justify* or *redeem.* The more concrete and simple your language is, the better you will be able to communicate.

Also, when you share about Jesus, make it a dialogue, not a monologue. Don't lecture others or give a 30-minute speech when all they wanted was a 30-second answer. You need to let the others set the pace. You can do this best by sharing in dialogue.

Sharing in dialogue just means normal conversation—only you're talking about Jesus. The other person asks a question, you respond briefly, the other person makes another comment, and so on. It's the way ordinary people talk, and much more comfortable than a lecture—for you *and* for the other person.

Guideline 5: Remain Nondefensive

Sometimes when you talk about Jesus others will disagree. This is normal, and you should expect it. Instead of getting defensive and telling others that they are wrong, you can ask them to explain more of what they mean.

Other times people will ask difficult questions about what you believe. If you know an answer that has made sense to you, share it. If you don't, that's okay too. You can simply say "I don't know" and offer to try to find out. You don't need to know all the answers. The important thing is to stay nondefensive—communicating love and respect for the other person.

It's funny, but sometimes people aren't nearly so concerned about your answers to their questions as they are about your attitude! Mike is a typical example.

As Mike and Ted developed an evangelizing relationship, occasionally they'd talk about God, and Mike would pepper Ted with questions. He wanted to know how a loving God could create hell; how God could condemn people who'd never heard of God; why people had to believe in Jesus instead of in Buddha or Mohammed; and how the theory of evolution fit with the Bible. Sometimes Ted could answer him; sometimes he wasn't able to. Mike seemed to enjoy coming up with the most difficult questions.

After several months of this, Ted was discouraged and frustrated. He didn't know if he was doing any good, caring for Mike. He went to visit him, and got a surprise.

"Do you know, Ted," said Mike, "I've been thinking over what you've said about Christianity for a long time, and I guess I'm interested. What do I do now?"

Ted was flabbergasted. "But— but—" he stammered. "What about all those questions I never answered?"

Mike smiled, *"Well, you couldn't answer some of them, but that's okay. I got to thinking, in all the time we've known each other you've always been there for me, even during the tough times. You always listened, even when I got mad or asked you tough questions. It seems like you have something in your life that I don't have, and I want it. So tell me how I can be a Christian."*

If you can stay nondefensive like Ted, and just keep on caring and listening to the other person, you may be communicating God's Good News far better than if you could answer every question ever asked.

Guideline 6: Be Prepared to Deal with Others' Responses to Your Witness

Now suppose that you've just finished telling a person about Jesus. What happens next? What can you expect?

Interest

Sometimes people will seem very interested in what you've been saying. If so, this might be a good time to offer them ways to learn more—perhaps by giving them a good book, or by offering to introduce them to a Bible study group. You may even offer to pray together or to have a Bible study involving just the two of you. You'll read more about how to respond to interest in chapters 15, 16, and 17.

As people continue to grow in their relationship to God, sooner or later they may ask you, "How can I get what you've got? How can I become a Christian too?" You'll read about this in detail in chapter 18.

Rejection

What if someone rejects the message? For many Christians, this is their worst nightmare about witnessing. You may feel personally rejected. You may worry about the other person's eternal fate. You may even blame yourself, thinking you failed God.

These are natural feelings, but they are also overreactions.

Sometimes rejection simply means that you were moving too fast. Maybe the relationship wasn't intimate or deep enough yet to talk about such personal issues. Maybe the other person hasn't had enough time to discover his or her own need for a Savior.

If you think moving too fast might be the problem, simply back off and continue to care for the person by listening. Work on developing the relationship, and let God make the other person ready in God's own good time.

As you recall, Margaret rejected an invitation to church when Andy moved too quickly. She hadn't had enough time to sense the caring behind the invitation, or to develop trust with Andy. But after Andy and Sarah concentrated on the relationship, Margaret gradually became more open to hearing about Jesus.

If the person you care for seems to reject your witness, it's possible that you might have slipped and gotten results-oriented. If so, you can get yourself back on track as a process-oriented evangelist, apologize, and concentrate on winning back the trust you've accidentally damaged. Most people are very forgiving of mistakes if they know you really care for them.

It's also very possible that the rejection has nothing at all to do with you. There may be something very painful in the person's past which is causing this reaction. By listening you can find out what the real reason for the rejection is. Then you can witness again at the right time.

And don't worry continually about the eternal destiny of the other person. One rejection of the Gospel does not mean that the person will reject God forever. Just think about how many times the Apostle Paul must have heard the message before God brought him to faith! God can reach even the most hardened people, and sometimes God chooses to take many years to do it. As Jesus said in another connection, "For God all things are possible." (Mark 10:27)

Neither Hot nor Cold

The most common response you can expect to receive is a non-committal one. People listen and think over what you have said, but they aren't ready to commit themselves one way or another.

Don't get discouraged! There are few people who come to faith the very first time they hear the story of Jesus. Most need to hear it more than once. They may need time to think it out. They need time to see if your life matches what you say.

As a caring evangelist, your job is not to push them into a quick response. Instead, you continue to care and share faithfully, as God gives you the opportunity.

Guideline 7: Remember, God's Love Is for Us Too!

The most important fact you can remember as a caring

evangelist is that God loves you too, just as much as God loves the people you share with.

Even when you make mistakes witnessing, God loves you. When you fall flat on your face, God picks you up and encourages you to start again. God knows your frailties and weaknesses. And yet God has chosen you. God prefers to work through *you* to bring the Good News message about Jesus to others.

Trust God and Relax

Knowing and practicing these guidelines can help make witnessing a positive and welcome experience—for you and for those to whom you witness. Be sure to listen in order to understand and respect the other person. Be sure to tell about Jesus, when the time is right, joyfully, and personally. And always remember, when you're witnessing, to trust God and relax.

Chapter 14

How to be an Assertive Witness

"You said to relax around Margaret, and that's fine." Sarah, Jim, and I were still talking about witnessing to Margaret. "I understand what you're saying about being ourselves and not pushing things," I said, "but the time will undoubtedly come when we need to say more about Jesus, and my question is, how do we do that without being pushy?"

Sarah said, "I want to respect Margaret, but I also want to witness to her."

Jim said, "Then be assertive."

"Oh, yuk," Sarah said.

Jim waited for her to say more.

"I have a friend who took a class in being assertive," Sarah said, "and she was the most obnoxious, pushy person for about two months until she got over it. She'd yell at waitresses and push her way into lines. She started telling everyone about their faults. When people challenged her, she'd say, 'If you can't handle it, I'm sorry. I'm just being assertive.'"

"She wasn't being assertive," Jim said. "The behavior you described isn't assertive, it's aggressive. Being assertive means caring for other people and respecting what they want, and at the same time caring for yourself, and respecting what you need and want."

"Tell me more about what that has to do with witnessing," I said.

Assertiveness is a way of relating and communicating that respects the rights and needs of others, as well as our own. This makes assertiveness an excellent model for our relating, communicating, and witnessing as caring evangelists.

Assertiveness is often misunderstood. If a person cuts in line at a movie theater you might hear someone describe the offender as "too assertive." Actually such behavior isn't assertive at all, but aggressive. Assertive behavior is different from aggressive and passive behavior.

In this chapter you will learn a definition of assertive behavior and see how it is different from aggressive and passive behavior. Then you will see how you can effectively care for others and communicate the Good News to them by being an assertive witness.[1]

Passive, Aggressive, and Assertive Behavior

Passive Behavior

People behave passively when they:

- fail to express their feelings, needs, or affection to others;
- don't say what they believe because they fear how others may react;
- fail to stand up for their rights because they are afraid;
- don't make decisions for themselves because they are afraid to exercise authority;
- are unable to say "no" to requests even though they really don't want to do something;
- are unable to say "yes" to requests even when they really want to do something; and
- constantly let others take advantage of them.

Aggressive Behavior

People behave aggressively when they:

- express themselves in a threatening, assaultive, demanding or hostile manner;
- disregard the rights of others—by taking advantage of them, pushing them around, or manipulating them to fulfill personal needs;

- sarcastically put down, insult, or belittle the feelings or opinions of others;
- take over the responsibility of making decisions without regard for others;
- make demands of others rather than requests; and
- label or pigeonhole others.

Assertive Behavior

People behave assertively when they:

- directly and honestly express their own feelings, needs, affections, and rights without resorting to aggression or abusing the rights of others;
- tell others what they think and believe without demanding that the others think or believe the same;
- assume or share the responsibility of making decisions and choices that affect themselves;
- say "no" to requests without feeling guilty;
- say "yes" to requests that they really want to meet;
- genuinely express warmth, affection, and appreciation to others without feeling excessively embarrassed; and
- view themselves as individuals with the same human rights, privileges, and responsibilities as everyone else, regardless of gender, race, religion, vocation, or social status.

Assertiveness and Evangelism

Just as there are three basic ways of behaving, so there are also three basic ways of witnessing.

Passive Witnessing

Sometimes Christians are very passive in their witnessing. They:

- don't express their opinions, beliefs, or feelings about God;
- keep their faith completely to themselves out of fear of offending others;
- fail to stand up for their beliefs because they fear ridicule or rejection; and

- behave in ways they would rather not because they allow others to make decisions for them.

An Example of Passive Witnessing

Look for these characteristics of passive witnessing in the following example.

Doug and Jeff had been friends for years. One evening they began discussing Christianity. Doug was confused. He said, "Christianity just doesn't make sense to me at all. I don't see how anyone can believe in a God that allowed himself to be crucified. Why do you waste your time on that stuff?"

Jeff thought, My faith isn't a waste of time, *but instead of saying that to Doug, he said, "Oh, I don't know, going to church isn't always great, but sometimes I get something out of it."*

Doug shook his head. "Jeff, it seems to me that you could do other things that would be a lot more fun."

Jeff started to say something, but Doug interrupted. Jeff was glad to let him continue—he really didn't know what he was going to say anyway. "Let's go play tennis together Sunday morning," Doug said. "I bet getting some exercise and being out in the sun and fresh air will be more fun than sitting in some stuffy old church building."

Jeff thought to himself, I promised my parents I'd go out to lunch with them after church, but if I say I'm going to church— Doug just won't understand.

"How about 9:30 Sunday morning?" Doug asked.

"Fine, I guess," said Jeff.

The Effects of Passive Witnessing

The communication between Doug and Jeff was not very beneficial to either of them. Because Jeff hid his real ideas and feelings, Doug never learned what Jeff believes about Jesus.

Their relationship faces trouble also, because now Doug will probably assume that Jeff's beliefs aren't that important to him. This isn't true, but because Jeff didn't say anything, Doug is left with a false understanding of his friend that could hurt their relationship.

Jeff himself has got a whole new set of problems. Not only does he have to break his commitment with his parents, but he probably feels guilty, frustrated, and angry at being pushed around.

Jeff may have felt he was doing Doug a favor by going along with him. But by not being honest with Doug, Jeff discouraged open communication and growth in their relationship. He didn't trust Doug enough to share his real feelings with him. Instead he assumed Doug would not understand and would perhaps make fun of him or think less of him.

The Assertive Alternative

Now see how Jeff could have responded assertively to Doug.

Doug said, "Christianity just doesn't make sense to me at all. I don't see how anyone can believe in a God that allowed himself to be crucified. Why do you waste your time on that stuff?"

Jeff answered, "I can see how Christianity would seem confusing. I used to have the same problems wondering how God could let himself be crucified. But then I started looking into it, and it made more and more sense to me."

Now Doug was puzzled. "What changed your mind?"

Jeff said, "Well, I looked into the reasons he did it. It's pretty easy to see that our world is in bad shape, and every time the scientists or government try to make things better, it just gets worse. My own personal life isn't so great, either. I find myself with problems I can't solve on my own. Sometimes I catch myself doing things I swore I would never do, but I just can't stop myself."

Doug nodded. "I know what you mean."

Jeff went on, "The Bible tells me that all these problems are related. Since we could never solve this huge problem on our own, God became one of us, a human being, to deal with it. The way he dealt with it was by dying on the cross and then coming back to life."

Now Doug was intrigued. "But how could God dying make things any better for me?" Jeff gently shared some of his own experiences with Jesus, and the conversation went on.

Aggressive Witnessing

Sometimes Christians are very aggressive in their witnessing. They:

- make decisions for others;
- don't allow others to say what they feel or think;
- tell others about Jesus in rude, intrusive ways;
- sarcastically ridicule the thoughts and beliefs of others;
- threaten others; and
- intimidate others.

An Example of Aggressive Witnessing

Here's an example of aggressive witnessing.

Jan knew Mary was a single parent, trying to raise four young children on her own. One day at work Jan invited Mary to go to church with her. "I'd like to go," said Mary, "but Sunday morning is the only time I have to get caught up on laundry and mending."

"I know you're busy, Mary, but that's really not a very good reason to skip church," Jan told her, ignoring the hurt look on her face. "I'm sure you can find another time to get those things done. Going to church is much more important than laundry or mending."

Without waiting for a response, Jan continued, "I'm busy, too, but I make sure my family and I are in church every Sunday. You just need to be more organized."

As Mary turned to walk away, Jan said, "Even if you don't care about where you are going to spend eternity, you could at least give your children a chance at eternal life."

The Effects of an Aggressive Witness

An aggressive witness can obviously leave very negative effects. In this case, Jan came off as uncaring, rude, and aggressive. Mary probably felt that Jan was attacking her, which would make her respond defensively.

Mary's relationship with God will probably also suffer. In this so-called witness, Mary didn't hear a word about God's love or care, even though she is in a situation where she needs a great deal of love and care. Instead, she was left with the impression that Christians, and maybe even God, are uncaring, rude, and aggressive. Mary is now much less likely to attend church or to seek help from God.

Aggressive behavior strains relationships because it destroys the trust and respect that are necessary for them to grow. Because aggressiveness hurts people, it discourages honest communication in the future. Jan's comments certainly hurt Mary, who is now much less likely to share sensitive problems with Jan in the future. Jan herself may regret what she said, realizing that she was insensitive to Mary's needs.

The Assertive Alternative

How could Jan have witnessed assertively to Mary, instead of aggressively? Here is one way.

Knowing that Mary was a single parent, trying to raise four children on her own, Jan looked for ways to care for Mary. One way she found was to listen to Mary as she "blew off steam" about the difficulties she faced.

Mary frequently talked about how lonely she was for adult companionship. "But," she would say, "I just can't spend any more time away from my children than I already do."

One day Jan said, "One of the things I really like about our church is the activities we have where a bunch of families do things together. I get to be with my children, but it's also a chance to get out and be with others."

"That sounds wonderful," Mary said, "but I'm already so busy. Weekends are the only time I have to get caught up with housework."

Jan thought for a moment, and then said, "I know what you mean about being so busy. But I was just thinking, if you'd really like to try one of the church's family outings, maybe I could come over and help you get caught up on housework so you could find the time."

Mary said, "You'd really do that?"

"I think I could make the time," Jan said, "and it seems like the kind of thing Jesus would want me to do. He really cared for people who were having a rough time, and I'm trying to live like he did."

Assertive Evangelism

Assertive witnessing is neither passive nor aggressive. When Christians witness assertively, they:

- tell others about their beliefs without demanding that others agree;
- take responsibility for their own beliefs and choices and allow others to do the same;
- take advantage of opportunities to share their feelings and ideas about God's love when the time is right;
- genuinely express care, affection, and concern for others;
- witness in ways that show care for others and for themselves; and
- sometimes choose to set aside their own rights in order to be of service to others.

An Example of Assertive Witnessing

Here's another example of assertive witnessing.

After work one day, Art invited John out for dinner. It was the first time they'd had an opportunity to talk since John's divorce. After they gave the waitress their orders and talked for a bit, Art asked John how everything was going.

John shook his head and looked down at his coffee cup. "I still can't believe it's over between Annie and me."

"It must feel strange being on your own again," said Art.

"It sure does." After a brief pause John continued, "I've joined a recovery group to try to control my drinking."

"That's great. How's it going?" Art asked.

"It's going okay, I guess. But it's really made me think about how rough I made it for Annie. I really put her through a lot. All the yelling and lying—I just didn't realize how my drinking was affecting our marriage and our family."

"You sound sorry for what happened," Art said.

John nodded. "I am. I really treated her badly, and I hate to think about what I put the kids through. I can't stop feeling guilty. It's really got me down. I hardly think about anything else."

"It really hurts to feel that guilty," Art said. "Sometimes I feel so angry at myself for the mistakes I've made. I don't know what I'd do if I wasn't sure that God forgave me."

John shook his head. "I don't think God can forgive me. I've caused my family too much pain. I don't deserve forgiveness."

"None of us do. But God loves you very much, John. So much in fact, that Jesus suffered and died for you. Because of Jesus, God forgives us," Art explained.

John asked, "You think that can help me?" Art answered him, and the conversation went on.

Benefits of Assertive Witnessing

There are several benefits to assertive witnessing. In this case, John felt listened to, cared for, and understood. John saw in Art a reflection of God's love and concern. John also had the opportunity to learn of Christ's forgiveness.

Assertive witnessing is very different from aggressive witnessing. Art was concerned about John and sincerely wanted to know how he was doing. He listened to John's feelings and acknowledged them. The concern he showed helped strengthen their relationship, and encouraged John to share how he really felt. In this way Art was able to understand John's needs and share the love of Jesus in ways that spoke to those needs.

Assertively Choosing Not to Speak

Christian assertiveness follows the example of Jesus, who was so free that he could choose to give up his freedom for the sake of others. Our Christian love for others can sometimes motivate us to meet their needs by denying our own. This is not a passive choice, however. It is self-respecting and consistent with who we are, and who we are becoming, in Jesus.

An important part of assertiveness is learning when not to say or do anything. For example, there will be times when all a friend needs is someone to show love and support by simply listening. Listening itself can be an assertive act, because out of love you deliberately choose to put others' needs first and deny your own. You haven't been forced to keep quiet—you have chosen it, out of love and respect for the other person.

How to Become More Assertive

Assertiveness is a learned behavior. With practice, you can replace passive or aggressive ways of relating with assertive ways of relating. Here are some ways to work on being more assertive.

- Ask for God's help.
- Observe your interactions with others and think about whether your communications and actions were passive, aggressive, or assertive. Think about how the passive or aggressive ones could have been more assertive.
- Keep an assertiveness diary, and record times you were able to deal with others assertively.
- Keep trying. Don't get discouraged or give up.
- Practice assertive communication in front of a mirror or with a trusted friend.
- First practice being more assertive in ways that are easy for you. Then move to more difficult assertive situations.
- Remind yourself that God loves you *and* those with whom you relate. God has made all of us valuable people who deserve to be treated with care and respect.

Assertiveness Is a Way to Care

Assertiveness is an essential part of your Christian witness. Learning to relate assertively allows you to share Christ's love with others in natural, sensitive ways. You will not witness aggressively, and turn others off. You will not witness passively, and fail to witness at all. Through assertive relating and witnessing, you will be able to care for others most fully—by respecting them as people, and by sharing God's Good News with them in caring ways.

[1]For a more complete look at Christian assertiveness see *Speaking the Truth in Love: How to Be an Assertive Christian,* Ruth N. Koch and Kenneth C. Haugk, (St. Louis: Stephen Ministries, 1992).

Chapter 15

How to Use the Bible in Evangelizing

Sarah and I went over to Margaret's house early Thanksgiving afternoon. We could smell the turkey roasting as we walked in the door. Margaret took our coats and invited us into the kitchen.

We went into her warm kitchen and sat at the table and talked while Margaret tended to several pots on the stove and prepared the salad.

"Where's your daughter spending Thanksgiving?" Sarah asked.

"Oh, she and her family are with her in-laws. They all live in California, and she can't afford to come back here very often. What about your children?"

Sarah answered, "Larry's working part time to help pay for college and he had a chance to work this weekend, so he stayed at school. He has some friends he's going to get together with today. Erica's with Nick and his family. Ever since they started going together it's been 'Hi, Erica,' and 'Good-bye, Erica,' and that's about all."

"I didn't think we'd have to face the empty nest for another year or two," I said.

"I really miss the kids," Sarah said. "Holidays are supposed to be family time."

Margaret stopped cutting the tomatoes for a moment and said, "Being with you two feels like being with family."

"We feel the same way about you," I said.

While Margaret and Sarah set the table, I got my coat and

walked around the backyard. The wind blew stray leaves around. It was starting to feel like winter.

Back inside it was warm and cheery. When we sat down to eat we all paused for a moment. Then Margaret said, "Andy, would you like to give thanks?"

I was surprised, and I guess it showed.

Margaret said, "I can't see a lot of sense in celebrating Thanksgiving without giving thanks to someone."

I said, "I can't argue with that," and said a simple prayer thanking God for food and friends and absent family members.

After supper we ate pie and drank coffee and talked together.

"I want you two to know that I've been thinking about the things we've discussed about God," Margaret said. "After that afternoon when we talked about the state of the world and sin and so on, I started remembering some of what I had to memorize from the Bible all those years ago."

I asked, "How did it feel to remember?"

"Oh, I suppose I remember in different ways . . . I've always remembered the facts. There's so much of the Bible in literature. Actually you can't understand a lot of the symbolism in literature unless you are familiar with the Bible."

"I remember that from college," I said.

"When I was a teenager I had to participate in 'Bible Quiz' contests. I never believed a bit of it, but I actually learned the content of the Bible pretty well. Even though I resented it, I still remember some of it. For example, how big did Noah build the ark?"

Sarah shook her head and I said, "I haven't a clue."

"'And this is the fashion which thou shalt make it of: The length of the ark shall be three hundred cubits, the breadth of it fifty cubits, and the height of it thirty cubits.' Genesis six, verse fifteen."

I asked, "What's a cubit?"

Margaret laughed. "I have no idea. They didn't make us memorize that. Here's another one: What was Noah's wife's name?"

I shrugged and Sarah said, "I don't know."

Margaret said, "Neither does anyone else. The Bible never says."

Then Margaret sighed and said, "I can remember all sorts of trivia . . . characters . . . facts. Especially from the Old Testament. That's just information and it doesn't bother me."

We were all quiet for a moment. Then Margaret said, "But there's the other way I remember the Bible that still brings back terrible memories." She stood up and said, "I'll be right back."

Sarah whispered, "Can you believe she knows the Bible like that?"

How to Use the Bible in Evangelizing

I shook my head.

Margaret came back carrying a new Bible.

"After we talked last month I kept thinking about it . . . about your explanation for the way the world is. Finally I decided that if I wanted to find out about God, I should go back to the original source of information. So a couple of weeks ago I went out and bought this."

I was so surprised I didn't know what to say.

"How long had it been since you'd read the Bible?" Sarah asked.

Margaret calculated for a moment and then said, "Not since I was eighteen. I left home to go to college and I've never read the Bible once since then until two weeks ago."

"But you've been reading it for two weeks?" I asked.

"No, I haven't. I started reading through the Gospel of Matthew, but I had to put it down."

"Why?" I asked.

"Because of all the bad memories it brought back. I know the Bible isn't a bad book, but I've seen it used in evil ways, and those memories are very painful."

"What do you mean?" Sarah asked.

Margaret paused and remembered for a moment. Then she said, "I was reading Matthew and I came to the point where Jesus says, 'Verily I say unto you, If ye have faith as a grain of mustard seed, ye shall say unto this mountain, remove from here to yonder place; and it shall remove; and nothing shall be impossible unto you.'"

Margaret took a deep breath. "The preacher at my father's church harped and harped on that verse. He said that when he was reading the Bible God had told him that our church was to have utter faith, and if anyone doubted, terrible things would happen to all of us. Then he used the Bible as a weapon to attack people. If anyone didn't agree with something he wanted to do he would accuse them of being unfaithful. He would threaten them. He would tell them that they were in danger of losing their salvation.

"There was a family in that church," Margaret said, "who had a child that became very ill. They asked for prayers for the child and the preacher and the elders went to the child's home and anointed her with oil and prayed for her. My father was one of the elders and he told us all about it. He quoted the book of James where it says, 'Is any sick among you? Let him call for the elders of the church; and let them pray over him, anointing him with oil in the name of the Lord; and the prayer of faith shall save the sick.' He said the little girl would be fine the next day.

"The next day she was sicker and her parents took her to the hospital. The following Sunday my father stood up and accused the family of unfaithfulness and the preacher drove them out of the church. The elders actually made them leave right in the middle of the service."

"How terrible," Sarah said.

Tears ran down Margaret's cheeks. "Soon after that my mother became very ill. She couldn't eat or drink anything without throwing it up. She kept getting worse until she was terribly sick, and finally my father brought the elders and the preacher over and they prayed for her for hours. I had never prayed because it all seemed so false and hypocritical to me, but that night I prayed too. I knew my father wouldn't allow my mother to see a doctor. I knew that the only chance she had was for these religious hypocrites to pray her back to health."

Margaret stopped and sat silent with her eyes closed.

I finally said, "Margaret, what happened?"

"Oh, she died later that week." Sarah got Margaret some tissues. Margaret wiped her eyes, and said, "It was so long ago, but it still hurts."

I said, "I'm sure it does."

Margaret nodded and then continued her story. "I didn't even stay for the funeral."

Sarah said, "Oh, Margaret."

"I couldn't stand to be with those people ever again. I couldn't bear the thought of listening to all their pious lies after they killed my mother. So I packed up and left home the day of her funeral. I went to live with my aunt and uncle on my mother's side. They hated my father and let me stay with them until I started college. My grandmother had left me the money to go to college, and I got some scholarships and loans. Anyway, that was the last time I ever opened a Bible or entered a church."

Sarah was crying. Margaret handed her another tissue. Then Margaret picked up the Bible. "So I don't know what I can do with this. I don't know if I can get past all those memories in order to read it again."

"Not all Christians use the Bible like that," I said.

Margaret nodded. "I know."

"If you'd like, we could read it together. Talk about it. Maybe that could help you get over some of the bad memories."

"I think I'd like that," Margaret said. "Thank you. I think I would."

How to Use the Bible in Evangelizing

Sometimes when we try to share God's Good News with others, we may find ourselves struggling to put into words all that God is and has done for us. How can we help our non-Christian friends to really see the God we have come to know?

The Gospel of John points toward an answer.

> Philip found Nathanael and said to him, "We have found him about whom Moses in the law and also the prophets wrote, Jesus son of Joseph from Nazareth." Nathanael said to him, "Can anything good come out of Nazareth?" Philip said to him, "Come and see." (John 1:45-46)

Sometimes words just aren't enough. We need to simply turn and point to Jesus. Obviously, we can't do this in the same way Philip did, taking his friend Nathanael into the physical presence of Jesus. But we can invite others to "come and see" Jesus in another very real way, in the Scriptures.

The Bible is where we learn what God is really like, what God thinks and feels about humanity. We see how God has met the needs of people down through the ages, and we find hope for our own needs. In the Bible's pages we encounter the living Christ and come into contact with his redeeming, remaking power.

Using the Bible to Evangelize Ourselves

Here is Paul's advice to Timothy about how to use the Bible.

> But as for you, continue in what you have learned and firmly believed, knowing from whom you learned it, and how from childhood you have known the sacred writings that are able to instruct you for salvation through faith in Christ Jesus. All scripture is inspired by God and is useful for teaching, for reproof, for correction, and for training in righteousness, so that everyone who belongs to God may be proficient, equipped for every good work. (2 Tim. 3:14-17)

To rephrase the saying, "Evangelism begins at home." We can't give what we haven't got. Every evangelist must turn to the Bible for his or her own sake, to learn God's will, to redis-cover his or her own need for Jesus, and to find God's promises of forgiveness and new life. As the Holy Spirit helps Christians grow in faith through this discipline of Bible reading, they become better able to share God's Good News with others.

Using the Bible to Evangelize Others

In Conversation

When you use the Bible, there are certain don'ts and dos to keep in mind. These guidelines will help make your witness much more caring and effective.

Don'ts to Keep in Mind

- Don't simply quote numerous Bible verses and expect this to solve the other person's problem. That is a results-oriented way of relating, and it appears very uncaring. Instead, listen carefully first, and when it seems natural, share a Bible promise or story.

- Don't use the Bible to prove you are right. In evangelism, avoid arguments. You are sharing God's Good News in order to care for the other person—not to prove that you are correct.

- Don't get sidetracked onto controversial issues like biblical inerrancy, evolution, biblical criticism, or the correct interpretation of Revelation. Interesting and important as these topics are, they are nothing in comparison to the message of God's love that you are trying to pass on. Stick to your main point.

A word of caution about the final "don't." In some cases the other person has real concerns about these issues that he or she would like cleared up. In those cases, you might want to talk for a few minutes about the issue or refer the person to a good book, or offer to check on it for him or her. But then return to the Good News, if the person is willing.

Occasionally you may find that the other person is only interested in talking about these side issues because he or she is trying to avoid the main issue—God's Good News. He or she is trying to sidetrack you. (The Samaritan woman at the well did this with Jesus.) If this happens to you, listen to the message these people are silently giving you—"I'm not ready to talk about the Gospel yet." Don't argue or force them to return to the issue of the Good News. Instead, go back to caring listening until they are ready—just as Jesus did.

Dos to Keep in Mind

- Do listen before you share a passage from the Bible; then you can make sure it relates to the other person's needs.

- Do use Bible stories. Telling a short Bible story that really fits the person's need is helpful for several reasons. Stories are always easier to remember than verses. Bible stories also allow the other person to see how God dealt with other people in situations similar to his or hers. They can offer hope. For example, a person struggling with guilt might hear the story of the prodigal son or the story of Jacob, and think, *If God treated him that way, there's hope for me too.*

- Do put it in your own words. You may know the Bible best in King James English, and that's fine. But for your non-Christian friends, be sure to tell the story in the clearest, simplest language possible. They are probably much less familiar with the Bible than you are, and your aim is to meet their needs.

Studying the Bible with Another

Occasionally in your relationships with others there will come a point when the other person is ready and willing to learn more about God, but he or she is not yet ready to visit your congregation. This is when one-on-one Bible study can be useful. As the two of you study the Scriptures together, your friend can ask all the questions he or she wants to without feeling embarrassed about not knowing the answers. Later, as your friend gains more confidence, you may be able to invite him or her into the larger Christian community of your congregation.

Having a two-person Bible study may seem intimidating at first, but it's actually very easy. It can also be a wonderful way to experience God's blessings through the Bible and through each other. Here are a few suggestions.[1]

Getting Ready

First of all, remember that your friend is probably as nervous as you are. Do what you can to lower the level of nervousness. You can do this by meeting in a comfortable setting, such as your home. You may want to have something to eat or drink ready.

Make sure you're using a Bible that is easy to read and understand, and have the same version for both of you. (Stay away from King James unless your friend feels most comfortable with it.) Also avoid small print or lots of distracting notes. It's an added bonus if you use two Bibles with the same page numbering!

Choosing Your Reading

An excellent way to start is by reading through one of the Gospels. A Gospel will give you a good grasp on who Jesus is and what he has done.

Take your reading in manageable chunks. A "chunk" is a single story or passage that seems to hang together. Don't feel obligated to read a whole chapter at a time. This is often too much to handle; instead, take your time, and enjoy.

Learning Together

When you sit down together, begin with a very simple prayer asking God to help you learn from what you're reading. Then open up the Bible and read out loud. (You may want to alternate reading verses or paragraphs.)

When you finish reading, talk over what you read. Here are some examples of questions you might ask:

- Do I understand what's going on in the passage? What is clear? What is unclear?
- With whom do I identify in this passage?
- What does God have to say to me in this passage?
- Where is the Good News for me in this passage?

Don't feel obliged to dissect the text verse by verse. This is okay for Christians who have been through the Bible many times, but it tends to confuse and bore newcomers. Focus on the story as a whole.

In your study time together, as much as possible seek to be a fellow explorer, rather than a teacher. Witness about how God is speaking to *you* through the passage. There will, of course, be questions that your friend asks you, and it's good to discuss these. But most of the time, you two are co-learners.

Watching for the Unfamiliar

When you study the Bible together, be sure to keep an eye out for things that may be unfamiliar to your friend. Remember that many people don't know how the chapter and verse system of the Bible works, or where certain books are located. If you have identical copies of the Bible you can refer to page numbers. Your friend will learn how to find his or her way around in the Bible as he or she becomes more familiar with it, but it's not necessary now. In fact, having to struggle with it too early could lead the person to give up reading the Bible completely.

Another unfamiliar aspect of the Bible is the culture of Bible times. Words like *synagogue, tax collector,* or *Pharisee* can be very confusing to a new reader. It's a good idea to read the passage before your meeting and look up any unfamiliar terms so you will be prepared to explain them to your friend.

Sooner or later your friend will ask you a question you can't answer. Don't panic. Just say, "I don't know, but I will try to find out for you," and make a note to yourself. Then you can check a Bible dictionary or ask your own Bible teacher or pastor to help you find the answer.[2] Be sure to have an answer for the other person the next time you meet, if possible.

What if nobody seems to know the answer? Then just say, "I'm sorry, I checked with several people, and none of us know. But if you ever find out, please let me know so I can tell the others." At least your friend will know you've tried.

Finishing Your Time Together

Finish your Bible study by praying together in whatever way makes your friend most comfortable. If he or she wishes you to pray aloud by yourself, do so. If your friend wishes to take turns, do that. Be sure to pray for the needs you both have at that time.

Agree together to read a portion of the book you are studying before you get together again. Over weeks and months God will use your Bible study to make faith grow—both yours and your partner's.

The Purpose of Using the Bible

The Gospel of John explains the purpose of using the Bible in evangelism when it says, "Now Jesus did many other signs in the presence of his disciples, which are not written in this book. But these are written so that you may come to believe that Jesus is the Messiah, the Son of God, and that through believing you may have life in his name." (John 20:30-31) God uses the words of Scripture to enable people to believe in Jesus and receive the forgiveness and new life God offers.

[1]There are many other ways of studying the Bible. Roberta Hestenes gives many good suggestions in chapters 4, 5, and 6 of her book *Using the Bible in Groups* (Philadelphia: The Westminster Press, 1983).

[2]Some study aids that may prove useful are Bible dictionaries, concordances, and commentaries. Your church library, adult education leaders, pastor, or local Christian bookstore might be helpful about specific titles.

Chapter 16

The Power of Prayer in Evangelism

Thanksgiving night Sarah and I lay in bed. In the dark I watched the dancing shadows of the tree outside our bedroom window as the wind blew through the branches. I couldn't go to sleep. From the way she was tossing and turning, I suspected she couldn't either.

"Are you awake?"

She answered. "Uh huh. I can't sleep. I suppose you can't either."

"No. I keep thinking about Margaret."

"Me too. What a day."

"Absolutely. You know what I've been thinking?"

"Tell me."

"I was thinking about how I've been praying for Margaret. Ever since last March when all this started."

"It's funny we don't talk more about this kind of thing," Sarah said. "I've been praying for her too."

"I suspected you were, knowing you."

"I'm not sure how much my prayers helped Margaret," Sarah said, "but often praying really helped me."

"How?"

"Sometimes I would feel discouraged about Margaret, especially over the summer when she was so sad all the time. Sometimes I just wanted to sit her down and tell her to believe in God and ask for help. I'd get frustrated by her when she was so depressed. But then I'd pray about it and then I'd think, 'No, give it more time.' I don't know if it was just common sense or if it was God talking to me somehow. Whatever it was, now I'm really glad I listened."

"Anything before this would have been too soon," I said.

"I know. What about you? What have you been praying for her?"

"I've just been praying the same prayer over and over again. 'God, take care of Margaret.' I was never sure what to do, but I know God knows. I just wanted God to use me in any way possible and protect Margaret from all my goof-ups."

Sarah said, "You're too hard on yourself."

"I know . . . Sometimes I wondered if praying was doing any good. A lot of the time it felt like I was talking to a blank wall. But I have to keep praying, mostly for my sake. I have to remember God is really a part of this, no matter what happens with Margaret."

Sarah turned over and pulled the covers up around her shoulders. "Maybe this will be the breakthrough for Margaret." She sounded sleepy.

"We can only hope," I said. "Well, I guess we can also pray, come to think of it."

It sounds like a paradox, but in evangelism, sometimes our most important words are the words that other people never hear. These are the words we use to talk to God—the words we use to pray. Prayer is a vital part of Caring Evangelism. Without prayer, any attempt at evangelism is likely to be weak and ineffectual.

Because prayer is so basic to the Christian life, it's not possible to try to say everything about it in one short chapter. There are many good books available that can guide your growth in prayer.

In this chapter, you will be taking a look at a few very important issues concerning prayer and the caring evangelist. First, you'll look at the benefits of prayer in your personal life, and cover some very basic ideas on how to pray. Then you'll look at how you can pray out loud in evangelizing relationships with others.

Jesus' Life of Prayer

Jesus knew how important prayer was in his relationship with God. He spent a great deal of time in prayer, sometimes entire nights. It's instructive to look at the life of Jesus and see where prayer is mentioned.

Often he would get up early and go out alone to pray (Mark 1:35; Luke 5:16). There's a reference to Jesus' praying all night just before he chose the twelve apostles (Luke 6:12- 13). It was an important decision, and Jesus prayed before making it. Jesus' transfiguration occurred on the mountain to which he had withdrawn for prayer (Luke 9:28-36).

Just hours before his arrest, Jesus sat at supper with his disciples preparing them for the terrible events about to happen. He warned them about his death and the impact it would have on them, and he comforted them with the promise of his resurrection. Then he turned to prayer. Jesus placed these disciples, who were so dear to him, in God's care (John 17).

Later that night Jesus prayed for hours in Gethsemane, until just moments before his arrest. Jesus turned to God through prayer in order to make his personal preparations for the suffering, death, and resurrection that awaited him (Matt. 26:36-45; Mark 14:32-41). Even on the cross, Jesus continued to pray (Luke 23:34, 46).

Jesus knew that prayer was important for others, too. When the disciples asked him to teach them how to pray, he complied (Luke 11:1-13). In the parable of the widow and the unjust judge, he taught the importance of praying always (Luke 18:1-8).

Following Jesus' example and teaching, the early church also made praying an integral part of their lives. The first disciples were meeting for prayer while they waited for Jesus to send the Holy Spirit to them from heaven (Acts 1:14). When Peter was in jail and under sentence of execution, the church prayed earnestly for him (Acts 12:5). Christians prayed together before sending out missionaries (Acts 13:2-3).

Our Life of Prayer

Prayer is just as important for us as it was for Jesus and the early Christians. Here are some reasons why.

Communicating with God Is Vital to Our Relationship with God

Relationships thrive on communication. When you love others, you naturally communicate with them. You want to share with them—thoughts, ideas, joy, and sadness. You want to understand the ones you love, and be understood by them.

When communication is blocked, relationships suffer. Imagine two people living in the same house who never spoke a word to each other, never gestured, never communicated in any way with each other. The relationship wouldn't last long. The two people would quickly become strangers to each other.

So it is with our relationship to God. If we fail to communicate with God—if we never pray—soon our relationship with God suffers. God becomes a stranger to us. We aren't in touch anymore.

But if we do communicate often and deeply with God, our relationship flourishes. We begin to see more and more clearly how much God loves us and cares for us. We learn to see things more and more from God's point of view, and we learn to love God more so that we want to do what pleases God. As Richard Foster writes, "In prayer, real prayer, we begin to think God's thoughts after him: to desire the things he desires, to love the things he loves, to will the things he wills. Progressively we are taught to see things from his point of view."[1]

Foster also shows that the ones who change most as a result of our prayers are us.

> To pray is to change. Prayer is the central avenue God uses to transform us. If we are unwilling to change, we will abandon prayer as a noticeable characteristic in our lives. The closer we come to the heartbeat of God the more we see our need and the more we desire to be conformed to Christ. . . . when we pray God slowly and graciously reveals to us our evasive actions and sets us free from them.[2]

Prayer Helps Us Evangelize

Not only is praying good for us personally, but it helps us when we evangelize others. Much of what we share as caring evangelists comes out of our own relationship with God. Without a life of prayer, without the closeness with God that prayer helps develop, we have very little to talk about with others. But when we do pray and draw closer to God, we will have much more to share with others.

God often prepares us to evangelize others while we pray. When we pray for people we're evangelizing, God can help us to know the right words or deeds to say or do. After all, God knows and loves them better than anyone else, and God can help us to meet their needs.

Sometimes, too, personal prejudices or weaknesses make it difficult for an individual to caringly evangelize others. God works on these problems, too, when we pray. It happened to Peter when God used him to evangelize Cornelius.

Peter was praying before lunch one day and he was very hungry. God showed him a vision—all kinds of animals and reptiles being let down from heaven in something like a large sheet, right in front of him. Then a voice said, "Get up, Peter; kill and eat."

Peter was shocked, because every one of those animals was on the list of creatures good Jews weren't supposed to eat. They were considered unclean. So he told God that, and received the answer, "What God has made clean, you must not call profane."

Peter was probably very puzzled. What kind of message was God trying to give him? The Holy Spirit told him to go downstairs, to meet three men who wanted him to go with them.

Then Peter figured it out. These men were Gentiles, people the Jews normally didn't associate with because they were also "unclean." And they wanted to take him to visit another Gentile's house.

Peter went. When he arrived at Cornelius's house he explained why he had come: "You yourselves know that it is unlawful for a Jew to associate with or to visit a Gentile; but God has shown me that I should not call anyone profane or unclean. So when I was sent for, I came without objection." (Acts 10:28-29a) Peter went on to share the Gospel with the people there, even though they were Gentiles and not Jews. This was one of the first real breakthroughs of Christianity into the non-Jewish world.

Like Peter, many Christians have preconceptions and prejudices that keep them from evangelizing in certain situations or with certain kinds of people. As they pray God works in them, removing these blinders and teaching them God's plans for their evangelizing.

In prayer, we have a wonderful opportunity to ask God to help in our evangelizing relationships. Earlier we read about how there are some things that only God can do—helping others realize their need for a Savior, creating faith, drawing others to Jesus. When we pray we ask God to do what only God can do. We can pray confidently, knowing that God will hear our prayers and answer them in the way that God knows is best.

This kind of prayer benefits the other person. But it also benefits us, because it reminds us that we aren't evangelizing all by ourselves, in our own power. It can be easy to feel responsible for the results of the evangelizing relationship, and blame ourselves if matters don't work out the way we think they should. Asking for God's help reminds us that evangelism is primarily the Holy Spirit's activity, not ours.

Personal Prayer Readies Us for Prayer with Others

Finally, personal prayer gives us experience and confidence, so that we can pray aloud with others later. Many Christians feel uncomfortable praying aloud with others. In our personal prayer we practice talking to God in private. This helps us find the courage to do so with others.

Ways to Pray

There are many different ways to pray. The list below is not meant to be exhaustive, but just to get you started with some ideas about how you might make prayer a deeper part of your life.

ACTS

ACTS is a commonly used acronym for Adoration, Confession, Thanksgiving, and Supplication. These four words can form an outline for prayer as you think about what to discuss with God.

Adoration means praising God. It is often well to begin your times of prayer by remembering how wonderful God is and how much God loves you.

Confession comes from a Greek word that literally means "to say the same thing." When you confess, you are agreeing with (saying the same thing as) God about how you should live, and you ask forgiveness for all the times you fail. You can confess confidently, remembering the promise, "If we confess our sins, he who is faithful and just will forgive us our sins and cleanse us from all unrighteousness." (1 John 1:9)

Thanksgiving is what it says—saying thank you to God for all the blessings God has given. This reminds you of God's care for you in the past and helps you find faith to expect the same care in the future. In fact, the Apostle Paul advised the Thessalonians, "Rejoice always, pray without ceasing, give thanks in all circumstances; for this is the will of God in Christ Jesus for you." (1 Thess. 5:16-18)

Finally, *supplication* means asking God's help, God's attention, God's blessing in specific situations. Supplication includes requests for yourself and for others. When you ask God's help and blessing you can do so believing that God hears you and will give you what you need (Matt. 7:7-11).

These four elements—adoration, confession, thanksgiving, and supplication—don't always go in this order in prayers. There will be times when you may start with a different element. In whatever order you pray, remembering the ACTS acronym can help you keep your prayers balanced—not only supplication or only confession.

A Prayer Journal

One good way to pray is to keep a prayer journal, in which

you list the persons or situations for which you are praying. You may want to write your prayers like a diary, or as letters to God. It can help concentration and make prayers seem more substantial to put them into writing. As time goes by, occasionally you will want to look back and reread what you've written. Then you can see how God has answered those prayers.

The Lord's Prayer

When the disciples asked Jesus how to pray, he responded by giving them a model—the Lord's Prayer (Matt. 6:9-13). This prayer is a great one to pray, either by itself or as a framework for further prayer.

When you use the Lord's Prayer as a framework, this means that you pray it slowly, meditating on it, thought by thought. At each phrase you stop to think about what it means, and to see how it applies to your life. You may also want to add thoughts that relate to that particular topic.

For example, when you reach the phrase "Give us this day our daily bread," you might stop and think about all the gifts God provides for you—family, friends, a job, rest, a place to live. You might then tell God about any of these that is of special concern to you. You might ask for help in finding a job, or for God's guidance in a relationship. Then you would continue with the next phrase of the prayer.

Listening to God

Another part of prayer that people often forget is listening. Søren Kierkegaard once wrote about a person learning to pray. "In proportion as he became more and more earnest in prayer, he had less and less to say, and in the end he became quite silent. He became silent—indeed, what is if possible still more expressly the opposite of speaking, he became a hearer. He had supposed that to pray is to speak; he learnt that to pray is not merely to be silent but to hear."[3] At its best, prayer is not a monologue. It is a true conversation, with times for speaking and times for simply listening in quietness. Often it is in your times of being silent that God is able to bring new thoughts and understanding to your heart.

Imaging Prayers

Prayer doesn't always require words. Sometimes your requests of God can take the form of seeing God in your imagination intervening in a particular situation.

For example, if you are praying for a person who is lonely, you might close your eyes and try to imagine Jesus right there with the person, comforting him or her. Imagine that person understanding that he or she is not alone and can never be alone when Jesus is with him or her. Of course you could use words to pray for the person, but sometimes you can picture in your mind's eye ideas you can't find words to express.

Constant Prayer

Paul says in 1 Thessalonians 5:17 to "pray without ceasing." Obviously, few people can completely retire from the activities of life to spend 24 hours a day in prayer. But everyone can learn to frequently bring daily concerns to God in prayer.

Here's an example. Dropping a child off in the morning at school, you think about the challenges he or she will face that day and turn those concerns into prayer. As you head for home or for your own job, you ask God to guide you and be with you as you tackle the work ahead of you. If you hear of a friend or co-worker going through a hard time, you immediately pray a sentence or two for that person. As the family gathers again at home in the evening, you quickly thank God for the love you share.

These kinds of prayers need not be long. Often they will be only a sentence or two. You may pray sitting still with your eyes closed and hands folded, or you may pray with eyes wide open while driving down the highway. What matters is that you bring every detail of your life and every need you see before God, realizing that God cares and wants to hear about it all. In that way you "pray without ceasing."

Quiet Times

Quiet time is the name many Christians use for a regular, daily time set aside for prayer. If you choose to pray in this way, it is best to set aside a short period of time to start with, perhaps ten minutes or even five. Then allow nothing short of a major emergency to interrupt. This time is only for praying.

Often, people who try this find it very difficult to sit still and pray, especially in the beginning. Thoughts about errands they need to do, phone calls they should make, and forgotten appointments they should attend to are distractions that can keep them from ever really praying. As much as possible, put such thoughts out of your mind and focus on God. Sometimes it helps to write down important but distracting thoughts as soon as they come to mind, so you don't have to worry about forgetting them later.

Quiet times of prayer require discipline and hard work.

They can be very beneficial, however, as you seek to draw closer to God through prayer.

The Holy Spirit Helps You Pray

Whatever way of prayer you choose, it is heartening to remember that you aren't doing it on your own. The Holy Spirit helps you pray, as Paul states:

> Likewise the Spirit helps us in our weakness; for we do not know how to pray as we ought, but that very Spirit intercedes with sighs too deep for words. And God, who searches the heart, knows what is the mind of the Spirit, because the Spirit intercedes for the saints according to the will of God. (Rom. 8:26-27)

You can also remember that Jesus himself is praying for you:

> Consequently he [Jesus] is able for all time to save those who approach God through him, since he always lives to make intercession for them. (Heb. 7:25)

Praying with Others

While our personal, private lives of prayer are of utmost importance, that is not all there is to prayer for caring evangelists. We also need to consider prayer with others—especially, with the people we care for in evangelizing relationships.[4]

The Value of Praying Aloud with Others

Praying together has clear benefits for others. When you pray with people you are evangelizing, they see what it's like to have a deep and intimate relationship with God. They see the love involved, and the trust. They see that you really believe God is concerned about people's daily lives.

This is often something they haven't been able to comprehend before. Even when you talk about your own relationship with God, they may not fully grasp it. But when they see the relationship in action, it can be very powerful.

If you pray for the others by name, they realize anew that you care for them. You care enough to actually bring them to the attention of God. They also see that you really think God can help them in their own lives.

Also, when you pray aloud with others, the others see that it doesn't take a degree in theology to pray. When others hear you using familiar words and simple, easy-to-understand sentences, they may gain the courage to try praying themselves.

Praying aloud together helps your evangelizing relationships grow deeper. There's something about praying together that brings people together. Once you've talked *to* God together it seems much more natural and comfortable to talk *about* God with each other.

Prayer Pitfalls

There are a few things to avoid when you pray with others. Below are a few dos and don'ts that can be very helpful.

- Don't pretend to talk to God when you're really talking to the other person. (For example, by saying something like "God, I know you want John to take better care of himself, to quit smoking and lose weight . . .")
- Avoid long, drawn-out, very intellectual or very emotional prayers. Do pray simple prayers using simple words that will be easy for others to imitate.
- Don't show off, draw attention to yourself, or try to impress others with how much you know. Do keep the focus on God and on the other person.

When to Pray Aloud with Others

So how do you know when to pray aloud with others? Probably you will need to be pretty far into the caring evangelism relationship before you are ready to pray. It takes time to develop the intimacy and caring that allow others to feel comfortable praying. For many people, prayer is a strange and slightly scary experience. For others, it is intensely personal. You should pray when it meets the other person's needs, not just your own.

When that time comes, gently ask the other person if he or she would like to pray with you. Chapter 17 will give some guidelines on how to know the right time to invite a person to pray.

How to Build a Prayer

So, you've asked, and the other person is ready and willing to pray. What next? It's not a good idea to just assume you know what others want to pray about. It's much better to plan what to pray about with the other person. You can do that by building a prayer.

You can build a meaningful prayer by asking questions, listening, and discussing the other's concerns.

Sometimes you may want to build a prayer quickly, because

you don't have a lot of time, or because you are praying with another Christian who has a lot of experience praying. Then you might use this question: "What would you like to pray about?"

Obviously, this is a very simple question. But it's a very good and quick way to learn what prayers will be most meaningful for the other person.

A Series of Questions for Building a Prayer

Other times you will have the chance to go into more detail building your prayers. Do this when you are praying with others who don't know how to pray, or who aren't sure what they want to say to God.

Here are some questions you can use with others to help build a prayer. Depending on the situation, you may want to ask any or all of them.

"What would you like to tell God?"

God is a wonderful listener. God is interested in the smallest details of our lives. If we feel confused, angry, sad, happy, excited, peaceful, or any other emotion, God wants to hear it. If we don't like what's going on in our lives, or if we do, God wants to hear it. If we are worried about people we care about, we can take that concern to God. We can also tell God how much we praise, adore, and appreciate God.

"What would you like to confess to God?"

If we feel guilty or troubled about something we have done, or just about life in general, we can share that with God. God will hear us, accept us, forgive us, and continue to love us.

"What would you like to ask of God?"

God wants to provide for our every need, and God wants us to ask for whatever we need, down to the simplest necessities of life. In the Lord's Prayer Jesus said to ask God for daily bread. God promises to hear our prayers and care for our needs.

"For what would you like to thank God?"

God always deserves thanks. When we stop to remember all that God has done for us and to thank God, it builds our love for God and our trust that God will continue to care for us in the future.

"What else would you like to say to God?"

This is a good closing question. It gives others the chance to mention things they didn't say earlier, and to bring up subjects you haven't asked them about.

How to Use These Questions to Build a Prayer

You won't necessarily use all of these questions as you build a prayer. Instead, choose the questions that are appropriate for the person with whom you are praying. As you ask these questions, you may think of others to ask also.

Choose which questions to use based on all you have learned about the other person. For example, if you know that he or she is carrying a burden of guilt, you may ask the question about confession. If that is not an important issue for him or her right now, however, just skip that question.

Be sure to discuss the questions and answers. It's not a good idea to quickly ask a series of questions as if you were checking them off on a list. Taking time for discussion and listening will help you understand the other's needs and how to build a prayer that meets them.

After you have asked and discussed the appropriate questions, include the other person's answers in the prayer. To help you remember, you might want to jot down a few notes during your discussion time, if it doesn't feel awkward to do this.

The Practical Details of Prayer Together

It's also important to talk over *how* you are going to pray out loud with others. You need to decide who will pray aloud. There are several possible choices.

- You can pray aloud, while the other person prays silently.

- The other person can pray aloud, while you pray silently.

- You can both pray aloud, first one person, then the other.

If you decide yes to the last option, then you also need to decide in what order the two of you will pray. Planning at the beginning helps avoid the embarrassment of not knowing who's supposed to do what and when.

Sometimes people wonder if they should hold hands while they pray. If it seems natural and comfortable for both parties, go ahead. If not, it's better to avoid making the other person uncomfortable.

What about kneeling or standing up during prayer? Probably the majority of people will feel most comfortable sitting. If, however, both of you want to kneel or stand, that's fine. In all of these decisions your goal is to help the other person feel comfortable talking with God.

Once you have worked out all the details of the prayer, pray! At first it may feel awkward or difficult, but go ahead and try it anyway. The more you practice the more comfortable you will feel. Many people have found praying aloud with others to be a wonderful way to express their faith in God and to enjoy God together with other believers.

Be Persistent in Prayer

Whether privately, or out loud with others, one of the most important ways we respond to the needs of others is by praying. Caring Evangelism is first of all God's work—in others' lives and in your own. Prayer is one way we invite the Spirit's work and put ourselves and others in a position to receive what God offers.

We can grow in our personal lives of prayer by finding ways to make prayer a discipline. This chapter only touched on the many different ways there are to pray. Discover others. Try out new ways to pray. Talk with others who are also learning to communicate more often and more deeply with God. Read books about prayer and blend what you learn into your own prayer journey.

Don't think you have to have a great mystical or emotional experience when you pray. Prayer is not a way to create ecstatic experiences. It is often an activity you discipline yourself to do out of love for the one with whom you are communicating. Over the months and years you will find yourself growing closer to your God, understanding God's will more completely, loving others more and more like Jesus did. Communication builds relationships and prayer is the communication we use to help build our relationship with God.

It's also quite possible to become more accomplished and more comfortable praying out loud with others. The simple secret is to practice. But don't begin practicing with people who aren't yet Christian. Start practicing with other Christian people, with members of your family or your church. And don't expect to feel fully competent or natural right off. Do expect to grow, to learn, to struggle sometimes, and to learn new things about yourself and your relationship with God. Then, when the

Holy Spirit gives you the chance to pray aloud with a person you are evangelizing, you will have the experience to pray aloud and to trust God to give you the words to say.

[1] Richard J. Foster, *Celebration of Discipline: The Path to Spiritual Growth* (New York: Harper & Row, 1987), pp. 33-34.

[2] Foster, *Celebration of Discipline*, p. 33.

[3] Søren Kierkegaard, *Christian Discourses*, trans. Walter Lowie (New York: Oxford University Press, 1940), p. 323.

[4] For a very practical look at praying aloud with others see Kenneth C. Haugk, *Christian Caregiving—a Way of Life* (Minneapolis: Augsburg, 1984), pp. 106-117.

Chapter 17

The Basics of Process-Oriented Inviting

We three studied the Bible together through the winter. We started with Mark and worked our way through Luke by spring. Margaret was a wonder as a Bible student. She could remember details and make all kinds of connections between one part of the Bible and the other. I'm sure Sarah and I learned as much about the Bible as Margaret did that winter.

There were times when Margaret became angry. "How in the world could they have been so stupid as to interpret that passage like that?" she'd ask. Several times we had to just put the Bibles up and listen as Margaret raged about some hateful way her father's church had twisted a particular passage.

In early April we started studying the Book of Acts. It was a blue sky day with a chilly breeze. We were so anxious to be outside after a cold winter that we put on our sweaters and sat in Margaret's screened-in porch behind her house.

We read about Jesus' ascension in chapter 1 of Acts. Margaret said, "I've been thinking about how important Jesus' resurrection is. When you read through the stories like we have and live the drama of Jesus' life . . . I found myself caught up in the same feelings the disciples must have had. The crucifixion made me feel dark inside, but the resurrection makes my heart feel light. And in this passage he even promises to come back."

"I can't wait to see what it will be like on that day," Sarah said.

I nodded and silently said a prayer of thanks for Margaret.

Sarah stood up to stretch. She said, "Look, your maple trees are budding."

We all looked at the new growth.

Margaret said, "They're so pretty every spring when they come back. But I think I like the red leaves of autumn better, even though it used to make me sad when the maples turned red. All I could see was winter approaching."

She was silent for a moment. "But this year I think I'll enjoy the beautiful red leaves. I'll just remind myself that spring always follows winter."

We went on to read the story of the day of Pentecost in Acts, chapter 2. We took turns reading out loud. When we came to the end of Peter's sermon it was Margaret's turn to read. She read aloud the question from the crowd and Peter's response.

"Now when they heard this, they were cut to the heart and said to Peter and to the other apostles, 'Brothers, what should we do?' Peter said to them, 'Repent, and be baptized every one of you in the name of Jesus Christ so that your sins may be forgiven; and you will receive the gift of the Holy Spirit. For the promise is for you, for your children, and for all who are far away, everyone whom the Lord our God calls to him.'"

Margaret stopped reading. "I suppose the question they asked is my question also. Is that the answer? To repent and be baptized?"

"What do you mean, Margaret?" I asked.

"I feel like those people who heard Peter's sermon," she said. "For the past year the two of you have been telling me about Jesus. We've read through two of the Gospels. It's been like hearing the story all over again, for the first time. Jesus has captivated me. So I want to know. What should I do?"

"What did Jesus say?" Sarah asked.

Margaret thought for a moment. "Repent . . . believe the Good News . . . be baptized . . . leave your nets and follow me . . . take up your cross . . ."

I laughed and said, "I don't think you have to do all that at once."

"I don't know if I'll ever do all that," Sarah said.

Margaret laughed. "I know. It's all too much to do at once. So what should I do? How can I begin?"

"I think you already have," I said.

Sometimes, as caring evangelists, we will have the joy of inviting others to grow closer to God. We might invite them to attend a church service, or a Bible study. We might invite them to pray or study the Bible together. We can invite others to borrow a special tape or book on a topic about God that they're interested in. And, most important, we can invite others to begin a relationship with Jesus.

Because process-oriented inviting is such a key part of Caring Evangelism, in this chapter you'll look over some basic guidelines that apply to all the inviting you do. You'll look at when to invite and when not to invite. You'll also see how you can stay process-oriented in your invitations. Then in chapter 18 you'll focus on inviting people to become Christians, and in chapter 19 the emphasis is on inviting people to church.

What Needs to Happen before You Invite?

A lot needs to happen before you invite. If these steps don't come first, your inviting may do more harm than good.

Build a Strong Relationship

Before inviting, there needs to be a high level of trust and respect between the two of you. One reason is *so they know you invite for their sake—not your own.* When you develop a caring relationship with others before you invite, then they know your invitation comes out of love. They know you're not just using them to get something you want—status, a reputation as a great evangelist, or anything else. They've already seen you demonstrate your trust and respect for them in the relationship and they know that their welfare is always your top priority.

Another reason to build a high level of respect is *so those you invite feel safe saying no.* The relationship also needs to be close enough that others feel confident you won't reject them, even if they say no to your invitation. When people fear rejection they may accept your invitation just so they won't lose the love and the care that they sense coming from you. They may be afraid that if they refuse to do something you suggest, you'll leave.

This isn't a healthy situation. People who come to church simply to make someone else happy are not likely to stay around long. The same is true of people who pray, attend Bible studies, or begin a relationship with Jesus in order to please someone else. It just doesn't last.

Even with the best of intentions, sometimes you may invite people to do things they simply aren't ready for. If they believe you love them enough to stay with them, they can find the courage to say no. Then, maybe months, maybe even years later, they *will* be ready—and say yes—for the right reasons.

Listen a Lot

Before you ever invite a person to take a next step in his or her relationship with God, you need to listen a great deal so that you learn about the other person's needs, history, desires, and fears. If you invite without first listening, you run the risk of hurting someone in a very sensitive spot that you didn't know about.

Andy had his heart in the right place when, at the beginning of the relationship, he invited Margaret to church. He thought it would draw her closer to God, whom she needed so much in her loneliness. But he made one big mistake—he didn't listen first. If Andy had listened first and built his relationship with Margaret, sooner or later she probably would have mentioned the way her father turned church into a prison for her as a child. Then Andy would have known he needed to listen and care for a much longer time before Margaret would feel comfortable thinking about church.

Witness

Another thing that needs to happen before you invite is to witness. It doesn't make much sense to invite people to begin a relationship with Jesus when you've never described what that means. How will they know what you are talking about?

Similarly, it's premature to invite others to church if you've never said a single word about your church and the role it plays in your life. How can they make a reasonable decision? They've never heard about the blessings you receive from being in Christian community. They have nothing to judge by.

Pray

You also need to have prayed for the other person before you invite. Ask God to show you what God wants you to do in the relationship. Is the other person ready to think about praying together? Bible study? Church? Beginning a relationship with Jesus? Is it time for you to invite, or should you hold off for a while and work on strengthening the relationship instead? The Holy Spirit can give you the understanding you pray for. As James writes, "If any of you is lacking in wisdom, ask God, who gives to all generously and ungrudgingly, and it will be given you." (James 1:5)

It's only after you have built the relationship, listened, witnessed, and prayed that you can start thinking about inviting. Otherwise you are likely to slip into a results orientation.

Knowing When It's Time to Invite

How do you know when it is time to invite? It's surprisingly simple. If you simply *listen,* the other person will tell you. He or she will express an interest in God that makes it only natural for you to respond by inviting him or her to grow more. Here's an example.

Jean had spent several months building a strong relationship with Rosa, her next-door neighbor. She had listened and cared while Rosa talked about the difficulties she was experiencing as a single mother raising two children alone. Rosa was also concerned about her relationship with a man she had been dating for several months, and how her children might handle it if she decided to remarry. Jean had been praying regularly for Rosa since their relationship began.

Rosa knew that Jean was a Christian from the beginning, but for months God was never a large part of their conversation. Then occasionally, Rosa started asking questions about the church. She asked Jean where she went to church, and when; she asked what the pastor was like. Rosa never seemed to want to talk very long about church; she would just touch on the subject, and then move quickly to something else. Jean didn't push her. Instead, she answered Rosa's questions as simply and gently as she could. Sometimes she would briefly mention what God and church meant in her own life. Rosa seemed interested, but noncommittal.

Then Rosa began to talk about something that really bothered her. She was raised Catholic, but after the divorce she didn't feel right about going to church, so she dropped out. Now she was concerned about the children, who were getting close to confirmation age. She wondered if she shouldn't go back to church for their sakes, but she wasn't sure what reception she'd get, especially since she was considering remarriage.

For quite a while, Jean simply kept quiet and listened while Rosa poured out all her concerns and anxiety about going back to church. Jean did her best to show that she cared for Rosa as a person, and when it seemed appropriate, told Rosa about Jesus and how he cared for her. Rosa seemed surprised to hear that Jesus could love her, just as she was. The third or fourth time Jean described Jesus' love, Rosa asked shyly, "But ... I'm divorced, and I haven't been going to church for a long time. I haven't raised my kids in the church. How could Jesus love me?"

Jean shared a time out of her own life when she, too, had felt that God could never love her. Then she told Rosa about the way Jesus treated others in the Bible, even people that everyone else looked down on. Rosa listened eagerly.

Then she asked, "But what about the church? I know I should go, but how could I ever go back?"

Jean knew that the local parish had started a divorce recovery group. She described it to Rosa, and asked, "What do you think? Would you want to try something like that? I'd be happy to introduce you."

Rosa looked a little alarmed, but then said, "Yes, I guess that would be all right if you went with me. I don't know any of those people." Jean and Rosa made plans to attend together.

How Did Jean Invite?

Notice that Jean didn't invite Rosa to church as soon as she met her—instead, she listened and built up the relationship. For a long time they didn't talk much about God at all. Instead, they focused on Rosa's feelings and needs.

When Rosa started being concerned about church, she knew whom to talk to—Jean. She knew Jean was a Christian. She also knew that Jean cared enough about her not to force religion on her, or criticize her for not being in church. Jean had proved her caring through those months of patient listening. So Rosa felt safe bringing up the subject.

Rosa didn't come right out and tell Jean what was on her mind, however. She started by asking general questions about church for Jean to answer. Rosa was testing the water—seeing if Jean would overreact.

As Jean continued to be caring and accepting, Rosa felt safe enough to express her concern directly: "I'm divorced, and I haven't gone to church for a long time. I haven't raised the kids in the church. How could Jesus love me? How could I ever go back to church?" At that point, Rosa was ready to be invited.

Notice what Jean did. She didn't just say, "Come on back to church, and everything will be fine." Instead, she showed that she understood Rosa's fears of not being accepted. Instead of suggesting Sunday morning mass, which could have been very scary to Rosa at this point, she suggested something smaller and more comfortable—a divorce recovery group. There Rosa could be sure that she would be with several other people who would understand her situation and treat her with acceptance. Jean also offered to smooth the way by introducing Rosa to the group.

Jean didn't use any high pressure tactics. It was clear to Rosa that, even if she refused, Jean would still love her and still talk with her. Jean's caring gave Rosa the courage to accept the invitation.

What about the future? As Rosa starts to feel at home in

the divorce recovery group, Jean will still be there for her, to listen and to witness. When Rosa is ready, Jean will invite her to further participation—perhaps this time in Sunday morning worship. However, everything will happen at Rosa's pace—when *she* feels ready. Jean knows that if the invitation doesn't proceed at Rosa's pace, it won't proceed at all.

Strong Interest

The time is right to invite when other people express a strong interest. People might express an interest in learning more about Jesus, or about the Bible. In that case, it might be a good idea to invite them to a Bible study group. Others might ask, "How can I become a Christian? How can I have God in my life like you do?" After listening to discover exactly what they mean, you might invite them to pray, telling God that they want to be part of God's family.

Sometimes People Will Even Invite Themselves!

Sometimes people even invite themselves! As you listen, witness, and care, others will sometimes talk themselves into taking the appropriate next step in their relationship with God. They might say:

- "I think I'm ready to try church again."
- "I've lived all these years without God—now I think it's time for that to change."
- "Didn't you tell me you are in a Bible study that meets on Tuesday mornings? That really sounds interesting."
- "I've seen recently how empty my life is without God. How can I give my life to God now?"

Remember, you are a process-oriented caring evangelist, and the Holy Spirit is the one who brings people to faith. You can trust the Spirit to use your caring and sharing as God wills.

The answer to the question of when to invite is a simple one: when inviting let the other person set the pace. Some people ask, "Do you mean I'm just supposed to continue caring for the person until he or she lets me know it's time to invite?" Strange as it may seem, the answer is yes! As the Holy Spirit continues to work in their lives, people will let you know when it's time to invite. Until then, you should evangelize them by caring for them, witnessing to them, and praying for them.

Be an Assertive Inviter—at the Appropriate Time

Whenever you invite, do it assertively, not passively or aggressively. Being assertive means that you invite others in a way that respects them and doesn't demean yourself or the message.

Passive, Aggressive, and Assertive Inviting

Sometimes people avoid inviting out of fear that others might reject them. Or, if they do invite, they apologize for it before, during, and after they invite. This is passive inviting. If you invite passively, others may decide either that you have nothing worthwhile to share with them, or that you are ashamed of what you have to share.

Sometimes people force an invitation on others who aren't ready for it yet. This is aggressive. It's also aggressive to criticize a person for not saying yes, or to keep inviting him or her every chance we get, even when the person has made it very clear that the answer is no. This is a lot like knocking on a turtle's shell in order to get the turtle to come out. Not only will the turtle stay inside, but it is likely to close the shell up even tighter.

Instead of inviting in either of these self-defeating ways, invite assertively. This means inviting gently, winsomely, and confidently, without either apologizing for the invitation or showing disrespect for the other person. It means accepting that the person has the right to say either yes or no without being attacked. It means that whenever you invite, you do it as an expression of care for the other person.

If Someone Refuses Your Invitation . . .

This is probably the most common fear that lurks in people's minds when they invite: What if the person refuses the invitation? Is he or she rejecting me personally? Is it something I did or said? Does this mean that the person is rejecting God?

First of all, if you stay process-oriented when you invite, people are much less likely to refuse. That's because you have listened, cared, and custom-tailored the invitation to suit their needs. You invite when you see them showing a strong interest in that area, be it church, Bible study, or beginning a relationship with God. You don't force an invitation on them before they show any interest at all. All these facts make it much less likely that people will say no when you invite them.

Sometimes, however, it does happen that a person says no. That's okay. If it does happen, don't consider their rejection of your invitation a rejection of you as a person. If you have been caring and process-oriented, you have no reason to worry about this.

Of course, if you look back and realize that you did invite in an insensitive, aggressive, or results-oriented way, admit your error and ask for forgiveness. Remember that you don't have to be perfect to be a caring evangelist, and most people are very forgiving if you're willing to apologize.

Find Out Why the Person Refused the Invitation

If it isn't a problem with your process orientation, then why do people say no? There can be any number of reasons. They could simply be afraid to say yes and risk the changes that would come with that answer. They could misunderstand what you're inviting them to do. They might even be reacting to a bad past experience that you don't know about.

So if people say no, don't give up, and don't blame yourself. Instead, continue loving them, listening to them, and evangelizing them. Try to learn specifically why they refused your invitation. Then you can care for them in ways that address that specific concern.

Remember that people change their minds. As you continue to care for them, they may work through the problem that caused them to say no in the first place. When this roadblock, whatever it is, is gone, it's time to think about gently inviting again.

If Someone Accepts Your Invitation . . .

Caring evangelists can be nervous when someone says no, but they can be even more nervous when someone says yes!

Be Prepared

Have a general idea what you will do if people say yes to your invitation. If you're inviting others to a Bible study group, you should have a particular group in mind, and know when and where it meets. If you're inviting them to attend church, you should have given thought to inviting them to the service (or congregation!) at which they would feel most comfortable. Be prepared to go with them to the service or Bible study. When people say yes, be prepared to seize the moment and follow through right then.

Let Others Be Part of the Planning

This is not to say that you should have every detail planned out. It's very uncaring to just impose your plans on others—plans that they might not feel comfortable with.

Here's an example.

After a long time of listening, caring, and witnessing, Dave invited Jim to begin a two-person Bible study with him. Jim accepted, and Dave was delighted. "That's really great, Jim," he said. "We'll go through the Book of John, and we'll do one chapter a week. I'll expect you to read it ahead of time at home. We'll use the Authorized Version. I'm going to lend you this copy, because it has good study notes. Then we can meet on Mondays at 7 P.M., starting this week. Don't forget to bring your Bible!"

Instead of imposing a completely planned course of action on others, make your plans together with them. Though you will probably lead, since you know the territory better, be sure to include them in the decision-making process.

Keep Caring

After those you invite say yes, do continue to treat them in a caring, gentle, process-oriented way! If you assume that you don't need to care or listen anymore, since they have accepted your invitation, you will do enormous damage. Others are likely to decide that all your caring and listening was just a sham, designed to manipulate them into doing what you wanted.

Keep Evangelizing

Remember that evangelism is an ongoing process for all of us. Even after we invite and others accept, they still need evangelizing. Christians continue to work their way around the Caring Evangelization Cycle all their lives. As we continue to caringly evangelize others, we help them to keep growing in Christian maturity, faith and discipleship.

Maintain Confidentiality

Always remember that a big part of caring is confidentiality. When you invite and others accept, it's exciting! You are overjoyed to see someone you care for growing closer to God. In that excitement and joy, you may be tempted to tell everyone you meet about the wonderful thing that has happened.

Resist this temptation. Often people are not ready to have their spiritual growth broadcast to the world. They may want to tell their family or the church in their own way and in their own time. It can be very embarrassing and painful for them to find out that their very personal relationship with God is common knowledge to everyone they know—courtesy of their evangelist. (If you want to tell someone—for example, your prayer partner or your spouse—about this new development in the life of the person you've been evangelizing, ask for permission before doing so.)

Applying the Principles of Process-Oriented Inviting

Inviting in a process-oriented way may be different than you expected. But it is important to remain process-oriented through the act of inviting. Otherwise you can quickly wreck the evangelizing relationship you have carefully built over months and years. In inviting, patience and trust in the Holy Spirit are extremely important.

In this chapter, you've looked at some basic principles that apply to all inviting. In the next two chapters, you'll take a very detailed look at two special steps you invite others to take: beginning a relationship with Christ and moving into Christian community.

Chapter 18

Saying Yes to God

"What do you mean, you think I've already begun?" Margaret asked.

The breeze had died down. I could hear two birds singing to each other, one in Margaret's backyard, the other in a tree next door.

"Just that I think the first thing is to believe," I answered.

"Believe what?"

Sarah answered. "To believe that God loves you, to believe that Jesus died and rose for you. God invites us to see that we need a Savior and to believe that Jesus meets our needs."

"Is that all?" Margaret asked.

"It's a beginning," I said.

"Then you're right. I believe that. I suppose I have begun."

Sarah stood and hugged Margaret. I had to wipe my eyes because tears blurred my vision.

Margaret looked so happy. She said, "Okay, what's next?"

"A next step might be to talk to God," I said.

Margaret said, "I haven't prayed in so many years."

"Are you willing to try?" I asked.

"I suppose."

"Then let's simply tell God what you've told us. What do you want to say to God?"

Margaret thought for a long time. I could sense that this was difficult for her.

"You know you can just talk to God like you talk to us. You don't need to say anything fancy," Sarah said.

"I know," Margaret said. "I just have such a jumble of

thoughts. It's hard to sort them out."

"Keep it simple," I said. "Would you like to tell God anything about what you're thinking or feeling now?"

"I'm feeling happy, joyful."

"Is there anything you want to ask of God? Or anything that's bothering you that you'd like to get off your chest?"

"I'd like to ask God to forgive me for a lifetime of neglecting him. I stayed away for so long. I'd like to ask God to accept me, to love me, to make me part of God's family. I want to say thank you to God . . . for Jesus . . . for loving me. I want to thank God for the two of you."

We talked some more and then we prayed. All three of us prayed out loud. Margaret prayed last, and when she finished I felt like jumping up and down and shouting—not because we'd somehow won Margaret over, but because I was feeling so grateful to God.

Sometimes as we care for others we will have the wonderful opportunity to invite them to begin a relationship with God. In this chapter you will consider when and how you can do this.

Two Important Considerations

First of all, there are two important considerations to keep in mind about beginning a relationship with God.

God Has Said Yes to You

Remember that God has already said yes to you once and for all in the life, death, and resurrection of Jesus. That fact is established forever. Long before you were born, God acted to save, love, and accept you.

If you remember this, you can see clearly that there is nothing you can do to add to God's work. God has done everything necessary for your salvation already. In fact, it would be terribly presumptuous of anyone to try to add his or her two bits to God's work in Jesus, as if God needed help!

So what does this have to do with beginning a relationship with God? Sometimes people think that becoming a Christian means doing a specific set of actions in order to earn God's love. They believe that God does God's part, and then they have to do theirs, or God won't accept them. It's as if what God has done isn't enough. It only works if it's combined with their actions.

But this isn't how the Bible describes conversion. According to Jesus, beginning a relationship with God is like being born. He tells Nicodemus, "no one can see the kingdom of God without being born from above. . . . no one can enter the kingdom of God without being born of water and Spirit. . . . The wind blows where it chooses, and you hear the sound of it, but you do not know where it comes from or where it goes. So it is with everyone who is born of the Spirit." (John 3:3, 5, 8)

No child earns the right to be born by doing something. Birth happens to the child. The mother is doing all the work. It is the same with spiritual birth. God is doing all the work. We receive the benefit.

Of course our lives will never be the same once God has saved us. We see and believe what God has done for us. We respond with lives of faith. When we believe in Jesus, it drastically changes the way we live.

We don't earn God's love, but we do have many chances to respond to the love we have been freely given. Praying, telling others about what God has done for us, repenting of what was wrong in our previous lifestyle, and being baptized are all biblical ways we can make a beginning response to the love God has already given us. Loving God and neighbor, caring for the poor and oppressed, being peacemakers, and telling others about Jesus are some of the many ways we can continue to respond to God's gracious gift of love. But our response is not like paying the cashier so we can carry away our merchandise. It is more like a young child who responds to the parent's love and care with stumbling attempts to obey and please the parent, to love the parent in return.

Conversions Are Individual

The second point to keep in mind is that all conversions are unique, just as all births are. God works in many ways. One person may become a Christian through a dramatic, life-and-death encounter with Jesus. Another may become a Christian so quietly and calmly that he or she can't point to the exact day or even the year it happened. Some people pray at their conversions; others respond to a Christian speaker's invitation. Still others simply begin going to church, and discover later that God has given them faith in Jesus through their encounter with God's Word in Christian community.

What does this mean for you as a caring evangelist? Simply that you shouldn't be surprised or worried when God chooses to work differently in different people. In the pages that follow you will learn one way to help others come to Jesus. This is not the only way people become Christians; it is simply a very common one. If you did not become a Christian this way, don't worry about it. Your relationship with Jesus is no less real. Similarly, if the person you are evangelizing doesn't seem to move in this direction either, don't worry, and don't feel that you have to force him or her into this pattern. Instead, just let the Holy Spirit work in the way God chooses.

How to Invite Someone to Begin a Relationship with Jesus

Knowing When

In chapter 17, you learned that the right time to invite is when a person shows a strong interest. This is also true for inviting someone to begin a relationship with Jesus.

Here are some of the ways people might express themselves when they are ready for you to invite them to begin a relationship with Jesus:

- "What's it like to be a Christian?"
- "Jesus seems to be really important to you. Why?"
- "Do you think Jesus would want me?"
- "Could God help me in my situation?"
- "You always seem to have a kind of strength and peace in your life. How can I get what you have?"
- "How can I become a Christian?"

What to Do When a Person Shows Interest

What do you do when someone asks you a question like those? The answer is easy—you listen and witness, just as you always do.

You listen to discover what others mean by their question. For example a person who asks, "Could God help me in my situation?" may mean any of the following:

- "Can God forgive me for the mistakes I've made and the way I've hurt my family?"
- "Will God take care of me and my family if we have to declare bankruptcy?"
- "If I believe in God will all my credit card debt immediately and miraculously disappear?"

Obviously you would respond differently to each of those possible meanings. The only way you can find out what the other person really means is by listening.

You can then witness about your own experience of God and what you know about God from the Scriptures. Your witness can help clear up misunderstandings others may have about what it means to be a Christian. Also, witnessing will often lead very naturally into inviting others to begin a relationship with Jesus. You may find yourself saying:

- "We've talked about Jesus a lot together, and I've told you what he means to me. Is this something you want in your life?"

- "It sounds like you're really interested in Jesus. Would you like to become a Christian?"

- "I've told you a lot about my own relationship with Jesus, and I'm just wondering—is a relationship with Jesus something you're interested in right now?"

Invitations like these come out very naturally in the conversation when you're already talking together about Jesus. It's much better than dropping them on people out of a clear blue sky.

What if They Say No?

What if they say no? That's not anything to be overly concerned about, if you've been caring and process-oriented in your witness. Remember chapter 17. Others may not be ready to accept such an invitation yet. There may be other things going on in their lives that you know nothing about. If others refuse your invitation, just keep caring, listening, and witnessing.

Remember that just because people decline your invitation to begin a relationship with Jesus doesn't mean that they are rejecting God forever. God continues to work with people, even when they seem to be rejecting him.

What if They Say Yes?

What if you invite others to begin a relationship with Jesus, and they say yes? What happens next?

Tell God What You've Told Me

One very simple way of helping them at this time is to pray together. Say, "Let's tell God what you just told me." It doesn't have to be a lengthy or elaborate prayer. It doesn't have to be in fancy words.

Here's how this might happen in a conversation.

Josh was evangelizing Philip, a neighbor of his. Philip's wife had died a year ago. In the beginning, Josh mostly listened while Philip talked about his grief and anger over her death. Josh prayed for Philip regularly.

Over time, Philip became interested in Josh and his faith. Sometimes he asked questions like "What do you think happens when a person dies?" and "How do you know what you believe is true?" Josh would explain what he had learned from the Bible, and Philip would listen. He didn't say much—just took it away to think over. Josh didn't press him.

As the relationship became stronger, Philip's questions got more personal. He asked Josh, "A lot of the time you seem so strong, so peaceful. I know you have problems, and you get frustrated and angry just like me, but you've got something to get you through those times that I don't have. What is it?"

Josh told him about Jesus, and what Jesus meant in his life. He shared one of his own experiences, a time when his son had to have surgery, and how frightened and upset he'd been. Then he told how Jesus had gotten him through that time.

Philip listened intently. Then he asked, "It sounds great for you, but would it work for me? I mean, I'm not a Christian or anything."

Josh gently asked, "Would you like to be a Christian, and have this kind of relationship with Jesus?"

Philip said, "Umm—I'm not sure I'm ready for that yet." Josh didn't push—he just returned to listening, caring, and witnessing.

About a month later they were talking again, when Philip said, "You remember how you asked me if I wanted to be a Christian? Well, I've been thinking it over, and I guess the answer's yes. I've seen what Jesus means to you in your life, and I want him in my life also. But what do I do?"

Josh suggested, "How about just telling God what you've just told me?"

"What?" Philip asked. "You mean just pray, and tell Jesus I want him in my life too?"

Josh nodded. Philip said, "But I don't know how to pray. I mean, I don't know all the fancy words they use in church."

"That's all right," Josh said. "Just use normal words, as if you were talking to your friend. It doesn't have to be long or fancy."

Philip hesitated, took a deep breath and then said, "Okay, I guess so." Then he prayed, "Jesus, I don't know you very well, but my friend Josh here has been telling me a lot about you, and I'd like to know you better. You seem to be friends with Josh, and I'd like you to be my friend also. I'd like you to be with me *in my life too." Then he asked Josh, "Did I do it right?"*

Josh smiled and said, "Sure." Then he said, "This might sound sort of funny, but I'd just like to say, I'm really glad that you're part of God's family too."

Faith and Experience

Occasionally you will have a person who says, "I don't feel any different. Am I a Christian, or not?" How can you answer this person?

First, remember that feelings don't matter when it comes to whether someone belongs to God or not. The only thing that matters is God's promise. In the Bible, God states:

- "Everyone who calls on the name of the Lord shall be saved." (Rom. 10:13)

- "For God so loved the world that he gave his only Son, so that everyone who believes in him may not perish but may have eternal life." (John 3:16)

- "Believe on the Lord Jesus, and you will be saved." (Acts 16:31)

On the basis of God's promises you can be absolutely sure that when you trust in Jesus, you belong to Jesus.

Feelings vary widely. Some people experience wonderful emotional highs at conversion. Others feel nothing, or even have negative feelings. C. S. Lewis describes how he felt at his conversion: "I gave in, and admitted that God was God, and knelt and prayed: perhaps, that night, the most dejected and reluctant convert in all England."[1]

Feelings don't last, either. They change constantly. That's why it's not safe to base one's confidence in salvation on them. But the promises of God stand firm forever, and people can be sure by God's promises that they truly belong to God.

Invitation into the Kingdom of God

Beginning a relationship with Jesus is just the start. You'll want to make plans together on what comes next—things like baptism, getting into Christian community, and Bible study. Don't leave a new Christian without guidance.

Consider William Abraham's definition of evangelism to see how the new Christian will settle into the Kingdom of God. Abraham defines evangelism as "primary initiation into the Kingdom of God." He says it must include:

- Assimilation—getting firmly grounded and settled in the church;

- Basic teachings—gaining at least an elementary understanding of Christian teaching so that they can explain what they believe as Christians;
- Living as Christians—learning about Christ's ethic of love for God and neighbor and beginning to live according to that ethic;
- Spiritual disciplines—learning about basic Christian disciplines, such as worship, prayer, and Bible reading, and beginning to practice these disciplines;
- Christian service—discovering and developing their Spirit-given gifts and beginning to use those gifts in service to others.[2]

Even after people come to faith in Jesus, keep evangelizing. There are many things you can do to help those you evangelize become more firmly rooted in the Kingdom of God. You can help them find a home in a Christian congregation, and, if necessary, help them be baptized. You can learn with them about the basic beliefs of Christianity and what it means to live as a follower of Jesus. You can pray with them and study the Bible with them in order to help them develop spiritual disciplines to nurture their relationship with God. You can help them figure out how the Holy Spirit has gifted them for service and help them get started using those gifts. Perhaps most importantly, you can continue to say to them the Good News that God loves them because of Jesus—they don't have to perform up to a certain level to earn or retain God's love.

Witnessing a Birth

If you ask a group of parents about the most wonderful experience of their lives, many will say it was when their children were born. They may describe the event in mystical terms, often calling it a miracle.

As a caring evangelist you may have the opportunity to be part of a similar miracle when another person responds to the love of Jesus and begins a relationship with God. It is a wonderful and humbling experience, as you realize that you could never have made this happen by yourself. You rejoice that God has used you to help bring this miracle about.

[1]C. S. Lewis, *Surprised by Joy* (New York: Harcourt, Brace and Co., 1955), pp. 228-229.

[2]William J. Abraham, *The Logic of Evangelism* (Grand Rapids: William B. Eerdmans, 1989), pp. 101-103.

Chapter 19

How to Invite Someone to Church

The next evening Margaret came over to our home for the first cookout of spring. We all felt so happy that we got a little silly, singing old songs, trying to harmonize and ending up terribly off-key.

After supper Margaret said, "So what's next? I've made a beginning. What do I do now?"

"Well I don't know if you'd feel comfortable with it yet, but what do you think about the idea of becoming part of a church?" I asked. "I'm trying to go about this differently than I did the first time I invited you to church. I promise not to invite you out to brunch."

Sarah groaned.

"It's different now, Andy," Margaret said. "You don't need to feel bad about what happened back then. A lot has changed since then."

"If you're interested, there are several different ways you could get started," Sarah said. "I mean, assuming you want to come with us to our church."

"Tell me about your church. I'll want to think about this," Margaret said.

We told Margaret about our congregation, about how much we appreciated Pastor Ed, about how he seemed to take the faith so seriously. We also told her about some of the different ministries our congregation does, in order to give her an idea of what's important to us.

"I don't know if you'd be interested in coming to the worship service on Sunday morning," I said, "but if you'd like to, please come with us, or sit with us if you like."

"Otherwise, there are other ways to get involved," Sarah said. "There's a prayer and sharing group that meets on Thursday evenings—."

I added, "You might be interested in a Sunday morning class we have where they read and discuss books together. Sometimes they're religious books, and when they're not they look at them from a Christian perspective. I was a part of that group for a couple of years."

"This is a lot to think about," Margaret said. "I want to mull this over . . . and also ask God about what to do. I don't want to make a decision right now."

"Let us know if there's any way we can help," I said.

Margaret nodded. We talked for a while longer and then we prayed together.

You know what Margaret decided. I think she already knew what she was going to do, but she wanted to surprise us by showing up at church on Easter morning. We had been hoping she would, but we left the decision up to Margaret and God.

Margaret joined our church a couple of months later. She went through an inquirers' class and even read several books about our church's beliefs on her own. She also spent hours talking with Pastor Ed before she finally decided that our denomination was one she could feel comfortable in.

Margaret has continued to grow in her faith, so much that now Sarah and I are learning a lot from her. We've continued getting together to study the Bible, but now our group has grown to five. Margaret has begun evangelizing a woman named Evelyn who lives down the street and was widowed just last year. Evelyn already goes to a church, but she still needs our care and fellowship.

One of Sarah's friends, Maggie, has joined us a couple of times. Maggie's not sure yet whether she wants to "be religious" as she puts it, but she comes to the Bible study every few weeks.

I have a new friend at work. His name is Carl, and he's in the middle of a pretty messy divorce. We've been having lunch together and talking, sometimes with Jim Hayashi too. I'm praying that he'll be the sixth member of our Bible study group pretty soon. I'm not pushing it, mind you. It's just . . . well . . . I never would have believed that I'd be an evangelist, but now that I've gotten into the habit I sort of enjoy it.

Why invite people to church, anyway? It's a common question

that most Christians have struggled with at one time or another. Why do Christians go to church? Why not worship in the privacy of your own home instead? Or, as the old cliche puts it, "Why can't I worship God just as well out on the golf course?" The seashore, a forest, or a meadow can be just as quiet and often more beautiful than a church building. What's the importance of going to church?

The Normal Christian Life

First and foremost, Christians attend church because it is a normal part of the Christian life. God never meant Christians to live alone, cut off from each other. God planned that we should live in Christian community. The Apostle Paul goes so far as to call all Christians part of one body.

> For as in one body we have many members, and not all the members have the same function, so we, who are many, are one body in Christ, and individually we are members one of another. (Rom. 12:45)

No part of the human body can live on its own, apart from the rest of the body. To be alive and healthy, each limb and organ must participate in the total life of the body. This is also true for us as Christians. If we cut ourselves off from the rest of the body of Christ, our life of faith will suffer. But if we cherish our relationship to the rest of the body, we will stay healthy and help the rest of the body of Christ stay healthy, too.

This isn't to say that all Christians cut off from the rest of the church by no fault of their own are going to wither and die. There are Christians in non-Christian countries, political reeducation camps, and prisons, who might not be able to meet with other Christians. God is well able to care for these special cases. But solitary Christianity isn't the norm. One of God's greatest gifts to us is the blessing of each other.

We also gather as a worshipping community because that's where growth in God takes place. In the Christian congregation we hear the Gospel, study the Scriptures, pray together, and receive God's gifts of baptism and the Lord's Supper. Through all these resources, God blesses us and helps us to grow.

Finally, in Christian community we discover our gifts for ministry and learn to use them. As Paul puts it,

> Now there are varieties of gifts, but the same Spirit; and there are varieties of services, but the same Lord; and there are varieties of activities, but it is the same God who activates all of them in everyone. To each is given

the manifestation of the Spirit for the common good. (1 Cor. 12:4-7)

It is in the church that we find encouragement to try out different ways of serving and discover which one God has gifted us for. Our congregation also helps us find ways to use our gifts for ministry and supports us in our service.

How Can You Invite Others to Church?

You've looked at some of the reasons why Christians gather together in community. Now let's look at how you can invite others to share in Christian community.

Inviting Begins with Witness

Normally you will talk about church before you invite others to visit church. When you talk about Christian community and the role it plays in your own life, others get their first impressions of what the church is like. When you talk to others about your congregation, there are two points for you to remember: speak personally about your church, and be sure to tell the truth.

When someone asks you about your congregation, speak personally and authentically. Talk about the aspects of your congregation that excite you. Talk about how your congregation affects your life. These are the aspects of the church that others care about.

Be sure to tell the truth about your congregation. Don't paint an overly rosy picture of the congregation—that will only lead to disillusionment when others find out that your congregation does indeed have flaws. This doesn't mean that you should dwell on the negatives of a congregation either. You focus on the positive while telling the truth.

Visit *Their* Important Places

It may sound strange, but you invite by your actions as well as your words. Sometimes you do your best inviting to church when you go with others to a place or gathering that's special to *them*.

Here are just a few of the places or events that could hold a special place in the hearts of those you are evangelizing:

- a movie theater;
- a favorite fishing or camping spot;
- their own homes;
- a club or bar;

- a golf course;
- a child's graduation;
- a birthday party or anniversary; or
- the meeting of a service organization.

When you go with others to their special places, you learn a lot about their interests, lifestyles, and needs. You also show that you care about them as persons, not just as potential statistics on the church rolls.

Sometimes people ask: but is it a good witness to go to a bar or to the home of a person with a bad reputation? What if other people see me there?

This is a decision that needs to be made on an individual basis. Jesus went to the homes of disreputable people. He got in trouble for it, but he didn't mind because he was so interested in spreading the Kingdom of God.

Within the bounds of common sense, accept others' invitations to go with them to special places and gatherings. This tells them that you find them valuable, and you want to share in their lives. This makes it much easier for them to consider your invitation to *your* special place—the church.

Know Your Congregation

Before you invite others to visit, you need to know certain details about your own congregation. You'll want to be sure what time the services take place. You'll also want to be aware of any activities your church offers that you might invite others to. If you belong to a small congregation, this may not be too difficult. If, however, you belong to a very large congregation, you may need to review your congregation's printed material that describes its programs and services.

Why is it important to know about these other activities? Some people you evangelize may feel very comfortable visiting a Sunday morning worship service, and that's great. For others, however, an invitation to Sunday morning service—especially at a very large congregation—might be moving too fast.

Some people may need a more intimate group where it's easier to get to know people, such as a Bible study. Others might benefit from an activity where they are actively involved in doing something, like the choir or a ministry group.

Usually congregations will have smaller groups or activities that can serve as "ports of entry" to the larger congregation. A newcomer can get started in one of these groups; then, as he or she comes to feel more comfortable, he or she can try Sunday worship. A port of entry can be a very good, nonthreatening way for a new person to get involved with a congregation.

United Methodist Bishop Richard Wilke writes about his former congregation's experience of evangelism:

> Laypersons invited newcomers to their church school classes, the choir, the youth program, the Bible studies, and a few were coming, taking part and learning what church was all about. Soon it began to happen that as I gave the invitation on Sunday morning, one or two people would come out of the choir, or out of an active relationship in a church school class, now ready to join the church. They first came, got involved, made friends, and then were drawn to a commitment. *They were assimilated before they were received. They were a part of us before they were converted.*[1]

Here are just a few possible ports of entry that exist in many congregations. You will doubtless be able to name more in your own congregation.

- The men's, women's, or youth groups
- Bible study groups that meet at church on Sunday morning or in members' homes during the week
- Special need support groups, like single parenting, divorce recovery, grief recovery, or 12-step groups
- Singles' groups
- Service groups, like those that serve the poor or homeless
- Prayer circles
- The church choir, brass ensemble, or other musical groups
- Athletic teams or events
- Children's programs
- Fellowship events, like potlucks, concerts, picnics, and church suppers
- Special worship services, such as Saturday night or weekday services
- Seasonal worship services, such as Christmas, Easter, or Lenten services

When to Invite

As you saw in chapter 17, you should invite others only after listening and relationship building. This is true for invitations to church, also.

You invite others when you sense an interest on their part. In the case of church, this might happen if a person kept bringing up the subject of church in conversation. You might respond to their interest by saying:

- "I notice that you seem to be very interested in what my church is like. Would you like to come visit and see for yourself?"

- "We keep talking about the Bible study group I meet with every week. Since you're interested, would you like to come to a meeting and see what it's like for yourself?"

- "A couple of times you've said how you think churches should have good music. When I heard about the concert we're having at our church next week I immediately thought of you. It's an excellent choir from a church college. Would you like to come?"

- "Speaking of church, we're having a special service next week [*describe very briefly*]. Would you want to come?"

Other times, the person may express an interest in a subject that you know your congregation deals with. For example, he or she might be grieving over the loss of a spouse or child, and you might know of a grief recovery group in the congregation. Or he or she might express an interest in a subject that one of the Bible study groups is discussing—better parenting, perhaps, or the problem of why there is evil in the world. It would be very natural to say, "There's a group meeting at my church that's interested in exactly that subject. Maybe you'd like to visit once and see how you like it."

If Others Say No

As you've read before, if others decline your invitation, don't take it personally. It usually isn't meant that way. Instead, just continue to care, listen, and witness. Listen to find out why they have refused your invitation. Invite them again whenever you think they are more open to the idea.

If Others Say Yes

Let Them Know What to Expect

If others are interested in coming, be sure to explain what goes on in the church service or group. Let them know what kind of clothes are appropriate and how long the service or meeting will last. If they will experience any customs or rituals that may be unfamiliar to them (such as the way your congregation receives the Lord's Supper, making the sign of the cross, or giving personal testimonies), be sure to explain these things ahead of time and what, if anything, will be expected of them.

Discuss Their Expectations

You may also want to discuss their expectations of Christian community. Sometimes newcomers (or even long-time church members) will have idealized visions of what the church is like, and they may suffer disillusionment when they find out that Christians are so much like everyone else. Give a realistic picture of what Christian community is like—one that is neither overly rosy or gloomy.

Go with Them

After the person has accepted your invitation to visit, go with him or her, so he or she won't have to face a strange new situation alone. It can be very frightening to visit a new church or Bible study by yourself! You can introduce the person to this new group, be someone for him or her to talk to, and help her or him form new friendships. Your being there can make the difference between whether the person feels comfortable staying or not.

Think about the little practical things, too. Can the person find his or her way through the hymnbook? Does she or he know where the restrooms are? How about Sunday School or baby-sitting, if there are children along? A little thoughtfulness can make your friend's visit more comfortable.

Talk about the Experience

Afterward, it helps to talk about the experience together. How did the other person feel? Does he or she have any questions or comments? Make time to listen to what the other person has to say about the visit. Your accepting care will free others from the burden of being polite, so that they can tell you the truth about the experience. You may even discover something you can do to make the next visit more comfortable.

Follow Up

Finally, you'll want to follow up. If appropriate, invite the person to return. Be sure to continue your caring relationship, whatever they decide.

As they continue to visit, keep caring for them. Don't leave

How to Invite Someone to Church

them alone. Too often people are so familiar with their own congregations that they forget how strange everything is to a newcomer. They may sit with their visiting friends and introduce them for one or two Sundays, but then they may think the others are ready to be on their own. Usually they're not.

Instead, continue to sit with them. Talk with them. Look to see if they made it to church or to Bible study this week. If not, call and see if everything's okay.

It's a good idea to continue to look after people for at least a year, to make sure they are getting acquainted with others and starting to feel at home in the church. New members who leave the church typically do so in their first year of membership.[2] As long as they have a relationship with you, they will be much less likely to drop out. They will sense your concern, and feel valued and wanted—not just by you, but by God and by the Christian community.

Well Begun Is Half Done

In his book *Assimilating New Members* Lyle Schaller says, "There is considerable evidence which suggests that at least one-third, and perhaps as many as one-half, of all Protestant church members do not feel a sense of belonging to the congregations of which they are members. They have been received into membership, but have never felt they have been accepted into the fellowship circle."[3] That is a sure recipe for people who become part of a congregation one year and drop out the next.

Here's another fact: about 80% of those who visit congregations do so because a friend or relative invited them. Evangelists like you are the ones making the biggest impact in getting people in the front door of the church. The care you put into your process-oriented inviting can help people who become members of the church remain members of the church. Because of your ongoing care they feel accepted and know they are a part of the congregation.

[1]Richard B. Wilke, *And Are We Yet Alive? The Future of the United Methodist Church* (Nashville: Abingdon Press, 1986), p. 69.

[2]Dean R. Hoge and David Roozer, "Research on Factors Influencing Church Commitment" in *Understanding Church Growth and Decline 1950-1978* (New York: The Pilgrim Press, 1979), p. 64ff.

[3]Lyle E. Schaller, *Assimilating New Members* (Nashville: Abingdon, 1978), p. 16.

Chapter 20

How Will *You* Be a Caring Evangelist?

You, an evangelist?

Yes!

In this book you've looked at a lot of good ideas on how to be a caring evangelist. You've seen that your evangelism begins when you yourself are evangelized, growing in your relationship with God. You've learned that evangelism must be process-oriented, allowing others to discover their own need for a Savior in their own time and way. You've seen how evangelism involves building relationships, listening, helping others sort through feelings and spiritual concerns, witnessing, and praying. You've learned to combine listening and witnessing in process-oriented invitations.

Now it's time to answer a question you've probably already been working on—how you are going to use your skills and understanding as a caring evangelist.

Discovering How *You* Can Be a Caring Evangelist

Caring evangelism can be done by anybody, in any life situation. Every caring evangelist has unique opportunities to care, to listen, and to witness. As a caring evangelist, you face the exciting challenge of discovering just how you can use the skills and ideas presented in this book to caringly evangelize the people you live and work with.

Below are five examples of how ordinary people serve as caring evangelists in their daily lives. These examples are meant to help you think of ways that you, too, can serve as a caring evangelist.

Jeannette

Jeannette is a hairstylist who's been working in the same shop for six years now. She has many special customers who prefer to get their hair cut and styled by her.

While Jeannette works, very often her customers talk with her—about their families, their work, and their friends. Jeannette is a good listener. Her listening and empathy have allowed her to develop several close continuing relationships with customers.

Sometimes these people will tell Jeannette about problems in their lives, concerns and worries that are really hurting them. Jeannette listens and prays silently for each person. Occasionally she has the opportunity to witness briefly to how God has helped her through similar times of trouble.

For Jeannette, work is more than just a place to earn a paycheck. It is also the place where she cares for people loved by God, and sometimes even gets to share that love by telling them the story of Jesus.

Duane

Duane came to the state university as a freshman. He lived on campus in a dormitory room which he shared with three other men.

Duane knew that, as a Christian in a secular university, he would probably have many opportunities to witness to others about Jesus. He decided that he would try to live the love of Jesus toward others, especially his roommates.

Duane's resolution was quickly put to the test. When his roommates arrived, he discovered that one, John, was a militant atheist. The other two, Alan and Lew, had no feelings one way or another about God, but they seemed to think Duane was a little strange for going to church on Sundays when he could be sleeping in.

What could he do? Duane decided that it would do more harm than good to argue with his roommates about Christianity. So, instead of confronting them immediately on the subject, Duane took the time to get to know them as people.

Duane was a little surprised to find out that John spent his weekends down in Mexico, working with children in an orphanage in Ensenada. Duane went with him one weekend.

In Ensenada, John showed him the additional schoolroom he

had built using donated materials. John's current project was putting up a swing set for the kids. Duane helped.

As they worked together, John began to talk. "I get so angry when I see how the kids here live," he said. "They don't have anything—not even a decent place to play. I keep trying to get some of the others at school to come down and help, but they all say they're too busy."

Duane nodded and listened. John went on to express his frustration with the apathy he perceived on campus. "Everyone talks, but no one wants to do anything," he said. "Even the religious groups don't do much. If they can't even live up to their own beliefs, it's no wonder people don't want to join them."

Duane knew that John was at least partially right, although Christian groups had a few projects going he knew about. But he didn't think it would help if he argued with John. So Duane just kept coming and working with John in Ensenada, hoping that he could show John that there was at least one Christian who followed through on his beliefs.

As their relationship deepened, Duane discovered that John was an idealist. He had dreams of making the world a better place, but he was continually frustrated by what he read in the newspapers and saw on TV about greed and corruption in politics. "If the politicians would only do their jobs . . ." John said. "But it seems like everyone's in it for what they themselves can get—money, power, or prestige."

Duane nodded. "I know. That's what the Bible says is wrong with the human race."

John was surprised. "I thought the Bible was only down on sex and drinking, things like that," he said. "You mean it talks about real problems like greed and corruption in politics?"

Duane and John had several conversations like this. After a few minutes, John would change the subject, letting Duane know that he had had enough of talking about religion. Duane never pressed.

One day, after a long conversation about Jesus and how he related to the poor and oppressed, Duane said, "You know, John, if you're interested, we could maybe do a little reading about this together. Right now I'm reading Luke, and it tells a lot about how Jesus dealt with people on the fringes of society."

John was doubtful, but he agreed. They've been getting together every few days to read a section from Luke and talk it over.

Audrey

Audrey is concerned about her parents, Barry and Kay, who

are not Christian. They are retired now, and they spend a lot of time with hobbies and social clubs. Occasionally they attend church, but they have made it clear that religion is Audrey's "thing," not theirs.

Barry expressed their attitude clearly: "Why should we go to church? I can live a good life without going to church or believing in a particular set of ideas. I don't think people should impose their beliefs on others, anyway. What counts is the heart. If I live a good life and don't hurt anybody else, religion doesn't matter."

Audrey didn't know what to do. She had tried arguing with her parents when she was younger, but it only made them more rigid in their ideas about religion. So for the last ten years or so she has concentrated on loving her parents, caring for them, praying for them, and waiting for God to work.

Recently Audrey's father has developed heart problems. He has had one bypass surgery, and he and his family know that he will probably have to have more surgery soon. It has been a difficult time for Barry and Kay. From things they have said, Audrey believes they are finally starting to face the fact of their own mortality, and it's frightening them.

Recently Audrey visited her parents, and was surprised to find them asking her questions about her beliefs. Sometimes her parents asked questions in an off-hand way—"So how are things at the church?" Sometimes they seem genuinely curious to know how Audrey could believe "all that stuff."

Audrey does her best to answer the questions without pushing her parents faster than they are ready to go. She hopes that soon her parents will be curious enough to find out about God for themselves—either by attending church regularly, or by reading the Bible with her. Meanwhile, she prays for them.

Lou

Lou is a retired mechanic, in his early seventies. He lives in a changing neighborhood on the verge of the inner city.

Lately Lou has noticed that a lot of the new families moving into his neighborhood are refugees. They come with very little in the way of possessions, and they speak a strange language. In the evening, the breeze carries the smell of the exotic spices they use to cook their supper.

Lou gets his exercise by taking long walks around the neighborhood. He makes a point of saying hello to any of the refugee families he happens to meet, because he figures they're probably lonely. He smiles at the children playing.

One day Lou saw a man looking under the hood of his car,

How Will *You* Be a Caring Evangelist?

apparently trying to figure out what was wrong with it. Through simple words and a few gestures Lou asked if he could take a look. He quickly found the trouble, and fixed it.

In broken English, the man asked Lou to come to dinner at his house that night. It was his way of repaying Lou for the help. Lou accepted.

He enjoyed the dinner very much, getting to know the family and a couple of neighbors who were there. A relationship began. Whenever the family or one of their friends had mechanical problems with a car or appliance, they would knock on Lou's door, gesturing to show him that they needed him. Lou always went home with a plate full of exotic food.

As time went on, Lou found himself helping in more areas than just the mechanical. He showed one father how to enroll his daughters in the local school. He helped a woman open a checking account. Several times he dealt with utilities and government agencies on behalf of families who didn't speak enough English to communicate clearly on the phone.

Even though Lou is becoming busier and busier in his neighborhood ministry, he still has time to play with the children of the families he helps. They call him "Grandfather" in their own language.

Several families have expressed surprise at all Lou has done for them. One man put it well: "It is much work, and we do not pay you. You are not our relative, and you do not have to help us. Why are you doing this for us?"

Lou smiled and said, "Because Jesus loves me and takes care of me. That is why I love you and take care of you." Later Lou found copies of the Gospel of John in the refugees' own language, and gave these to the families. "This is the Jesus I am talking about."

Lorna

Lorna works in a dentist's office as a receptionist. Over the period of a year she has developed an evangelizing relationship with Judy, who works in the same office as a dental assistant. Judy moved from another state, and she's still having a hard time getting used to the new area.

"Everything goes so much faster, here," she said. "I just don't feel at home yet. And it's hard to get used to the weather."

Lorna listened and sympathized. Over time she found out that what was really bothering Judy was being away from her family and relatives. Back home, everyone knew her. Here she knew only her husband Fred and the people at her work.

"I'd just like to find a place where Fred and I can meet some nice people. I'd like us to socialize a little."

Lorna suggested, "If you like, I could take you to visit my church on Sunday. There are a lot of really nice people there you could get to know. We're having a church picnic afterward."

Judy said, "We used to go to a church, years ago. I'll talk to Fred."

Judy and Fred came to the picnic and enjoyed it. Lorna introduced them to some people she knew had similar interests. When they discovered that Fred had a good voice and loved to sing, they asked him if he'd like to join their choir some time. He said he would.

Judy and Fred spoke so positively about the church that Lorna invited them to attend worship the following week. She also continued her personal evangelizing relationship with Judy. As Judy and Fred got involved with the church, they began to learn a great deal about God. Judy would often save her questions to ask Lorna.

"Why do you say Jesus is the Son of God?" she asked one time. Another time, "Pastor was talking to us about baptism. What is that all about?"

Judy and Fred grew quickly as Christians. Lorna was happy to see that they were finding ways to get involved, serving God and others. She continued to keep an eye on how they were doing, and called to see how they were doing whenever she noticed they hadn't made it to church. They appreciated her caring, especially when Fred broke his leg and couldn't get out for several days.

Several months later, Lorna looked up after service to see Judy approaching with another woman at her side. "Lorna, this is Maggie," she said. "She's my next-door neighbor, and she does a lot of gardening. I know you love gardening, so I thought you might like to meet each other."

Lorna couldn't believe it; Judy was building an evangelizing relationship with Maggie! Lorna smiled at Maggie, and they got into a conversation about roses.

Five Examples

These are just five examples of how ordinary people can serve as caring evangelists. God opens up unique opportunities for each of us. You may find your caring evangelism happening at work, like Lorna and Jeannette; at school, like Duane; in your neighborhood, like Lou; or in your own family, like Audrey. Your evangelism may mean primarily listening and witnessing, as it did for Lorna and Audrey, or it may involve a large proportion of physical help, as it did for Duane and Lou. The

How Will *You* Be a Caring Evangelist?

evangelizing relationship may progress quickly, as it did with Judy, or slowly, as with Audrey's parents.

Yet, no matter how different your ministry, one thing will always be the same. As a caring evangelist you will work with the help, comfort, strength, and guidance of God's Holy Spirit. God is the real evangelist.

Getting Started

So how can you get started? Below are some very simple, concrete steps you can take to begin serving as a caring evangelist.

First of all, pray. Ask how God wants you to serve as a caring evangelist. Ask for the courage to listen, care, and witness honestly and authentically.

Second, look around. Is there one obvious person that you could establish a caring evangelism relationship with? This might be a relative, roommate, or co-worker.

If not, ask God to send you the person God has in mind for you to care for. Then keep your eyes open. One caring evangelist tried this, and the next day there was a blackout at her school. She ended up listening and witnessing (in the dark) to a new friend for almost two hours!

Third, establish the relationship. You can do this by using your skills of listening and empathy, as well as offering physical help when needed and welcome. Remember to stay process-oriented. Focus on the other person. And don't forget to pray for him or her!

And Now . . .

This book has no conclusion. That's because if this book is truly useful, its continuation will be written in the lives of people like you, who go out to serve as caring evangelists. You are writing the rest of this book. God will bless you in it.

Two Ministry Systems from Stephen Ministries®

1. STEPHEN SERIES®

A complete system for training and organizing laypersons for one-to-one caring ministry in their congregations and communities

Congregations from over 75 Christian denominations in the United States and 10 foreign countries are using the Stephen Series to care for hurting people and people in crisis. Since 1975 Stephen Ministries has been committed to maintaining and delivering a quality lay caring ministry system. The Stephen Series IS distinctively Christian caring.

To learn more about the Stephen Series you might want to order one of the following information videos.

THE HEART OF STEPHEN MINISTRY

The heart of Stephen Ministry is "Christ caring for people through people." The stories in this extraordinary ten-minute video show the healing, joy, and renewed lives that God brings through Stephen Ministry—not only for those who receive care but also for those who serve as Stephen Ministers and Stephen Leaders. The Heart of Stephen Ministry helps people catch the vision for lifechanging lay caring ministry—not only with their eyes, but also with their hearts.

THE GIFT OF STEPHEN MINISTRY

This 20-minute video explains how any congregation can benefit from the many gifts the Stephen Series offers through lay caring ministry. People who have known the gifts of the Stephen Series—pastors, lay leaders, Stephen Ministers, care receivers—share their stories, telling how God has blessed them, changing their lives and giving them hope, and how other congregations can share in those blessings.

2. CHRISTCARE® SERIES

A comprehensive system for leading and organizing lay small group ministry that enables congregations to care for the spiritual growth and needs of their members

This complete ministry system offers congregations the opportunity to build Christian community through small groups by helping members care for one another, engage in Biblical Equipping, join together in prayer and worship, and extend themselves outward to help others through missional activity. Carefully researched and extensively tested, the ChristCare Series offers a detailed, well-integrated system for developing and delivering a small group ministry that works.

To learn more about the ChristCare Series you might want to order the following information video.

THE CHRISTCARE SERIES AT WORK
This 20-minute video describes ChristCare Group Ministry through the words of those who know it best—the pastors and other leaders who are directing this system of small group ministry in their congregations. This presentation helps pastoral groups—boards, committees, even the congregation as a whole—understand the ChristCare Series, why this system of small group ministry works, and how this system can further spiritual growth and community within individual congregations.

Courses From Stephen Ministries

CARING EVANGELISM: HOW TO LIVE AND SHARE CHRIST'S LOVE

A 16-hour course that equips Christians to be caring evangelists in their daily lives

This is evangelism training for people who never thought they could be evangelists. Course materials include the *Leader's Guide, Participant Manual*, and *Administrative Handbook*. Participants read the book *Me, an Evangelist? Every Christian's Guide to Caring Evangelism.* Developed over a period of five years, the course equips God's people to fulfill the Great Commission.

CARING FOR INACTIVE MEMBERS: HOW TO MAKE GOD'S HOUSE A HOME

Designed for use by church staff, lay leaders, and members

This course on church inactivity provides a comprehensive congregational approach to inactive member ministry. 10 to 14 hours of course work address the issues of preventing inactivity, caring for inactive members, and welcoming inactive members back to God's house. Participants learn a caring approach to an often sensitive situation. Course includes the *Leader's Guide, Participant Manual,* and text, *Reopening the Back Door: Answers to Questions about Ministering to Inactive Members.*

ANTAGONISTS IN THE CHURCH
A course on how to identify and deal with destructive conflict

This practical course helps participants identify and deal with church members who attack leaders and destroy ministry. The book *Antagonists in the Church* and the companion *Study Guide* teach participants how to recognize, prevent, confront, and halt antagonists in the church.

**CHRISTIAN CAREGIVING
A WAY OF LIFE**

**The definitive approach to
distinctively Christian care**

Based on the *Christian Caregiving—a Way of
Life* book and the accompanying *Christian
Careqiving—a Way of Life Leader's Guide*, this 20-hour course
answers many questions about putting faith into action.
Participants learn how to use Christian resources, such as prayer
and the Bible, in their everyday caring and relating.
Distinctively Christian caring really can be a way of life!

**DISCOVERING GOD'S VISION
FOR YOUR LIFE: YOU AND
YOUR SPIRITUAL GIFTS**

**An 8-hour course designed to help
members discover their gifts and
mobilize them for ministry.**

This complete set of resources, including a *Leader's Guide* and
Participant Manual, helps congregation members understand
their own spiritual gifts for ministry, gives them a solid
foundation in the theology of Christian ministry and discipleship,
and motivates them to use their spiritual gifts in service to
others. Additional resources help congregation members prepare
for the course and put the findings to practical use in ministry
afterward.